BILLION

DOLLAR

START-UP

BILLION

THE TRUE STORY OF HOW

DOLLAR

A COUPLE OF 29-YEAR-OLDS TURNED $35,000

START-UP

INTO A $1,000,000,000 CANNABIS COMPANY

ADAM MIRON, SÉBASTIEN ST-LOUIS & JULIE BEUN

Published by ECW Press
665 Gerrard Street East
Toronto, Ontario, Canada M4M 1Y2
416-694-3348 / info@ecwpress.com

Editor for the Press: Jennifer Smith
Cover design: Michel Vrana

LIBRARY AND ARCHIVES CANADA CATALOGUING IN PUBLICATION

Title: Billion dollar start-up : the true story of how a couple of 29-year-olds turned 35,000 into a 1,000,000,000 cannabis company / Adam Miron, Sébastien St-Louis & Julie Beun.

Names: Miron, Adam, author. | St-Louis, Sébastien, author. | Beun, Julie, editor.

Description: Includes index.

Identifiers: Canadiana (print) 20200362801
Canadiana (ebook) 20200362844

ISBN 978-1-77041-586-7 (HARDCOVER)
ISBN 978-1-77305-648-7 (PDF)
ISBN 978-1-77305-647-0 (EPUB)
ISBN 978-1-77305-649-4 (KINDLE)

Subjects: LCSH: HEXO—History. | LCSH: Marijuana industry—Canada—History. | LCSH: Marijuana—Law and legislation—Canada—History. | LCSH: New business enterprises—Canada—Case studies. | LCSH: Entrepreneurship—Canada—Case studies. | LCSH: Success in business—Canada—Case studies.

Classification: LCC HD9019.M382 H49 2021
DDC 338.1/7379097I—dc23

The publication of *Billion Dollar Start-Up* is funded in part by the Government of Canada. *Ce livre est financé en partie par le gouvernement du Canada.*

PRINTED AND BOUND IN CANADA

PRINTING: FRIESENS   5   4   3   2   I

MIX
Paper from
responsible sources
FSC
www.fsc.org   FSC® C016245

Adam: To Sébastien, from whom I learned more about business than from anyone else. Thank you for forever changing my life and for what we did in the last little while of my dad's life. To Meena — the perfect partner. No matter how good of an idea that was pitched, it could never have been possible without your support, confidence, and love. I'm lucky to have you. Mom, without the confidence you instilled in me, with endless love and support, I neither could nor would have even attempted anything like this company. Michael, Jay, Vincent — thank you for taking a chance on us (and sticking with us). To all the employees — you took this dream and made it real, please be very proud of what you've done. To our agent, Lloyd, thank you for making this book a reality. To Julie, you are one of the best writers I know, and it is an honour to have produced this book with you. And to my daughters Iyla, Nalina, and Sohana, you girls are my life.

Seb: To my parents, Lise and Jean, for their unwavering support, guidance, and love. To my business partner, Adam, and to Michael and Vincent, thank you for taking the risk and seeing it through. To Max, this is all your fault, man. To every employee and every single person who's worked with me to build this thing at HEXO, I thank you for the heart you have put into every hour of this journey. To my beautiful wife and my children, you have all my love.

Julie: To my kids, Jed and Hayley, thanks for understanding when I disappeared into my woman-cave to write. Thanks, too, goes to my faux-bro, Brendan McNally, for being an unflagging supporter and early editor, and to my besties Janet Wilson, Mauri Brown, and Measha Brueggergosman for patiently listening when you could have legitimately zoned out. To Adam and Seb, you goddamn rock stars. What a ride it's been. Thanks for having me in the passenger seat and trusting me to write about this crazy journey. To my former OG HEXO and Hydro squad, there'll always be the Taj.

Disclaimer

This account describes events covering HEXO's early years, between 2013 and 2019. Yet the HEXO story continues to evolve and change, just like the industry it helped create. In fact, even between the end of our story and this book hitting the shelves, anything — literally anything — may have happened. The company could have become the world's largest cannabis producer. It could have been sold. It could have been taken over by highly evolved, cannabis-consuming sentient beings from another universe whose five-year mission is to chill. Who the hell knows? In the cannabis industry, anything seems to be possible. (Except that last one. Obvi.) The point is, the reader should approach this story as a snapshot in time — in crazy, colourful cannabis years, of course.

In some cases, the names of those involved have been changed. These are denoted with an *.

TABLE OF CONTENTS

FOREWORD

A few years ago, I told Sébastien St-Louis and Adam Miron that they were amongst an elite group of entrepreneurs who'd managed to dramatically turn a start-up into a company with a billion-dollar valuation within their lifetimes. In fact, I added, they were two of only a handful of Canadians who'd ever achieved such success.

It sounds impressive — it IS impressive — but that simple statement of fact doesn't tell the story of the sacrifices, the enormous personal risks, the roller coaster ride they jumped on when they became cannabis entrepreneurs. It also doesn't talk about the personalities of these two people, or their deep bond of brotherhood and friendship.

There are millions of entrepreneurs around the world, and in my experience, they all share similar characteristics. They are risk-takers. They are dreamers with a streak of hard-nosed pragmatism. And, when the rest of the world tells them over and over that what they want to do simply can't be done, they ignore the naysayers and *do it anyway*.

Sébastien and Adam have all those qualities. They're also two very innovative leaders who steered HEXO to winning awards for products like Elixir and Decarb and changed the game with large format, value-priced products like Original Stash.

From the moment they incorporated in 2013 to now, they've remained committed to each other and their friendship, even when things go very wrong. (Seb told me he once covered payroll on his credit card — talk about commitment and personal risk!)

They took chances and made some wrong turns along the way. But I don't call that failure. In business, failure leads to gaining experience. If you never try anything, you never fail — but you never do anything important either. A majority of entrepreneurs never get anywhere, but those like Seb and Adam, the ones who stick with their ideas and are flexible enough to adjust when plans don't go as predicted, often turn out to be winners.

That's the bottom line in *Billion Dollar Start-Up*. It's the story of how a couple of guys with next to nothing put together their own little empire in a brand new and unpredictable industry. It is the North American capitalist dream in action.

For entrepreneurs reaching for this book as you struggle to get your ideas to market or attract financiers, this story should make you feel that anything is possible, and that you, too, can do something out of the ordinary.

Don Wright
Chairman, RF Capital Inc.
(Formerly GMP Capital Inc.)
October 2020

A Cannabis Timeline: A Potted History

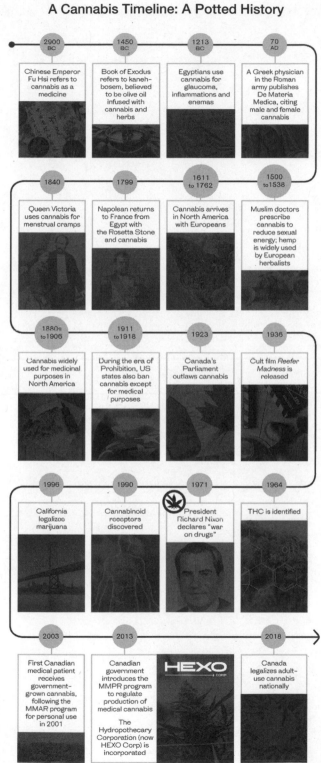

2900 BC — Chinese Emperor Fu Hsi refers to cannabis as a medicine

1450 BC — Book of Exodus refers to kaneh-bosem, believed to be olive oil infused with cannabis and herbs

1213 BC — Egyptians use cannabis for glaucoma, inflammations and enemas

70 AD — A Greek physician in the Roman army publishes De Materia Medica, citing male and female cannabis

1840 — Queen Victoria uses cannabis for menstrual cramps

1799 — Napolean returns to France from Egypt with the Rosetta Stone and cannabis

1611 to 1762 — Cannabis arrives in North America with Europeans

1500 to 1538 — Muslim doctors prescribe cannabis to reduce sexual energy; hemp is widely used by European herbalists

1880s to 1906 — Cannabis widely used for medicinal purposes in North America

1911 to 1918 — During the era of Prohibition, US states also ban cannabis except for medical purposes

1923 — Canada's Parliament outlaws cannabis

1936 — Cult film *Reefer Madness* is released

1996 — California legalizes marijuana

1990 — Cannabinoid receptors discovered

1971 — President Richard Nixon declares "war on drugs"

1964 — THC is identified

2003 — First Canadian medical patient receives government-grown cannabis, following the MMAR program for personal use in 2001

2013 — Canadian government introduces the MMPR program to regulate production of medical cannabis

The Hydropothecary Corporation (now HEXO Corp) is incorporated

HEXO CORP

2018 — Canada legalizes adult-use cannabis nationally

PROLOGUE

"Hey. What's up?"

What is up is that Ottawa is in the depths of one of its hellacious blizzards.

Adam Miron is on the speaker in his car, headed down Autoroute 50 out of the Gatineau farmland around Masson-Angers and back to his home in central Ottawa. But, being Canadian and given that a blizzard is a weekly occurrence from December to March, he is on the phone with his colleague Julie Beun, speeding a little in his clapped-out Mazda 3 and doing business anyway. In this instance, however, there's something electric in his voice.

"Yeah. How are you? I'm good. You got a minute?"

Small talk is not Adam's strength when he's excited, so he blows past waiting for an answer.

"Listen, I just have to tell someone. Today is the day we became a billion-dollar company. Any way you cut it . . . we have 218 million fully diluted shares outstanding at $4.95. That's $1.08 billion. Today is the day."

She can tell he is grinning down the phone.

"We did it."

But let's not get ahead of ourselves.

While it's true that day was a banner day, so too was January 18, four days earlier.

That night, in Montreal's chic Hôtel St-James, Adam and his brother-in-law, Sébastien St-Louis, held their first annual general meeting as a publicly traded company named Hydropothecary. Standing together, greeting investors with boyish grins and manly slaps on the back in the lush surrounds of XO Le Restaurant, with its grand staircase and thick white pillars, they looked nothing alike. (Their wives, on the other hand, are sisters who share the same perfect complexion, bright-eyed curiosity, and insightful wit that make them near replicas of each other.)

Admirers often describe Sébastien as a "young Tom Cruise" — or at least, the marquee Tom Cruise. Broad-shouldered, devastatingly intelligent, at turns affable and charming, steely-eyed and blunt, he moves between conversations quickly, the look on his face saying that he is anticipating most of what the speaker has to say before they've thought of it. But he lets them say it anyway.

Standing at Sébastien's side was Adam, his eyes darting around the room. A master of a quiet word in the right ear, Adam is Seb's perfect foil: a brilliant tactician who learned the fine art of getting into the right rooms at the right times through his work in politics. He is the ebullient and visionary architect of the company's brand. Where Seb almost exclusively wears athleisure wear and flip-flops, Adam pulls from his collection of ascots, tailored suits, and the kind of footwear bankers should be compelled to take as collateral. Yet, because they are as close as two brothers-in-law and friends can be, it works. And it works well.

At the appointed time, Seb stepped up on stage with Chief Financial Officer Ed Chaplin and board chair Dr. Michael Munzar. A hush fell over the XO, which had been cleared of tables and set up as an ad-hoc meeting room. It was packed with investors keen to meet the two brash 34-year-old entrepreneurs behind the company. A dozen staff and VPs loitered at the edges, pride and trepidation written all over their faces. Amid the exclusive atmosphere, they and the shareholders listened, rapt, as Sébastien, CEO and co-founder, expounded on the company's ballsy vision for the future like a seasoned politician rallying the troops.

For this company, he told the mesmerized audience, it will be a case of "Today, Quebec. Tomorrow, Canada. And then the world." Hydropothecary (later renamed HEXO) was in the midst of building a 250,000-square-foot greenhouse and had just announced plans to add another 1 million-square-foot facility by the end of 2018. Overall, he told the gathering, the company would produce 108,000 kilograms of dried bud annually.

Dazzling? Bold? Decisive? You bet.

But anyone in the room who had followed Seb and Adam's trajectory over the previous few years couldn't have been surprised at the audacity of their plans. Having listed their company on the TSX Venture Exchange in March 2017, the two men were just two months shy of its one-year anniversary on the public markets.

That in itself isn't remarkable — other companies went public that same day. But since that day, few have done what Adam and Seb have achieved. Five years earlier, in a 175-square-foot basement office, the two brothers-in-law had embarked on a mission.

They believed in it. They invested all of their money, as well as any that their friends, families, and banks were willing to send their way. They churned through paperwork, landed in debt, and turned to each other when doubt reared its head.

They worked 20-hour days. They made mistakes, nearly lost it all, took leaps of faith, lived on their wives' incomes, and went without sleep.

But that's the magic of business.

It's the entrepreneurial spirit in its rawest form, a distillation of Big Hairy Audacious Goals coupled with chutzpah and pigheaded tenacity.

Adam and Seb had that in spades. Within five years, they had turned their dreams — fuelled by $35,000, followed by $1.13 million rounded up from friends and family, mostly in $10,000 and $15,000 increments — into something else altogether. They had, as Adam gleefully told Julie during his juggernaut drive in the blizzard, created a very big something out of almost nothing.

Within five years, the two brothers-in-law had created a billion-dollar, award-winning, take-no-prisoners Canadian cannabis company called HEXO.

How did they do it? That's what comes next.

INTRODUCTION

The Canadian cannabis industry moves fast.

So fast, they say, it's like high tech or the semiconductor industry. Or even the fun, money-making bits of the dot.com bubble.

But like so many other things in life, "they" have no idea what the hell they're talking about.

Where those industries evolved over time, driven by technological advances made in incremental steps, the Canadian cannabis industry has been a greyhound running flat out, ears back, right out of the gate.

After all, this is an industry with a ready-made market. By the time the federal Conservative government turned over the production of medical marijuana to licensed producers in 2013, cannabis had already been a thing in Canada for more than a hundred years, whether it was legal or not. Before that, it was definitely a thing dating back to 2900 BC, when Chinese emperor Fu Hsi raved about its medicinal properties. (That may be an overstatement, but he was a fan.)

An estimated 7,024,000 Canadians will be cannabis consumers by 2021, says the Office of the Parliamentary Budget Officer. Thanks to the federal Liberal government's legalization of cannabis in 2018, it'll generate around $7.17 billion in sales, according to a 2018 report by Deloitte.

That's a lot of Canadians, but despite what we may want to believe, we don't own the industry worldwide — at least not yet. Around the world, lots of people consume cannabis, mostly under strict legislative restrictions. But should Europe, the United States, and Latin America, as well as the pharmaceutical, alcohol, health, and pet care industries, all follow Canada's lead (a great thought, isn't it?), the international market could be valued at US$130 billion by 2028, according to a 2019 report by the US investment bank Jefferies Group.

In short, this is a bullish industry.

The numbers say a lot. They tell a tale of a young prime minister determined to go further than any other politician has when it comes to marijuana. They speak to a groundswell change in public attitudes. And they record how a federal government — not public markets — unleashed a brand-new industry.

But that's not what this book is about.

The tale herein is about how two eager 29-year-old brothers-in-law and friends from Ottawa, Adam Miron and Sébastien St-Louis, grabbed hold of a bold moment in Canadian history and, with just $35,000 in credit, turned their basement start-up into a billion-dollar corporation in just five short years.

Put like that, it's a dazzling achievement. And it is an incredible piece of financial brinkmanship, to be sure. But it wasn't easy. They made mistakes and errors in judgment. And they nearly lost everything, more than once.

This account takes in events that occurred from 2013 to 2019, yet the HEXO story continues to evolve, and indeed, even within months of the events described in the final chapter, much changed in the industry and for the company.

The first part of this book, "Escaping the Basement," is a story straight from the *Big Book of Start-Ups*: the struggling entrepreneurs, the romance of the basement office, the horrifying realization that every friend they ever had could lose their investment if they fail. There are ups, there are downs, and there's a lot of pizza and beer.

Part 2 is called "We Bought the Farm." The title is no exaggeration. It's all about peril, loss, and anxiety. And having babies. Having committed everything to their nascent cannabis company, then called Hydropothecary, Adam and Seb found themselves riding a white-knuckle trajectory on their way to their first $50 million valuation. But in the end, the challenges they and their growing team faced became some of their finest and most memorable moments.

Finally, in "Hitting a Billion," the clouds part and the sun comes out. Well, sort of. Its exponential growth, driven by the two men's relationship, shared vision, and dedicated team of employees, pushes the company (now HEXO) out of its all-hands-on-deck start-up mentality and into a mature corporation. Like leaving the teenage years behind, it is awkward and noisy at times, but ultimately worthwhile.

Throughout Canadian history, fewer than a hundred Canadians have started a company that surpassed a billion-dollar value in their lifetimes. Two of them are Adam Miron and Sébastien St-Louis.

This is their story.

PART 1

ESCAPING

THE

BASEMENT

CHAPTER 1

5 P.M., JUNE 28, 2013
COTTAGE ON LAC MCGREGOR
VAL-DES-MONTS, QUEBEC

Like many a great Canadian business story, this one starts with a campfire at a cottage.

At least, that's the company lore. Campfire yarns being what they are, they are either the victims or happy recipients of embellishment. Especially when there's beer and weed involved.

So, that evening five years before HEXO was a billion-dollar company, there was a campfire — at some point. There was beer, this being the Canada Day long weekend and the location being someone's rustic cottage at Lac MacGregor, in rural Quebec. And the two key players in the story, Sébastien and his childhood friend, Max Cyr, were definitely talking about cannabis.

Max had grown up with Sébastien, or at least hung around Seb, his older brother, and best friend Will in Blackburn Hamlet, a working-class Franco-Ontarian suburb in east Ottawa. Even now, years later, Max maintains that Seb has not changed since childhood: confident, outspoken, no sugar coating, no filters.

"If someone orders soup and it arrives cold," Max remarks, "Seb doesn't rest until the restaurant manager makes it right. When he was in grade 3, he made a speech referring to adults as 'old dinosaurs,' which really pissed off our teachers. I've never forgotten that. But it's Seb. Out with the old, in with the new."

Early on Friday afternoon, Max left his Health Canada job in Gatineau and headed to the cottage, which consisted of a main house and a collection of random, ant-infested outbuildings that had nevertheless been the site of many happy gatherings. Max was hoping to have a quiet conversation with Seb alone, before their friends and partners arrived later that evening.

He definitely had something on his mind. Max's job was getting more and more complicated. The Conservative government was moving from the Marihuana Medical Access Regulations (MMAR, under which registered patients could grow their own bud) to Marihuana for Medical Purposes Regulations (MMPR, under which patients could no longer grow cannabis themselves or have it grown for them). Their rationale was, in part, that this would tightly regulate the health and safety concerns around cannabis. As a result, Max had to train frontline Health Canada staff on the legislative changes and application process, plus oversee the client services call centre, ministerial correspondence, and the Police Services Unit.

The MMPR meant that any company with enough time, money, and knowledge could apply to become an LP in the nascent medical marijuana industry. Registered patients would no longer have to go through a government contact. They could choose their LP, order their product directly from them, and have it delivered by courier to their homes. It was a brand-new industry — admittedly conceived of and run by the federal government — but it opened endless possibilities for making lots and lots of money.

Funny thing about marijuana, though. It has a stigma that lingers like spilled bong water.

Invest in the weed industry? No one seemed interested, judging by the few applications recorded by Health Canada at that time. No one, Max thought, except perhaps Sébastien.

Formerly a regional manager at Export Development Canada (EDC), then a senior account manager at Business Development Canada (BDC), Seb knew business. He'd worked as a chief financial officer for a manufacturing firm, doubling sales to $10 million in a single year while preparing it for public sale. He had real estate investments and knew his way around a boardroom.

After a celebratory beer by the campfire, Max and Seb headed inside. There, at the cottage's battered wooden dining table, Max shared what was on his mind. Everything was public and in the press at that point: Seb had been dimly aware of the government's regulatory changes, mostly through Max grizzling about his workload. He wasn't exactly sharing the Conservative government's state secrets.

Max scratched his bristly mop of hair and looked at Seb. "It's like no one wants to be a millionaire in this country."

Anyone who knows Seb can picture what happened next, even without witnessing it first-hand. Seb grilled Max, asking about everything from how many buds he thought a plant could grow to how much those buds might sell for and what kind of infrastructure Health Canada was expecting from interested companies.

Before long, Seb was surrounded by paper, running scenarios, looking at numbers, and figuring out how much money they needed to get skin in the game.

People started showing up at the cottage, ready to party for the weekend. As friends asked what they were talking about, the conversation grew until it was the only thing being discussed. Jobs? The weather? The drive up? No, no, and no.

The next morning, Max stumbled into the kitchen, looking for coffee and aspirin. The first night at the cottage, he thought — ouch. And there was Seb, at the kitchen table, just where he'd left him late the night before. As Max told the story later, he wasn't even sure Seb made it to bed.

But the numbers were there. Seb had calculated that they needed $250,000 to get started. He would pitch in $100,000; Max and his brother would contribute what they could. The rest would have to come from someone else.

For the rest of the weekend, whether they were around the campfire, at the kitchen table, floating on pool noodles out on the lake (with someone occasionally dock-bombing cans of Coors Light out to Seb), marijuana was pretty much the only thing worth discussing. And it stayed that way for the next five years.

Meena and Aruna Rajulu are as close as sisters can be.

Watching them finish each other's sentences, seeing the shared merriment in their glances, it's hard to believe they're not twins. Everything, from their bon mots to their delighted laughter, comes from a deeply held place of knowing exactly who one is and who is one's blood. Born in Los Angeles of South Indian parents, they were raised to be tight, to have each other's backs, and to be indelible in each other's lives.

Not surprisingly, meeting each other's potential life partner was going to be a big deal. Sisters who spend that much time together, whose every thought references "What would she think, say, or do?" know their partners also have to like each other.

That night at Absinthe wasn't encouraging.

Aruna and Seb had been dating seriously since they met over the May 2009 long weekend at a wedding for people they didn't really know. "Well, he looks interesting," Aruna thought when she spied him sitting with two elderly people she mistook to be his parents. And once he hit the dance floor, sparks flew. A Mexican friend had once told Seb to "ignore your instincts when it comes to dancing" and showed him how to lead with his hips. The results were impressively sensual enough to catch Aruna's eye. By the end of the evening, Aruna recalls, "I knew he was the most interesting person I'd ever met. He was an absolute lion. And I felt something in my heart." They spent the next few days together and, within a few dates, they decided to be exclusive. Or rather, Aruna (equally a lioness) told Seb, "If you're dating anyone else, break up with them. We don't have to get married right away, but we need to be on the same path."

Within a month, Seb introduced Aruna to his parents, Jean and Lise, both deeply caring teachers and activists for French-language rights in northern Ontario. On a swing in his parents' backyard a short time later, Lise delicately queried Aruna about her intentions toward her son. The elder St-Louis rightly adored their brilliant son and had done all they could to give him an engaged and joyful childhood, even encouraging him to believe in Santa Claus till he was 12, despite good-natured teasing from his friends. They'd been hands-on parents who both set the guard-rails to life and involved themselves in every way — Jean was both his teacher and his Scouts leader for two years of elementary school.

Lise was determined that Seb's love interest pass muster. By the end of the evening, she and Aruna were bonded over shared outlooks and love of Seb.

Adam had met Meena only a month earlier at a charity speed-dating event she and Aruna had organized. Over the years, the sisters had raised more than $30,000 for various charities on the premise that love conquers all. And it did: their speed-dating events eventually became the stuff of legend, resulting in four marriages, several partnerships, and 10 babies.

When baby-faced Adam walked in that particular night, a wag-gish friend of Meena's took one look at him and drolly asked if Meena thought he was old enough to be there. He was very young looking, Meena thought, but that was pretty much it. When Adam — quite smitten — called her a few days later, she was charmed by his person-ality. After five dates in which it became clear even to Meena's friends that they were serious, she decided it was time for the "double date test" with Aruna and Seb.

Absinthe is one of those restaurants everyone in Ottawa ends up at eventually, especially on date night. Located in the city's hipster-central Wellington West Village, it has cool bred into its location. Plus, aside from the delicious, coronary-inducing French dishes drowning in bacon, cream, and confit, it offers a mind-numbing array of absinthe. The green fairy, as it's called, is the original social lubricant, though it is no longer brewed in its addictive form.

Drinks were ordered, menus perused. Meena and Aruna chatted and laughed confidently, secretly side-eyeing Adam and Seb.

For the first hour, the signs were not good. As affable as Adam was, as charming as Seb appeared to be, the tension was palpable.

To Seb, Adam was little more than a cheap braggart of a salesman punching above his weight. The more Adam talked about his success in business, the less Seb liked him. Meena and Aruna shifted nervously in their chairs. These two women clearly liked a certain type of man, but could men of that type like each other?

And then the green fairy intervened.

"By the end of dinner, a little absinthe later," Adam recalls, "we realized we were a lot alike."

Both men were 26 years old. Both were serial entrepreneurs. While Seb worked his way through EDC and BDC, and made real estate investments, Adam was a bright light in the media space. He had co-created Ottawa's premier online political newspaper, *iPolitics*, which was sold to the *Toronto Star* in 2019. He was well known and well liked in political circles, having worked as the Liberal Party of Canada's national director of the federal commissions. And now, he had his own media consulting company, earning six figures.

Not only were they a lot alike in the ways that mattered to them, they liked each other's energy and world view. Although it took weeks, even months, for them to truly find common ground, and a few years to build the implicit trust they'd need to go into business together three years later, the seeds were sown that night at Absinthe.

They came from completely different backgrounds — Seb is the only child of Franco-Ontarians and Adam is the eldest son of West Coast family, his parents divorcing when he was 16 — but it was the quality of their minds, and their willingness to vault into bigger dreams off each other's ideas, that drew them together. It's unlikely Meena and Aruna gleefully rubbed their hands together that night, but they undoubtedly shared a delighted glance.

For the next few years, the men grew closer, bonding over ideas and whisky. Combined holidays would be planned and taken; meals would be enjoyed over bottles of wine. Eventually, Adam and Meena married in September 2011 and had their firstborn, Iyla, in 2013. Seb and Aruna married in May 2013, with Lise telling the wedding party, as her father-in-law had done for her years earlier, that with Aruna, "Now I have my daughter." Life unfolded as it should.

For two weeks straight, Max's electrifying words at the Canada Day cottage weekend buzzed around in Seb's head. "It's like no one wants to be a millionaire in this country." But Seb did. And maybe he could convince Adam to think about marijuana, too.

Over the years, the two future brothers-in-law had spent countless hours talking business ideas. Adam wanted to do high-end everything. Seb was always looking at the bottom line. One by one, they eliminated possibilities. Not all of their ideas were serious, much less winners.

Pushed along by Scotch-fuelled nights, they'd shoot the shit and Seb — a firm believer in keeping business diaries — would note down the ideas. Yoga Pub was to be the happy intersection between yoga, beer, and babes. The Wet Desk would be a temperature-controlled water chair you sat in that was cold enough to force your body to burn fat and shed kilos as you worked. There was Expedia for financing and Tupperware delivery for lazy bachelors. Clean containers would arrive by mail every week and the dirty ones sent back.

But this time, Seb knew the idea was a winner.

On a hot and sultry night in early July, the couples and their friends gathered for dinner at a friend's small fifth-floor apartment in downtown Ottawa. After dinner, the couple chatted with Aruna while Meena tended to Iyla. Seb asked Adam to step out onto the balcony for a word. Adam instantly felt a sheen of sweat on his face as a result of the sticky breeze. "Goddamn humidity," he muttered. The dry heat of his native Kamloops was so much more manageable. But he was intrigued by Seb's barely contained excitement. As a marketing guru, Adam loves the setup, the build up to the pitch. But this was Seb, so screw the preamble. Seb started right in.

"Listen, I figured out what we'll do in business together. We're going to grow marijuana."

In a matter of seconds, Adam's face ran through all the emotions: "Marijuana? Is he fucking kidding me? Uh, wait, this is Seb. Seb doesn't kid about money. But mari — fucking — juana? That's insane."

True, the two men had dreamed up some fanciful business ideas. It was a sort of game, but a serious one they had played even as children.

When Seb was 14, Lise opened her son's first stock-trading account in her name. He and his best friend, Will, invested their life savings — the princely sum of $200 each. They had wanted to invest in a payment processing company called IVI Checkmate Corp. but accidentally bought stocks in a similarly named but worthless chicken-feed company, which remains in Seb's stock portfolio to this day. By the time he was 15, Seb was reputedly one of Future Shop's top three warranty salesmen in Ontario. (Six months into the job, he quit, unhappy at what he saw as the lack of value to customers.)

Over in British Columbia, Adam's mother, Ann Ramage Kootstra, had always assured her son that he would be the best at anything he tried. Astronaut? Yes! Truck driver? Of course! (Once, he tested her by saying he wanted to be a hairdresser. She was all in.) His earliest business, suggested by his father, Gaston Miron, was hilarious: Adam encouraged his younger sister, Ashley, to stand in a lake. He collected leeches off her legs and sold them to passing fishermen.

Although his father never told him outright what to do, he would nudge young Adam toward DIY opportunities, like when the pair started Adam's Bike Shop out of their garage. A round of dot matrix–printed "spring special" flyers distributed at Adam's elementary school netted him $100 in business on the first day.

Soon after that adventure, the town's hospital asked Gaston to purchase two or three computers, but the nearest place to buy them was in Prince George, two and a half hours away. So instead, he set up AAA Miron Computer Services ("AAA" standing for Ann, Adam, and Ashley) and sourced parts from a Vancouver/Chinese supplier. He had Adam at his elbow every step of the way, even encouraging him to attend business meetings. As the small computer company grew, Gaston rented the back lunchroom of the local realty office and hired staff. Adam soon became interested in software and, before long, was building websites for their clients for between $2,000 and $3,000. At 16, he was a budding sovereign of software.

In short, neither Seb nor Adam were risk-averse. They were raised to be that way. Nevertheless, the business model had to be rock solid and not subject to emotional reactions. Now Seb was suggesting they jump into a seemingly sketchy, black market–ridden and untried industry that hadn't even learned to crawl, much less prove it had legs.

"Absolutely not. I'm not into pot — you know my feelings on that when it comes to family. Not interested."

As a 14-year-old, Adam had moved from Alberta to the tiny village of McBride in the mountains of British Columbia (population 586). That summer, during a sleepover with a friend in the backyard, he tried his first joint. It was the classic age to try something like weed: old enough to experiment, but young enough to still think sleepovers were pretty cool.

Even so, he was nonplussed when his friend pulled out a clear cassette tape and tugged out some dried bud to roll. "Wanna smoke some weed?"

It seemed so illicit, so dangerous, yet there he was casually handling drugs — illegal drugs! — like they were lawn clippings. Adam thought about everything he'd heard from kids around town about people getting the munchies, giggling endlessly, some even going a bit crazy. Watching his friend carefully and inexpertly roll the joint, he couldn't imagine what dangers lurked in a little tuft of weed.

For the next hour, the boys chatted and laughed, letting the silence and warmth of the day blanket them as they waited for the THC to loft them away. And waited. And waited some more.

"I'd like to say it was the time of my life, but it wasn't. It was utterly underwhelming. Eventually, I rolled over and went to sleep, wondering what all the fuss was about," Adam recalls.

A few months later, emboldened by his newly acquired sense of cool and puddle-deep well of drug culture insight, he got in touch with a kid he knew sold pot. In his head, the scenario would play out like any Hollywood film. They'd meet behind a dumpster, exchange brief, knowing glances, and almost imperceptibly, the money, before going their separate ways.

To say that it was conspicuous for a slightly older teen to meet a baby-faced 15-year-old behind a dumpster in a town that looked like it had been lifted from the set of *Heidi* is underselling the whole thing. Looking back, anywhere else would have made more sense: a quiet nook at the public library, a football field, even Adam's bedroom. Their body language was so obvious, they might as well have held up signs that read "Drug Deal Occurring Right Here."

This time, using the older kid's advice to exhale the smoke into a balloon if he wanted to share it with a friend, Adam did get high. Very high. Like a teenager deciding a mickey of vodka would be a good first drink, it was too much. And it was terrifying enough to scare him off weed for a long time.

"Definitely not," Adam told Seb again, shaking his head. "Not interested."

Out on that hot balcony, the rest of the dinner party still inside, Seb was undeterred. He'd expected resistance. Relished it, even. Nothing like a great argument backed with irresistible bottom lines to get the salesman in him going. And he'd done his homework. He'd looked at what was happening in the industry, how much competition for licences there was on the table, and how many of those potential competitors would fail before they'd ever planted a seed. He'd considered funding models from every angle. The idea had been swirling around in his head ever since that night at the cottage and he was vibrating with excitement.

He put his glass down on the balcony table and leaned confidently on the railing. "No, listen to me, Adam. I've done the projections. This will work. It's perfect. We don't need a lot to get started, believe me. And we could be a family-owned, $20 million company within 20 years."

Adam's eyes widened. He liked the sound of that. A lot. One thing he and Seb had in common other than fabulous life partners was a driving ambition to be wealthy, born from childhoods that were not always the textbook Canadian dream. And so, as with the conversation at the cottage, marijuana swept the two friends into a state of entrepreneurial bliss.

Adam was naturally hesitant about the idea — the anticipated reaction by their shared South Indian mother-in-law momentarily sent a shiver down his back — but when Seb asked Adam to sit down with him a few days later to go through the proposal carefully, Adam promised to do so with an open mind.

Of course, the whole thing had to make it past Meena first. Pushing the stroller on the walk back to their house after the party that night, Adam broadly sketched out Seb's idea. He was hesitant. After all, his younger sister was living with a guy who was growing pot plants in their apartment, which made him equal parts nervous and angry.

"It sounds crazy. I mean, he said it is legal, commercialized production. I know there'd be a demand for it, but it's weed! How the hell do you market that anyway?"

Even as Adam enumerated his objections, his rational mind quietly asserted a few facts. Adam trusted Seb. Trusted his business nose. As BDC's senior account manager, Seb had assessed more than three hundred businesses in Ottawa and Calgary, putting them to the test before he would authorize a loan. He had a good eye for opportunities. And what's more, when Seb said he had a business idea, people stopped what they were doing and listened.

Meena walked beside Adam in silence. At her job as a Canadian Air Transport Security Authority adviser, Meena was used to listening, assessing, analyzing, and untangling emotions from fact.

"It does sound crazy. But I think you should hear what he has to say. You know he's not shooting from the hip. Anyway, sleep on it."

8:30 A.M., JULY 17, 2013
ADAM'S HOUSE, CENTRETOWN
OTTAWA, ONTARIO

Two days later, Seb showed up at Adam's two-storey red-brick Victorian row house on a quiet, partly gentrified street. It was in a vibrant neighbourhood increasingly at odds with its history. The north side of the area was once part of a tough working-class neighbourhood called Lebreton Flats. Now home to the Canadian War Museum and modern high-rise condos of dubious beauty, Lebreton Flats was, until it was torn down in the 1960s, a sprawling spiderweb of tenements, taverns, and corner stores populated by families working at the gritty, dangerous lumber mills and factories along the river. After the Great Fire of 1900 levelled the area, the lumber barons rebuilt their mansions along the adjacent escarpment, while some workers relocated a few blocks to the south in what, from 1911, was an ad-hoc Chinatown, courtesy of a few hundred Chinese immigrants. Chinatown remains — after nearly disappearing in the 1940s, it grew and became its own Business Improvement Area in 1989 — but the hardscrabble workers have long gone. They have been replaced by hipsters with ironic facial hair and young urban families.

Seb took the front steps two at a time, knocked on the front door, and then let himself in. He had come ready for battle, armed with spreadsheets, ideas, and a hell of a lot of enthusiasm.

"Let's do this in the basement. Quieter down there," said Adam. The baby, Iyla, was making her naptime objections known upstairs and her displeasure resonated throughout the house.

In a revisionist telling of the HEXO story, the basement office would be spacious, warm, and wood-panelled. A fireplace stocked with fragrant cedar and applewood would burn brightly between two leather wing chairs and elbow tables set out for discreet lamps and cut-crystal glasses of Scotch: the good stuff, not the safety bottle. A mahogany desk would be nearby, tidy and ready to do gentlemanly work. Because when you dream of wealth, that's where it's made.

In truth, the stairs to the basement office were narrow, uneven, and in fact downright treacherous. Its low-hanging ceiling had been the cause of so many barked foreheads and shouted expletives that the words "Watch your head at the bottom!" would come out of Adam's mouth more often than "Help yourself to a soda in the bar fridge." As an office, it was more of a corner of the basement on its way to somewhere else, like the furnace room or a storage space crammed with university-era furniture too ugly to use, but too marked by memory to wantonly discard. Stark white paint and a single clerestory window did their best to brighten the space, which was so narrow that one long IKEA desk was all that could be used to support computer monitors, laptops, and teetering piles of books on business and marketing.

It was just 176 square feet. But considering what was about to happen, it might as well have been a boardroom on Bay Street.

"Here, grab a seat." Adam pulled out two chairs from the desk and looked intently at Seb. He was excited to hear the pitch, the real pitch. After giving the matter some thought, he'd come to the conclusion that if Seb was sure, he could be convinced, too.

Seb pulled up a spreadsheet on his computer. He had done a lot of research and given the project hours of thought. Even at first glance,

Adam could tell it was a business. A real business. Seb had almost finished a master's in quantitative finance and had an MBA specializing in finance. He had forecast everything, starting with a 2,000-square-foot micro-cultivation site, funded by $250,000 in start-up money. Neither had that kind of money stashed in a sock under the mattress, but it could be found if they tried.

At the time, Seb was living off his real estate investments, some of which could be liquidated or remortgaged. Adam had stepped away from the operational side of *iPolitics* and was running his own media consultancy. He had equity in other digital properties that were becoming valuable. Meena and Aruna both had well-paying government jobs to support them, at least for now. And, if they put together this proposal compellingly enough, they could raise money organically, through family and friends.

Two hours later, they were still talking. And Adam was already convinced. He had done his own research before Seb's visit and he now understood. This was it. This was the moment they would join forces and make millions.

But there was also something else happening at the basement meeting. Something perhaps more powerful than the plan itself.

When it comes to taking an idea out of a box and giving it oxygen and room to grow, you need the right people and the right timing to succeed. You need hard work. You might have a great idea, executed by the wrong people. Or the right people at the wrong time. But with the combination of the right people, the right time, and hard work, almost anything is possible.

"Almost" anything, because when it comes to working with people you are related to, or even like enough to call a friend, trust becomes as much a currency for success as using individual skill sets to their best advantage.

But trust can be deceptive in business. It often happens with goodwill but for the wrong reasons. Went to the same school as your business partner? Lived in the same neighbourhood as kids? Laugh at the same jokes, enjoy the same movies, and have a similar appetite for risk? Humans inherently gravitate to those like us, through unconscious bias. And, although same thinking likely developed as an early survival method, it's probably not a great idea when it comes to making money.

A 2012 Harvard University study looking at friends and family in business together found that when partners are too similar, they often fail. Two investors who earned their undergraduate degrees from the same institution were 20 percent more likely than those who attended different universities to partner in business, but 22 percent less successful at it. Why? People with similar backgrounds who like each other and tend to think alike also agree with each other, rather than challenge ideas, identify potential hazards, and risk upsetting a friendship. In other words, difference is good, but even so, one person's bumps have to fit the other's grooves.

So when complementary skills are bound by trust, juggernauts can happen. Microsoft was founded by childhood friends Bill Gates and Paul Allen. Ben & Jerry's became a household name in the late 1970s after Ben Cohen and Jerry Greenfield — who met in grade 7 gym class — took a $5 correspondence course on how to make ice cream. In 2000, they sold the company for US$326 million. Whole Foods was started when friends John Mackey and Renee Lawson Hardy opened a natural food store in Texas with US$45,000 they managed to cobble together.

In many ways, Adam and Seb were that perfect combination of same but different, brought together by family and shared ambitions but with completely different skill sets. Where Seb speaks in numbers, Adam understands people. Where Adam inherently gets the value of ephemeral notions around brand, Seb is watching its ROI. They complement each other and, more importantly, value the expertise each other brings. The differences are not so much papered over as respected and given space.

Adam didn't fully understand how powerful that aspect of their relationship would be until that day in the basement.

"Adam, I need someone who can sell this, put a company together. I need you. We'll split the burden, the workload. Doing it together mitigates the perceived risk."

Adam was one part excited, one part taken aback. More than thrilled by the opportunity, he was moved by Seb's show of faith. Later that night, talking over the pitch with Meena, Adam reflected on the moment. "I genuinely believe that is one of the sincerest ways anyone has told me what they thought of me. To say they want you to be part of their great idea and give you half? It's an incredible thing."

The next day, Seb and Adam Inc. were in business.

Billion Dollar Lesson

"When you're working with family, you have to remember that, first and foremost, you're business partners before anything else. There are ups and downs. Individuals will falter, but to know that your partner is going to grab you, that you're not the one faltering when your partner falls, that's key. You make sure you grab your partner, and you get him back on that mountain again, because you'll need him to have a hand to reach for when you fall. Give him that benefit of the doubt and put the energy in when the other partner can't achieve the goal. It's not about 50/50 all the time. The effort level will vary during a relationship. It's natural and normal. Every day, that mountain that looked big before doesn't look as big now because you know you have a top rope and how to tie it." **— Seb**

Quickly settling on the basement as a headquarters — it was also two blocks from Adam's favourite watering hole, Pubwells — they started making lists and figuring out the critical path. Problem was, where do you actually start a pot company? The enormity of what they were about to do hit them for a moment. Neither had a green thumb or any agricultural experience, but they knew one thing: they would figure it out.

And they realized one other thing. This was a race against the clock. The wheels within Health Canada's licensing branch may have been turning at a barely perceptible pace, but the number of companies applying to become licensed producers was accelerating. And although there were only six LPs at the time, more licences were inevitable. And that meant more competition. They had to hit the ground at a clip, and they had to start now.

Adam and Seb obtained a copy of the MMPR — the Marihuana for Medical Purposes Regulations — two hundred pages defining all the rules, plus the massive application to grow medical cannabis. There would be others, later, like a licence to store and a licence to sell. It was intimidating, to say the least. But they did what would later become their classic business approach to any problem: pull it apart, get it to a granular level, split the work, make a to-do list, and dive in.

Working around the clock, they researched, cross-referenced, and wrote. Other hopeful LPs were no doubt busily hiring firms who made it their business to understand the minutiae of things like Good Manufacturing Practice in Cleaning and Sanitation (GMP cleaning), but Seb and Adam wrote the first arduous draft of the Standard Operating Procedures themselves.

Within a gruelling two weeks, they were as done as they could be. They sent in the 150 pages to Health Canada and waited. In the meantime, they were running at top speed on the hundred other things they would need to do, think about, or act upon once the licence was granted. Financing, share structures, land acquisition, buildings, employees, brand development, strains, marketing, publicity. Like nesting dolls, every task they unpacked resulted in secondary and tertiary lists of action items, all needing to be done right that second. Hours blended into days, leaving them exhausted yet still palpably excited because this, at last, was a vision, a direction with the kind of exuberant possibility they'd been waiting for.

Two weeks later, Health Canada wrote back. More information was required. Seb and Adam thumbed through 12 pages of questions, each more technical or involved than the last. If their hearts sank, they didn't show it, at least not to each other.

Over the previous two weeks of non-stop conversation and strategizing, they had come to dimly realize that, together, they had something unique. More than just two related entrepreneurs, they were driven. They were smart. They trusted each other's opinions and skills. They could take on the world. Setbacks? Just another mountain to climb up, climb around, or blow up.

Once again, they locked themselves in Adam's basement and worked around the clock for 36 hours to answer every question. They sent in the paperwork. Health Canada sent back another 10 pages of queries, which were promptly answered. Then another nine pages arrived. More answers were returned. When, a few weeks later, they received only five pages of questions, they celebrated with beer and pizza. Here, then, was progress. Considering they were working in a basement in downtown Ottawa, some of the details required creative thinking. Did they have SSOPs (Sanitation Standard Operating Procedures) for Room D, Building 2?

Adam laughs now, but at the time, the stress was real. "Room D didn't exist. Building 2 didn't exist. We didn't own land or even know what a SSOP was. But they wanted to know how we would clean this room, how would we wipe the counters, with which products, and for how long. It was so unfathomable."

Six weeks after deciding they'd get into the marijuana business, they had a thick orange binder with their completed application. There were a few other pieces to wrap up, but it was done, and just in time. The two families were due to leave on a joint holiday, to visit the in-laws and attend a family wedding in Coimbatore, a South Indian textiles city of 1 million. In the rush to finish the application, the trip became a bit of an afterthought, but now they were looking forward to it, mostly because they could continue to work and plan while travelling. It was just the kind of lifestyle Adam had always dreamed of having. Pop the baby in the backpack, move from one awesome location to another, eat fine food, and gather passport stamps along the way. There was no money — at least not yet — but when it came, and it would, that's how he'd want to roll.

As Adam, Meena, and Iyla flew out of Ottawa, Seb finalized the application to become an LP. It was momentous: they would become the 90th company to apply for a licence in Canada's shiny new medical cannabis industry. If there was a stepping-off point into the unknown, this was it. Seventy-two hours after Adam left, Seb carefully packaged up the binder, took a selfie, addressed the package, and walked to a Canada Post outlet in a convenience store on the corner of Bell Street and Gladstone Avenue.

He pulled out his phone and attached the photo to one of his notoriously brief and understated emails.

"Adam, application is mailed. See you in a few days."

He slid his phone back into his pocket, turned on his heel, and walked the few blocks home. He was already thinking ahead to what awaited around the corner.

But that's the trouble with anticipating the future in business. Like stepping into traffic, sometimes you can't see what's about to hit you until it's too late.

CHAPTER 2

11:30 A.M., SEPTEMBER 2013
ARYA AMED BEACH RESORT
AMED BEACH, BALI, INDONESIA

Meena reclined on the crisp white hotel bedspread, air conditioning on "arctic blast." She was flipping through a magazine while the baby slept. Every now and then, Iyla would make sweet little snuffling, grunting noises, followed by a sigh. For a six-month-old, she was a pretty good traveller. Meena smirked to herself. It helped that the kid was so damn cute — part Rajulu, mostly mini-Miron. Every time she peeped those big, brown eyes at people, they practically shoved each other out of the way trying to elicit a gummy smile from her. Total future princess, Meena thought. As it should be.

During the previous four weeks in India, Iyla had been the centre of her own travelling universe, populated by her doting Indian grandmother, Reva, as well as her aunties, uncles, and extended family. And that was a good thing, considering how much time Adam and Seb had spent together, talking, planning, and scheming about what they would do once their application to become an LP was approved. Once Seb and Aruna showed up in Coimbatore, the guys basically disappeared into their own world. It's not that they were intentionally inattentive or not present, they were just being Adam and Seb.

Plus, a conversation took place on Seb's first day in India that made it all okay.

Indian weddings are not quick afternoon events in which the "I do's" occur 10 minutes before the end of the ceremony. Rather, they are life celebrations incorporating three days of feasting, dancing, blessings, and parties, highlighted by everything from a groom on a white horse and a parade of dhol drumming to a women's day of mehndi, dizzyingly intricate henna patterns drawn on hands and feet. There was plenty to do, plenty to eat, plenty of family to see. The groom's father had managed to borrow a wealthy colleague's luxurious three-bedroom apartment. The well-appointed condo, with its beautiful art and grand rooms, was big enough to house both couples, the baby, and Grandma Reva, who had travelled from her home in Edmonton.

The morning after everyone flew in, Reva and Seb both awoke early, around 7 a.m., bleary-eyed and restless from travel. They liked each other and, over the years, had fallen into a comfortable relationship punctuated by long, interesting conversations. Seb was a dynamic straight shooter, and Reva admired her son-in-law for it. That morning, the topic turned to Seb's latest business venture. As he enthusiastically discussed the plans he and Adam had come up with, Reva's face crumpled first with anxiety, then into tears. Taking risks in business was one thing, but marijuana? Wasn't it illegal? And run by gangs?

"I wanted you and Adam to be as close as brothers," she wailed, "but I never saw it like this!"

Seb pressed on. If he needed anyone's blessing, it was that of this strong, intelligent matriarch who'd raised her equally independent daughters on her own. He quickly went through an abbreviated version of the pitch he'd given Adam a few months earlier, adding that both men were putting in $100,000, and that Rajan Uncle — her trusted and successful brother-in-law, Rajan Govindarajan — was already investing some of his wealth earned as a valve manufacturer. Rajan too? By then, Reva's tears had dried, her fears allayed. She listened intently to Seb, asked a few questions, and listened some more.

"Okay," she finally said. "This sounds like a good idea. I want to invest. If you succeed, you get an inheritance. If you fail," she said, half sternly, "you get a mother-in-law living with you." Seb's eyebrows shot up, then he grinned in delight. Their own mother-in-law, an investor! The conversation had gone full circle before anyone had even had breakfast.

With Reva's blessing, Adam and Seb were able to grab what time they could from the wedding and family visits to focus on getting the company on its feet. For the moment, it was okay just with the two of them — three if you counted Seb's dad, Jean, back in Canada volunteering to translate documents into French — but if this was going to work, they'd need staff. They needed a place. And they needed a name.

And so, they broke it all down in between wedding festivities, battling time zone challenges, the spotty internet, and the limited charms of a tablet. Still, they managed to find a small HR firm in Ottawa, discussed what they wanted for company culture, wrote and rewrote their mandate, and did video meetings in the middle of the night with people back in Ottawa. It wasn't ideal. They were used to working in their narrow slice of a basement, with their roomy computer screens and whiteboard. But Adam and Seb made it work.

Flicking the magazine shut, Meena flopped onto her back. When Iyla woke up, they could head down to the restaurant for lunch and, later, a dip in the cooling pool. Or maybe the beach. Amed is a series of seven seaside fishing villages on the northeast side of Bali, strung together by that famous black volcanic sand. Walking along the shore, she'd spotted countless jukung, the traditional outrigger boats. And plenty of newlyweds and divers, too, all eager to explore the offshore wreck of the USAT *Liberty* cargo ship torpedoed in 1942, or snorkel the reefs, looking for seahorses, manta rays, and coral. It was an interesting cross between modern tourism and traditional fishing village life — the locals got phone lines only in 2003.

But, oh Lord, it was humid. And hot. Meena rolled over and peered at Adam on the balcony, his forehead and face glistening in the 35°C heat. He was talking to Seb in Canada by video call outside on the balcony, so he wouldn't wake Iyla. Meena sat up to watch him more closely. When Adam is listening — really listening — he has the intense gaze of a hypnotist, the focus in his brown eyes piercing. He had that look now, despite the heat and humidity from the adjacent jungle.

"Fuuuuuck, this is hot." Adam mopped his brow to avoid the sting of sweat in his eyes. He could tell he was bright red. Heat was definitely not his friend. But that wasn't the only reason for his flush. He looked back at Seb, his sweat-free head and shoulders appearing on the tablet's screen. Ottawa was not much better. The city was experiencing an end-of-summer heat wave, with most days hitting 27°C. At least Seb was inside an air-conditioned room for their regular check-in meeting.

"Adam. I've been working on this whole thing and did some remodelling. We need to think bigger. Much, much bigger. So we are going to need more money. Like, $450,000. Can you do half?"

Whoo-hoo, okay, Adam thought. That's a serious change of plan. He glanced briefly over at Meena, who was reclining again. "Look," Seb was saying, "I'll break it down for you. I've done all the research . . ."

A property, staff, infrastructure, lights, tables, lawyers. And that was just to start. While Adam was still on holiday, Seb had reviewed and reworked the business plan to reflect a 24-month profit-loss scenario based on an 8,000-square-foot growing facility. Sure, they'd already incorporated, but Seb's line of credit had just $35,000. It was the only ready cash they could get their hands on, at least for the moment. They were both working 12-hour days, even on holiday, but they weren't generating any income. Seb knew his plan was solid, but he needed Adam's buy-in.

Adam wiped his forehead again. "Okay, let's do it."

"Good. You sure? This is more than we bargained for, but the good news is we'll be a $20 million company in 10 years, not 20. And we'll still own the whole thing."

"Let's do it. I'm in. No question."

And there really wasn't any question. Even though the new plan meant they'd have to double the investment, Adam felt good saying yes out loud. He trusted Seb implicitly and liked that he, Adam, could broach tough conversations with him, confident in Seb's receptivity. In truth, it would be the first of countless talks Seb would start by saying, "Adam, there's been a change of plans," followed by "but the objective remains the same; this is how we'll do it, and this is what it'll cost." And just as many times, Adam would listen and immediately respond with, "Okay, let's do it." As time went on, events and even some calamities would put that mutual trust to the test, but it would always remain intact.

Finishing the call, Adam slowly peeled his thighs off the plastic chair, stood up, and slid open the balcony door. The cooler air was a welcome relief that instantly triggered gooseflesh. He stepped inside and half whispered to Meena.

"Just spoke to Seb. Change of plans. We'll have to invest more. A lot more. But it'll mean we'll be richer quicker."

Meena looked steadily into Adam's eyes.

"Okaaaay."

There was a question in the acceptance, but not enough of one to bother uttering aloud. Adam would explain. She would listen. She trusted Adam.

NOVEMBER 2013
ADAM'S BASEMENT OFFICE, CENTRETOWN
OTTAWA, ONTARIO

Canadian Medical Services.

It was bland. It said nothing, really, about anything. What kind of medical . . . catheters and IV units? Which sort of services? Personal care workers helping the immobile and elderly? As the brand architect, Adam had assured Seb it was the perfect name for a medical marijuana company, because although more and more Canadians were realizing they could get reliable and safe access to medical cannabis under the new legislation, not everyone was behind the idea.

Outliers and early adopters like Adam and Seb could imagine where the money trail would lead and were, in fact, paving that trail for others to follow. But everyone from the banking industry on down were lockstep with imagining medical marijuana companies to be little more than an excuse for stoners and couch surfers to legitimize being baked for a living. Never mind that entry into the industry required an enormous amount of money. Never mind that it demanded extensive business experience. Never mind that hard work had to happen. Never mind all that. It's just what people wanted to think.

Canadian Medical Services, Adam reasoned, sounded like the antithesis of stoner culture. Here was something bland, yes, but it positioned the company as medical, perhaps even vaguely pharmaceutical. And if the industry ended up doing business in the conservatively minded United States, a reassuringly stalwart name like that would be necessary.

But even before the notion of Canadian Medical Services could harden onto letterhead, two things happened that forced them to reset their approach. The first proved to be near fatal. The second was more of a stumble forward.

Before they'd left for India, Seb and Adam had fretted over a complete lack of feedback from Health Canada. They were waiting for a response on a submission application, and while the government wasn't normally a chatty correspondent, the information they were waiting for was time sensitive. What's more, they were on the hunt for a farm or other property to buy or lease in anticipation of being awarded a production licence. Yet none of the realtors or property managers was getting back to them. In fact, the more they thought about it, the stranger it seemed. Complete radio silence by email? How was that even possible? They'd signed up with an incredibly secure email service out of the United States to avoid communication failures of this kind, yet contacts were now phoning them to report bouncing emails. What the hell was going on?

The Edward Snowden controversy was going on. Headlines around the world were trumpeting the news that the former CIA employee had copied and leaked classified information from the National Security Agency. His public and embarrassing overshare that the Americans had top secret and very much non-consensual global surveillance programs had turned the intelligence world into a dumpster fire.

In the aftermath, there was even more scrutiny and questions about what governments were gleaning through everything from email servers to laptop computer video cameras. Suddenly, companies just minding their own business were being watched. One of those called into question was the highly secure American email service that Adam and Seb had been using. In a note to customers, the CEO explained that the government had ordered him to hand over all their customers' emails and data and had issued a gag order barring him from speaking about it. No doubt with Snowden's grand gesture in mind, he wrote to say that rather than hand over a client's information to any government and not tell them about it, he'd rather torpedo it and go to jail. So that's exactly what the CEO did.

Seb and Adam read the CEO's note. And then read it again. It was all gone. All their emails. They had backed up old emails, but anything new, any news from Health Canada, was gone. While they could recreate some email trails, the most recent correspondence about their work over the past few months had disappeared into an abyss. It was almost as if Canadian Medical Services had never existed. They'd have to gather all that information again from scratch.

And, according to an accountant they consulted about incorporating after they returned from India, it never would. The name is too vague, he said. There's no IP protection. It's like Acme Corporation in *Road Runner*, he sniffed. Perfect for Wile E. Coyote, but not for real life.

That day, Seb and Adam got up and stood in front of their basement office whiteboard, markers poised. In the face of chaos, they loved a good chart, along with a solid list, and maybe a few breakout boxes in different colours. Watching them talk through problems, skipping ahead and then circling back to an earlier half-thought is a master class in verbal and non-verbal communication between family in business. Facing a problem, they dispense with recrimination or hand-wringing and get down to work. True, this was a disaster, but even the wreckage caused by a tsunami can be put to right with enough effort.

Billion Dollar Lesson

"There is enormous value in finding the right partner, both at home and in business. I've always been supported positively by my wife at home, but business is also about having a complementary skill set with your partner. Sometimes, I stumble and Adam is there to keep me from falling down. You don't need the same skill sets, but you do need to fit together seamlessly." — **Seb**

For the next few days, Adam thought about company names. If Canadian Medical Services was too meh, he'd brand the shit out of this thing. He considered what the other LPs were doing. Tweed — their neighbours over in Smiths Falls — had taken a clever play-on-words approach. Others were treading the well-worn and far more predictable path of using West Coast trigger words, like "organic" and "natural." Each offered their own style, but when it came right down to it, those brands were all so close in tone, they were setting themselves up to compete for the same customers.

But not this company. Health Canada's cannabis rules on advertising, marketing, and basically letting potential customers know the details of what you were selling before they bought it were so restrictive it was like offering someone a white box wrapped in a ribbon and saying, "Trust me, this is good. I can't tell you what it is, but you need it. And it's worth the money."

Huh, Adam thought. White box, eh? Having grown up without a lot of money, he appreciated beautiful things. He loved not only luxury but the superb branding that came with it. Exquisite branding is a red sole that sells a pair of high heels that hurt as much as any other. Smart branding in an icon is what convinces consumers to buy one smartphone over another, though they are identical in any way that matters. What he wanted, he reasoned, was beautiful branding. He wanted this company to be the Chanel of marijuana. Artisanal. Hand-crafted. High-end and exclusive. It's where he wanted to be in life.

If you want to make money, you need to look like money.

After working for a few hours in the basement that day, Seb and Adam emerged just before lunch, hoping a change of scene and a bite to eat would spark creativity in coming up with a new name for their venture.

Adam threw together his favourite, a thick, tinned ham and mayo sandwich, paired with a diet cola. So salty, so sweet, so good. "Okay," he said, taking a bite, "here's what I'm thinking . . ."

He outlined the key words he had in mind, segueing into what he saw as the place in the market where no LP existed: luxury. If all the other LPs were aiming themselves at the middle and low-end of the market when it came to look, feel, and pricing, they would go high-end. Sure, it was marijuana, but it would be the best damn weed anyone had ever consumed. And it would come packaged so beautifully, it would immediately appeal to the demographic he was after.

For the next few hours, they tossed around words and concepts. Adam had grabbed a notepad and was making lists, charting the key ideas and noting things that appealed the most. One word that consistently came up was "apothecary." It was derived from the ancient Greek word for pharmacist, so it had an established, historical feel. And because an apothecary makes and sells drugs, it also denoted an old-fashioned craftsmanship he really liked. Still, it wasn't enough. It needed to be a compound word, even a made-up word that would suggest artisanal growing without actually saying it. Finally, one of them suggested "hydro" — another ancient Greek word — as in hydroponics. Not that this company would ever use hydroponics, but Adam liked the association with water and the science of cultivation.

But how could they stitch it together? Adam industriously scribbled down names and letters, but nothing seemed quite right. Finally, Seb said the two words together. "Hydro apothecary." Adam took a swig of his diet cola. That wasn't it, he thought. He said it out loud, to check the mouthfeel, so to speak. Nope, too clunky.

Seb tried again. "What about if we put 'hydro' and 'apothecary' together, like 'hydropothecary'? That sounds okay."

Seb grabbed his phone and started texting. "Let's see what Max thinks."

Max pinged back immediately. "Love it."

Good. It would do, thought Adam. It might mean educating people on how to say it easily, but once it stuck, it had the potential to be as memorable as Adidas and L'Oréal.

It was settled. Their company had a name. They were the Hydropothecary. Soon after, they'd become the Hydropothecary Corporation so that if they ever went public, the ticker would be, appropriately, THC.

A made-up name without a logo is just a quirky word, so Adam quickly found a local branding agency to do initial discovery and development. The brief was clear: the brand had to be visually strong, clean, and architectural. It had to be regal, classic, and timeless. Oh, and it had to look medical.

One evening a few weeks later, and Seb walked the few blocks from Adam's house to the second-floor branding agency office over an all-you-can-eat sushi restaurant in Chinatown. Upstairs, the walls were covered with funky art; Drake was playing on the stereo. The agency team presented their concept, a beautiful and arresting image of an imperial Indian elephant, decked out in traditional jewelled headgear. Adam loved it. It was exactly what he wanted the brand to be: noble, established, monied. But, on the other hand, he also wanted something clean, simple, and immediately recognizable to anyone who could be influenced into brand loyalty. He could imagine the "H" of Hydropothecary as a main design element, like the "H" of hospitals signs. A stylized marijuana flower could be incorporated, but so subtly you'd have to know what you were looking at. And the whole thing — the big, black "H" with the cannabis bud as the crossbar — could be stamped on plain white boxes, tied with a broad, black satin ribbon. They could have Hydropothecary-branded clothing, with the "H" as recognizable as the interlinked "C"s on every Chanel clutch. Any customer receiving their order would be under no misapprehension that they were getting the best product on the market. But that would come, he thought. First, they needed to nail this down.

Over the next few days, the Hydropothecary logo took shape. A strong black serif "H" with a stylized dried cannabis flower interwoven where the crossbar would normally be. It was elegant. It was classic. Was it Coco-worthy? Most definitely. Now they just had to do the paperwork.

10 A.M., OCTOBER 28, 2013
ADAM'S BASEMENT OFFICE, CENTRETOWN
OTTAWA, ONTARIO

Adam and Seb sat side by side at the basement office's long white desk, like high school kids who'd been dating for three months and still insisted on sitting beside each other in the cafeteria. They needed to lawyer up. Now that they'd decided to essentially liquidate their lives to go forward with their bigger plans — Adam had taken investment capital from his other business interests to pay his bills while Meena was on maternity leave; Seb was keeping them afloat with the line of credit — they needed to raise lots of money. To do that, they needed to have all the framework such an endeavour requires: a bank account, incorporation, a charter, trademark, and a subscription agreement, among other things. They also needed to move very quickly if they were going to attract investment capital to establish their business.

Yet, somewhere between starting their phone calls to law firms with "We are forming a medical marijuana company" and the arrogant/bored/harried voice on the other end responding with, "Yeah, we're a busy firm; it'll take three to five weeks to make that happen," they were getting nowhere. Surely there had to be a damn lawyer in Ottawa who wasn't so busy they couldn't take on a new client with a short time frame? Jesus, it was frustrating. As Adam typed "corporate lawyers" into the search engine, Seb called and talked. They were impatient in the way young men with full heads of steam often are. And they weren't going to wait for some asshat in a mediocre suit and bad shoes to decide they had time to help them out.

"Here, Seb, try this one." Adam read out the number for a law office off O'Connor Street in downtown Ottawa. It was for an external general counsel who worked with a lot of small and medium-sized businesses in a bunch of industries, one who had a first-class honours degree from Queen's University and a law degree from Western University. Seb dialled, then put the call on speakerphone.

"Hello. Karl* speaking." A man's voice answered. Adam looked at Seb and shrugged.

"Yeah, hi. My name is Adam Miron. I'm on speaker with my business partner, Sébastien St-Louis."

The voice on the end sounded distant, a bit distracted.

"Hello. What can I do for you gentlemen?"

Adam's voice dropped into the sotto voce he uses when imparting something that is either terribly important or he wants you to view it that way.

"We have a start-up, in the medical marijuana space. We need to raise $1 million to get things underway, and we need the usual documents to make that happen."

The voice — this Karl guy — sounded more interested now.

"Yup, makes perfect sense. Why don't you come by my office and we'll take it from there."

"Uh, yeah, one other thing. Every other law firm we've spoken with says this will take three to five weeks to get done. Time is of the essence in this industry, and we have to move much quicker than that. How soon can you get that paperwork ready?"

"Lemme see." A keyboard clicked in the background. "How's next Wednesday? If I don't sleep, I can do it by this Friday."

Adam grinned at Seb.

"Do you sleep often?" he asked. Beside him, Seb laughed quietly.

A few days later, the two men pulled up near Karl's offices in Seb's four-door Pontiac Grand Am. He loved that car. Growing up in the Outaouais, it was the coolest set of wheels any young Franco-Ontarian could ever desire. And he owned it in white, the best colour of all. It was racy and quick, but more stylish than expensive. Adam, on the other hand, drove a battered, gas-powered Japanese skateboard of a vehicle that beggared belief by somehow passing safety inspections. For someone who loves elegance and tailoring in his clothes, Adam had a mode of transportation that was utilitarian. For the next few years, every meeting they went to, every trip to the airport to pick up an investor, they went in the Grand Am.

Karl's office was unprepossessing, to say the least. Back then, he was a one-man show renting space in a low-rise corporate building near the courthouse district, populated by every kind of lawyer in every possible specialization. Still, who cared what his office was like? If he was qualified and could do what they needed done in the time frame they wanted it done in, he was their man.

Karl ushered Adam and Seb into a conference room furnished with a few chairs and a round, laminated table. They all sat down, and Seb and Adam started talking. They were like evangelists for the medical marijuana industry who had somehow found themselves door-knocking in Ottawa's Lawyerville.

Adam recounted the cottage story, described their vision and how they would be game changers. Seb added his financial insight, fully illustrated with charts and spreadsheets. Karl asked questions and listened. Bottom line, they said, was that the paperwork had to be done as expediently as possible.

Karl nodded. Sure, he could do that. In fact, he could do one better.

"Yeah, I can put this all together for you pretty quickly. Actually, I can have it all ready so you can start taking investor cheques next week."

Adam and Seb nodded. Happy nods. But Karl wasn't done.

"And the first cheque you'll bank is mine. Guys, I'm impressed. I'd like to invest $25,000 in your company."

Adam and Seb's grins got even wider, if that was possible. He was their first investor aside from friends and family. And it came to them so unexpectedly. They may have driven away in the Grand Am, but they were floating on air.

10 A.M., EARLY OCTOBER 2013
INVEST OTTAWA OFFICES, BAYVIEW ROAD
OTTAWA, ONTARIO

Mark Zekulin stood up from his desk and shook hands with Seb and Adam. At just 33, he was Tweed's new general counsel. That summer, he'd quit his job with an international trade company, spent four months networking, and by autumn, was having lunch with Tweed's then CEO, Bruce Linton. Shortly thereafter, he signed on as the newly formed company's fifth employee. (After the dramatic ouster of Linton from Canopy Growth Corp. in 2019, Zekulin briefly held the CEO title, from July to December 2019, before he, too, left the company.) But he was more than that. He was savvy and entrepreneurial and had the kind of debonair good looks that stood out, whether in a greenhouse or a Bay Street boardroom.

The get-together was nothing formal, just people in the same industry comparing notes. Although he was professionally reserved, Mark was open about how Tweed's application still hadn't been submitted to Health Canada. Rather, he said, the company had six executives working on the file, thinking through the whole process from the top down. Seb's eyebrows shot up. Really? Six executives to do what he and Adam had already achieved on their own? He was floored by the approach. When he and Adam climbed into the Grand Am, they were chuckling in disbelief.

"We couldn't get over ourselves that we were going to win. They hadn't even submitted their application and already had six-figure guys on the payroll," recalls Seb. "We left thinking we were so much better at saving money than they were and that we'd get our licence first."

That's what should have happened.

But the Hydropothecary story is full of should-haves that took a hard-right turn straight into a brick wall before setting off in a new direction. While Adam and Seb waited to hear from Health Canada, Tweed received its production licence — a month after the meeting with Mark, on November 18, 2013 — making it the first publicly traded and federally approved cannabis producer in North America. Seb and Adam were in utter disbelief when they heard the news, and then they grudgingly marvelled at the wisdom of Tweed's approach.

"We were thinking big but spending small. There's a responsible way to spend, but we were at the opposite end of that spectrum. When we eventually hired a real executive, we saw the difference they made and the value they brought. And from that point on, the rule was 'Get the right people, get the right team, and go with the top-down approach,'" Seb says. "We still say, 'Remember that time we underestimated Tweed?'"

Billion Dollar Lesson

"To succeed, you have to fail fast and empower individuals to proceed. And you have to focus. You want your team to take risks and fail. The failure is on all of us; the success is on all of us." — **Seb**

10 P.M., NOVEMBER 24, 2013
AD-HOC NIGHTCLUB IN A DISUSED WAREHOUSE
AMSTERDAM, THE NETHERLANDS

If they were going to get into the cannabis industry in a real way, Seb and Adam had to immerse themselves in the culture. And that meant going to the epicentre of canna culture in Europe, the Amsterdam Cannabis Cup. Less than a month after hiring a lawyer, Adam and Seb got on a plane across the Atlantic. They thought they knew what to expect, but Amsterdam over-delivered from the first night they arrived.

Seb and Adam could smell the party before they could see it. Pot smoke wafted through the air, streaming out of window cracks in a disused warehouse on one of Amsterdam's docks. Electronica reverberated throughout the whole area, punctuated with seizure-inducing flashes of colour and strobe lights. This was, after all, the opening night and everyone who was involved in the European marijuana industry was there: dreadlocked hippies, expert cultivators, cannabis accessory company executives, happy young consumers, weed celebrities, and media of every stripe.

Amsterdam had hosted the international event that had grown to sprawl across multiple venues ever since *High Times* magazine founder Steven Hager launched it in 1987. This was be the last year before it became the Amsterdam Unity Cup, and everyone was determined to go out in a blaze of smoke. Now that Hydropothecary had a name, a lawyer, and a logo, this was the place to start looking for people, ideas, and suppliers.

Adam tugged nervously at the button of his blazer. He and Seb had arrived in Amsterdam late that evening, laden with a suitcase full of "We're hiring" cards and Hydropothecary-branded printed materials. They'd dropped everything off at their rented loft in the city, where they planned to hold meetings and interviews. But before any of those took place, they would first mingle, dropping their cards on every available surface, and getting a bead on their targets.

Looking around the booming nightclub with its mishmash of counterculture savants, patchouli-scented armpits, and pot enthusiasts, Adam realized the blazer wasn't going to work. He darted a look at Seb, who lived in athleisure clothes and running shoes and didn't really give a shit what anyone thought of it. Adam scanned the crowd, looking for someone — anyone — in a blazer. Even a tailored vest or a tie would do. Nothing. He looked like a Young Liberal who stumbled into a 4/20 protest expecting a cocktail party fundraiser. He vowed to hit an H&M the next day and buy something more youthful, like a grey knit sweater with toggles. Maybe a brown vest of some type. Until then, he thought, he'd just have to try to blend in.

Deeply unhip clothing choices aside, he was there with Seb to figure things out. The Cannabis Cup was the highlight on the marijuana calendar. Part massive celebration, part awards night to honour the best seeds, hash, concentrates, bud, and coffee shop flowers, it was held in two locations, but pop-up parties and try-and-vote events were everywhere. And they were going to try it all. Following the crowd along the waterfront, past a french-fry stand and up to a third-floor space over a shawarma shop, they found themselves in a brightly lit, bubble-gum pink room dotted with metallic silver lounges and big screens playing a movie. They found a spot on one of the couches and sat stiffly, feeling more out of place than they'd thought possible. Before long, a parade of bikini girls came into the room with a 10-foot-long plastic volcano bag filled with smoke, which they passed around the crowd.

"It's legal," Seb shouted over the noise. "Let's give it a try."

He immediately questioned the decision when the guy ahead of them not only put his lips on the bag but his entire tongue as well. When the bag was passed to Seb, he wiped the plastic nozzle with a look of disgust, closed his eyes, and inhaled. Adam followed.

After so many years as friends and family, Seb and Adam had developed a certain style in social situations. Adam would sidle up to strangers, find common ground, and talk. If Seb knew the crowd, he would confidently stride in. Otherwise, he sat back, watching, then engaged when he felt the time was right. But that night, as the weed quickly took hold, those roles were reversed.

Seb was observing everything, talking at the speed of light and showing no signs of slowing down. Whatever that weed was — and they would vote on it later — he became Sébastien the Verbose and Erudite. Nothing escaped his notice, and everything was worthy of a remark. From his own haze, Adam could hear the non-stop commentary: Did you see what that girl was wearing? How many people do you think are here? I can't figure out that movie. Oh man, this smoothie is incredible! — and just wanted it to stop. Shhh, he whispered. Time was contracting and expanding, he could feel the blood pulsing in his veins, and even if someone were to pull the fire alarm, he felt too paralyzed to move. Shhh, he said again, this time vaguely batting a hand. Just fucking shhhhhh-hhhhhh. His brother-in-law was at 11 and he needed him at a 5. If this was jumping into cannabis culture with both feet, he thought, I'm taking one foot out.

For the rest of their two-day stay, they talked to people, listened, asked questions, and, more than anything, felt wildly out of place. They had come to Amsterdam expecting this . . . this crazy, weed-fuelled love-in . . . and while it was an education, they realized it wasn't their demographic. Neither knew enough about the cannabis culture to participate in it, and both respected the pioneers who'd established it too much to even try to mimic it.

If there was an a-ha moment on that trip, it was this: cannabis counterculture already had its own demigods, outliers, icons, and points of reference. What Hydropothecary wanted to do was remove the stigma associated with stoner culture and figure out how to sell medical marijuana to people who didn't fit in with it. They wanted to market their cannabis to people just like themselves.

Billion Dollar Lesson

"One of the great strengths of start-ups is their absolute belief that they have a great idea that will be a winner. You trust your gut instincts and the dining-room-table focus groups of friends and family. But if your market research stops there, so will your idea. Building a consumer brand means really getting granular about who you are building the brand for and why they need it." — **Adam**

9:30 A.M., DECEMBER 2013
BRIDGEHEAD COFFEEHOUSE, CENTRETOWN
OTTAWA, ONTARIO

Back in Ottawa and supported by their lawyer, the guys realized it was time to level up. Seb, a lifelong board and video-game enthusiast, had begun using the gamers' term for next-level when it came to the business. No matter what sacrifices they made or successes they had, there'd always be another level to attain. It was an infinite game, they realized, but every time you level up, your resources and tools become more interesting as the tasks become harder. They were playing a game with no end. And until now, they had been playing with certain abilities, tools, and knowledge. After the fog of Amsterdam, it became clear that they'd need more, much more, if they were going to get this company into the space it belonged.

That also meant entertaining serious investors. The first was Dr. Michael Munzar, a respected clinical researcher who'd served as medical director and vice-president for a number of medical and pharmaceutical companies. His pedigree was impressive. Seb's first meeting with him to discuss money was not. With Adam busy with his baby, Seb decided to meet with Michael and another man, who said he was a financial adviser. To grow pot, they had to have a master grower, but so far their lead candidate wanted more money than they could pay. So, over coffee at a flashy new Bridgehead coffee shop on the border between Chinatown and Little Italy, Seb hoped Michael would come up with another suggestion, as well as some investment money.

"I don't think Seb even had money for coffee," Michael reflects years later. "I had been looking for opportunities that involved medical marijuana. I'd had incredible experiences with patients who got amazing relief from cannabis. It fulfills the five Hs of health, from a simple point of view. It can make you hungry and happy, it's harmless — and helpful. And, if you're lucky, it makes you horny. So I brought along someone I knew who was very knowledgeable to meet Seb."

Within minutes of meeting, Seb felt a wall of resistance from Michael's companion, who grilled him for the next hour and a half. "He cut me up over and over," Seb recalls of the man shooting out questions, dismissing the answers and getting in Seb's face. But two things became clear to Michael. First, neither Seb nor his adviser could work with one another. Second, Michael did want to work with Seb.

"He shared his vision with me, and I told my wife I was going to invest. She thought I was crazy, but I was very taken with their vision and their ability to execute. They floored me," Michael says. "I was convinced that they were realistic and had a vision which I wanted to be a part of."

Afterward, Seb walked the two blocks to Adam's house, still reeling from the interrogation. Although Michael had agreed to another meeting at Adam's house, Seb was convinced that the possibility of a financial injection was low.

A few weeks later, Michael drove from his home in Montreal to Ottawa. The Hydropothecary office was temporarily moved upstairs to the dining-room table, where all three men could sit comfortably and look over Seb's financial pitch.

That was the plan. But the baby was having none of it. Upstairs, Iyla wailed, her lung capacity surprising even to Adam. A bright child, curious about every single thing in the world, she found naps an absolute affront.

Downstairs, Adam and Seb shifted in their chairs, irrationally hoping Michael's hearing wasn't as good as theirs. They talked over the noise, smiling apologetically. Whether Michael sensed their discomfort or recalled his own children's inopportune distractions, he reassured them.

"You know," he said, "the mark of a good parent is knowing when to let their baby cry in a controlled manner. It's fine."

That afternoon, Michael agreed to invest $250,000, instructed his lawyer to proceed, and the good doctor became one of their most important and trusted facilitators, confidants, and friends.

As 2013 wound down, Seb and Adam went into overdrive, talking about the company, where it would go, and what it could do. With their lawyer Karl's money tucked into the bank, together with family investments, the two men spoke to every friend, and their friends' friends, about investing in the company. They spoke to their groomsmen. They talked to Adam's old friends from the Young Liberals. Another friend invested his entire life savings, despite having near faint-inducing anxiety over it. He'd arrived at the basement office with his hands shaking so hard he could barely sign the subscription papers before he handed over a cheque for $15,000. Adam poured him a shot of whisky. The friend downed it quickly and bolted out the door, the look on his face saying, "I've done it, now get me the fuck out of here."

It was both an incredible testament to the belief people had in them and a crushing burden, having to hold themselves accountable for other people's life savings. It also brought the partners even closer together. Every Monday night, Adam and his friends would typically gather for a hilarious, beer-driven trivia night in which they could crack jokes at each other's expense, commiserate about inept bosses, and stand witness to each other's day-to-day existence. But, after most of those friends became investors, trivia night became an ad-hoc shareholders' meeting in which everyone wanted the latest update. Adam was no longer free to dish on his frustrations like everyone else. On the upside, it drew him and Seb even closer together.

Billion Dollar Lesson

"Getting money from family and friends is critical, because it's also kind of your money. If I'm looking at a young company coming to me for money, my first question is very frank: Is your brother in? Is your mother in? Did you put them at risk before you put me at risk? Are you at risk?" — **Seb**

11:58 P.M., NEW YEAR'S EVE 2013
ADAM'S HOUSE, CENTRETOWN
OTTAWA, ONTARIO

Adam's Spruce Street house was a long and narrow warren. No more than three short-person arms widths across, it rambled from front parlour to dining room, kitchen, and family room, stitched together with a shotgun hallway. Despite its size, it had been the scene of countless parties so over-populated, it was a wonder the fire department was never called.

That New Year's Eve was no different. The house was packed with pretty much everyone Adam knew, including his mother-in-law, Reva. Food was plentiful, the booze was flowing. As the clock inched toward midnight, the chatter grew louder, the laughter more spontaneous, and the glad-eyed, cheerful glances more frequent.

They were headed into 2014, but this wasn't just a New Year's Eve party. This was a night to remember. Earlier that day, on December 31, 2013, Seb and Adam closed financing for Hydropothecary, having raised $1.1 million from friends, family, and a few investors.

It was a moment to celebrate, and everyone there felt it. There's no greater bond in creating a tribe than knowing that you've all bought in, you're all sipping the Kool-Aid together, and it tastes just fine, thank you very much.

The moment and its significance were not lost on Adam. "Holy shit," he thought. "Holy shit." He took a swig of Scotch. "We did it."

Six! Five! Four! Three! Two! One!

Noise erupted afresh in the house, friends clasped hands, partners and lovers held each other close. After a few minutes, Adam held up a hand and a bottle of prosecco.

He had a few things to say. Looking around the room at the expectant faces, he realized those who'd gathered represented half of their investors. He had a grateful, yet bowel-loosening realization that Hydropothecary had its tentacles in every aspect of his life.

Practically everyone they knew had invested. Anyone who could be a buffer to them being homeless had invested. They had a million bucks to get started, but if anything went wrong, they'd wipe out their credibility and maybe even friendship with anyone who'd bought into it.

Adam cleared his throat. "I just want to say that this has been an amazing year for me and Seb," he said, looking around. "And that's been in great part due to you. We wouldn't be here without you. And we wouldn't want to be either."

He shimmied the fat cork out of the bottle, poured a glass and held it aloft.

"Guys . . . this one's for you."

CHAPTER 3

Seb and Adam were born to hustle. They knew it. Their parents knew it. Everyone around them knew that, of all people, they'd be the ones to make serious money. But to make money, you have to make mistakes, learn from failure, push the boundaries of what's possible . . . and in Seb's case, never be late for dinner.

Although the St-Louis family came from a long line of lumberjacks and miners, some of whom struggled to make ends meet, Seb's parents were middle class. He was an only child, and the last in his father's family line. So if his extended family had less than his friends' families, he never noticed because the adults in his life told him he could do and be anything he wanted. That engendered a certain amount of ego, which in turn taught him a valuable lesson about scarcity.

Family meals were hurried and peppered with bursts of the usual St-Louis family rant, in which food was digested vociferously with a side dish of hot takes and opinion.

One night at such a family meal at his grandparents' 800-square-foot home in Sturgeon Falls, in northern Ontario, 12-year-old Seb was called to dinner. "No," he thought. "I'll wait for my TV show to end." Eventually it did, as had dinner. And there was nothing left for him to eat. His five uncles just laughed at the sight of his stricken face. "Well," one pointed out, leaning back in his chair, "that'll teach you to not come when you're called."

If scarcity and a rock-solid ego fed by his family's undying belief in him were recurring themes in his life, they were also drivers for Seb's success. At age 16, after his stint at Future Shop, Seb and his best friend, Will, started their first company, a 3D computer simulation business and landed third place at the Toronto International Film Festival's teen event for their feature-length film, *The Island of Dr. Twig*. (Will and his wife, Renée, eventually started a company in Toronto called Secret Level Films.) A year later, at age 17, after a conversation in Will's basement the summer before grade 13, the friends decided grade 12 was enough education, at least for the moment. Seb's thirsty mind wasn't being filled quickly enough, or with the stuff he wanted to know. So instead of attending grade 13, they landed contracts doing 3D computer work like wire-mesh rendering on projects for the Canadian Space Agency (CSA) and MDS Aero. They were pulling in $1,000 a day each.

Even then, Seb's chutzpah was legend: when their CSA contact turned down their $45,000 pitch after months of building the relationship, Seb immediately pivoted. If their contact didn't have the signing authority for the whole job, he wondered aloud to the head honchos, what about a reduced contract for just the wireframe at, say, $15,000? Walking out of the meeting with a cocky grin and a contract, Seb could feel Will shaking in an attack of nerves beside him.

When Seb did eventually return to formal education, he first did part-time business classes, then completed most of his three-year bachelor of arts in 17 months by cramming his schedule full of courses in both English and French. Later, he studied for, but was an essay and a few classes short of, earning a master's in quantitative finance, but did complete an MBA in finance at UQAM Outaouais, despite limping through grade 12 math. Seb's remarkable ability to quickly learn, assess, and apply information at lightning speed was being finely honed.

"It was about creating my own destiny," he recalls. "To succeed, you have to fail. I learned that early. Now, return on failure is one of our core principles and drives our decision making. You need to fail fast, focus, and proceed."

That attitude dovetailed with Adam's. On the other side of the country, young Adam was learning his own lessons about business and ego. His father, Gaston, was an electrician who playfully created endless opportunities for his young son to discover, learn, and figure out how to earn his own money.

It was a far cry from Gaston's own childhood in the northern Franco-Ontario town of New Liskeard (now Temiskaming Shores, population 9,920), where his parents had moved their 13 children after their property in Hull, Quebec, was appropriated for municipal improvements. The family found a small, two-story home on a secondary highway outside town and, leveraging the French Canadian hard-hat genes, found work in construction. Life was challenging financially — supper was sometimes just a big pot of mashed potatoes — and socially, too. Bored with school and life in general, the Miron boys formed a leather-jacket patch-wearing gang with their cousins, dabbling around the edges of legality with entrepreneurial schemes to earn quick cash. Whatever it was, recalls Adam, "you had to find a way to make some money to get by."

Like his son would years later, young Gaston's enthusiastic spirit of innovation led him to grow cannabis plants, albeit illicitly. (Once, his mother found a plant and, tsk-tsking over its anemic state, unwittingly revived it on the sunny windowsill of her bedroom, never once guessing why her children found it so funny.) Gaston's enterprise soon landed him in trouble with the local constabulary. Walking along train tracks with friends one day during the summer after grade 9, they were stopped and frisked; Gaston had enough dried weed to be charged with possession.

Perhaps fed up with his wayward sons or maybe embarrassed to be the object of public censure, Gaston's father was anything but supportive of his second youngest boy. When the judge asked him, "Monsieur Miron, what do you suggest we do?" after the prosecutor laid out the case, he responded harshly, according to family lore, "Your Honour, I am having a hard time teaching not just this boy but my other boys. I encourage you to give him the stiffest penalty possible. Maybe you can teach him a lesson I can't."

Gaston turned 16 during his six months in juvenile detention. His irrepressibly upbeat nature helped him survive the ordeal, but his problems did not end with his sentence. His father picked him up on the day he was released, but rather than driving home, where Gaston was looking forward to seeing his mother and having a home-cooked meal, his father drove out of town to the nearest truck-stop diner.

Standing in the centre of the room with his stunned teenage son, he asked, "Is anyone here headed out west? I hear there are jobs."

One trucker put up his hand. "I'm taking a load of oranges to Calgary."

"Good. Will you take my boy?"

Shocked to tears, Gaston stood riveted to the spot, barely able to understand the turn his life was about to take. But his father didn't wait for him to collect his thoughts. Pulling out his wallet, he handed over $50. "You get your life together before you call."

Clutching a bag with his only possessions, Gaston watched his father walk quickly from the restaurant. They wouldn't speak to each other for many years, but the impact of the moment — of being abandoned, rejected, excommunicated from his family — would later shape his own parenting.

Gaston was enthusiastically, almost pathologically, a homebody who loved spending time with his kids. He built them the Buckingham Palace of treehouses, made from free and found materials. Once, he lugged home a spare chest freezer and, in the dead of winter, filled it to capacity with soft, fluffy snow. During a particularly hot spell the following spring, he told Adam and Ashley to invite their friends over after school on a Friday. When the crowd arrived, Gaston threw open the freezer and shovelled the contents onto a waiting tarp so the kids could have a summertime snowball fight.

That sort of forward-thinking made a deep impression on Adam. "He never gave me the drink, but he always led me to the creek, when it came to exploring business ideas as a kid. That worked time and time again, to the point where it really started to dawn on me; now, one of my favourite things to do is talk about an opportunity or problem and find a way to turn it into a business," he says.

Although his family wasn't well off, Adam's grandmother did have some funds, scraped together through frugality and real estate investments. Those savings soon became a parachute out of the chaos unfolding the year he turned 16.

The family was in utter shambles. His parents were divorcing. His father had moved out, into a friend's basement. To add to the drama,

Gaston was declaring bankruptcy and about to have their house repossessed. They lost everything — the car, the computer business. It was a messy end to what had been a star-crossed love story.

Ann and Gaston had been together for 17 years, marrying seven months before Adam was born. Although their relationship soured, it started off as the salvation for Gaston.

Soon after the 16-year-old arrived in Calgary, courtesy of the trucker and his load of oranges, he was on a bus and spotted a beautiful 18-year-old girl with shimmering red hair, struck up a conversation, and persuaded her to meet him for a date. Fate intervened and he couldn't make the date, but when he coincidentally ran into her again on a bus, he asked her out again. Her name was Ann — and she flat out refused. She had an education and a good office job. And she didn't need this long-haired whippet of a boy complicating her life.

But Gaston hadn't just spent six months in juvie without learning a few things about persuasion and charm, so he worked on Ann the whole of the bus ride. Eventually she relented and later accompanied him to a party, where she suggested they arm wrestle. Having seen his lean, muscled frame, she knew she wouldn't win. But she did have a point to make about being stood up earlier. Having settled into their stances and about to start, she pulled back her right fist and bopped him on the nose.

It must have been the language he needed to hear because before long, Ann was pregnant with Adam. Life was extremely challenging, despite Ann's reliable income. One apartment was so cockroach-infested, Gaston's visiting brother Marcel caught dozens of the insects, putting them in a pickle jar to leave on the landlord's doorstep in protest. Ann's supportive and generous father, Steve Ramage, often deposited money into their bank account — not that it always found its way into their cupboards via the grocery store. Once, Gaston stopped in at the bank to withdraw cash, saw there was a tidy sum in his account, and spent it all on new stereo speakers.

The disintegration of the marriage and indeed their entire life was too much for teenage Adam to manage emotionally. He needed to escape, and if it took running away from home to run toward his future, so be it. He researched boarding schools and put together a presentation for his grandmother. It would cost about $30,000 a year for St. Michaels

University School in Victoria — and his grandmother was the only one who had the money to pay for it.

If he had any uncertainty about leaving his imploding home life, it dissolved the minute he stepped foot on campus with Ann and his godfather, the Venerable M. Edward Simonton. A highly educated, worldly, and monastic Anglican priest who'd left behind his wealthy Southern family to be a missionary in Canada's North, Edward was one of the most influential people in Adam's life. "Without Edward, I'd almost certainly be working for a logging company in northern British Columbia," he recalls. "He opened up the world to me."

And it started at St. Michaels. At McBride Secondary, where the guidance counsellor had laughed at Adam's expressed desire to attend Stanford University, attending would have seemed incredible. Wearing his only suit and a rather shiny blue tie, Adam walked across the campus in wonder. Students in natty blazers strolled from class to class, held in ivy-covered redbrick buildings. There were sporting facilities, a cricket pitch, and a sense that Disney had designed the whole thing. It looked like the success it promised: 95 percent of graduates went to the top 30 universities in the world. Adam immediately formed a burning and violent desire to wear one of those blazers.

His entrance exam proved he'd have to earn it. Having told the administrators that he wanted to be a doctor, they handed him a math exam. His heart sank to his feet. One of the first questions was to determine the square root of 347. "What the hell is a square root?" Adam muttered. The facilitator spoke. "Remember, it's less about the answer than the process." Adam hunkered over his paper. "Process?" he thought.

Deciding he'd be better at guessing than trying to work out the "process," he wrote the exam, handed it in, and went for lunch. Then he met with an administrative clerk.

"So, Mr. Miron, we have an interesting situation here. You say over here," he said, pointing to Adam's application, "that you want to be a science student." He paused and picked up the math test. "And yet, here's your exam."

After graciously offering Adam a chance to explain his hopes for the future, the clerk asked Adam if he'd consider humanities, as science and math didn't seem to be the right fit. Having done a few first-year psychology courses, with Edward coaching him, while in high school, Adam jumped at the opportunity. A few days later, Adam was formally accepted into the school. That started a trajectory into learning that took him across the world to a summer program at Cambridge University, then to Cape Breton University, and finally, home to Kamloops's Thompson Rivers University. Although Adam accrued an astonishing number of credits for all his transfers, they were so diverse — theoretical formalized logic! Biology! Political science! — he never earned a degree. Adam's dreams of attending Cambridge as a full-time student ended with Gaston's bankruptcy. His grandmother's largesse would not quite stretch to post-secondary studies overseas. Nor would the income from any part-time work hours he managed to grab at his job at Staples or, later, at a lumberyard in Kamloops, be enough to support his educational ambitions. But both jobs did teach him significant lessons in the value of customer service. At Staples, where he was a floater, standing in for colleagues on lunch breaks, he was so adept at handling customer queries that he got a five-star rating from the Secret Shopper assessment program three times in one month, as well as a letter of commendation from the company's national general manager.

Although Adam and Seb grew up almost a country apart, their childhoods and upbringing, their egos and their drive, got them their first $1.1 million in investment money from friends and family. All of that life experience boiled down to this moment when they had the backing of true believers who saw their potential. That money meant more than an investment. It also meant that, for better or worse, they were on a trajectory into something they couldn't fully anticipate. And they knew it.

Billion Dollar Lesson

"The only way to learn customer service is on the floor. Seb did it at Future Shop, and I did it at Staples, which ended up being one of my favourite jobs. Dealing with people day in and day out teaches empathy, which is an essential skill. When hiring, I always value work experience in customer service, no matter what kind of job is on offer. I've told my three daughters that when they are 15 or 16, they could choose where, but they'll all work a customer service job for at least a summer. It doesn't just make you a better person, it makes you a better co-worker, employee, or entrepreneur." — **Adam**

OCTOBER AND NOVEMBER 2013
VARIOUS REAL ESTATE LOCATIONS
EASTERN TOWNSHIPS, ONTARIO

Months before the $1.1 million investment was even a possibility, Seb had gone property hunting for Hydropothecary's permanent home. He wanted something rural, but with established and reliable access to water and electricity. He needed skilled people to employ. Kemptville, a small town of 3,900 souls south of Ottawa in the United Counties of Leeds and Grenville was one of the first places he looked. It was a 45-minute commute from Ottawa, but as a rural community with an established workforce, it had a lot going for it. And the town had been founded by Seb's kind of guy: a shrewd businessman and Loyalist named Lyman Clothier who had bought a hundred acres of land in 1812 for a yoke of oxen and a flintlock rifle. He set up a lumber mill and sawmill to clear the land, built a few houses, and, when his micro-industry became a waypoint along the Ottawa-Prescott Road, he and his four sons expanded into a grist mill and a hotel. Thus, Kemptville was born.

Seb combed through the Leeds-Grenville real estate listings and considered the options. Of course, the nascent marijuana industry was still viewed with distaste and even hostility by many municipalities, so even if Seb and Adam found the ideal location, there was no guarantee they'd be granted a business licence or permits. And who could blame those municipalities? Sure, the federal government was mandating an industry, but no one knew who would be running it. It was so new and fraught with questions that misinformation and speculation were rife.

When Seb eventually did find the right property, it wasn't anywhere near Kemptville. In fact, it was not even in Ontario. Casting his net wider, he had landed on an undeveloped plot in an industrial park in rural Gatineau, near Ottawa. The owner-builder had just broken ground on the construction. It was nothing more than a dirt pit the first time Seb visited it, but what he saw was possibility. They'd have a little over 8,000 square feet, which was part of their plan. It was ideally located off Autoroute 50 on Rue Bombardier, not far from the growing Gatineau executive airport. Plus, its location near the city of Gat, as it's locally known, guaranteed a skilled workforce. Best of all, the company's return on investment (once the company started growing) would benefit from Hydro-Québec's inexpensive electricity.

"On the downside," thought Adam when he eventually went with Seb to inspect the site, "I've never commuted a day in my life." He looked around the unlovely industrial park, with its Purolator distribution warehouse, glass suppliers, and logistics centre. It was so basic, there wasn't even a chip truck.

But a lack of places to eat would turn out to be the least of their worries. They were about to enter the most stressful period they'd experienced to date.

Seb and Adam had already commissioned an office layout and began planning the planting tables. They had spent around $80,000 so far, and having an actual building was the first concrete and significant sign of progress. Challenging as it was and long as the days were, they were vibrating with excitement at the thought of finally getting out of the basement office and into a brick-and-mortar establishment. As the concrete truck backed up and started pouring the cannabis storage vault's foundation, Adam snapped a photo and proudly posted it on a cannabis Reddit thread.

Yet, something was wrong. Very wrong. Their business licence application with Gatineau was being met by a barrage of questions, some so obscure or pedantic that it seemed like someone, somewhere, was stalling.

What was up was a lack of certainty about how to proceed at the municipal level. While Adam took the lead on brand development and products, Seb was fronting up at Gatineau's Hôtel de ville to deal with the two clerks handling their file. The main sticking point was that the company wanted to start an agricultural business in an industrial zone. Did they mean to grow and sell? What was the square footage of the growing area? Where was their licence from Health Canada? Would they consider making their company a cannabis R&D company, with no actual plant production, to get around the zoning issue? The more Seb answered, the more questions came up.

And Seb had a few of his own. "How long is this process going to take? Why is it taking so long? Is there anything we can do to speed things up?" On the other side of the counter, the clerks shrugged their shoulders and assured Monsieur St-Louis that they were doing their best.

Meanwhile, conversations with Health Canada were drying up. Every few weeks, it sent Hydropothecary a formal request for more information, most of which seemed ludicrous. Oddly excited when they arrived, Adam and Seb nevertheless were caught between confusion, frustration, and uncertainty. It was like being lost at sea in a boat. Sometimes, you just have to pick a direction and start rowing.

Billion Dollar Lesson

"Once you're past the start-up phase, you'll realize the first thing you should have done is build up your team. That's not realistic when your pockets are empty. But when you have nothing, you still have force of will. It may be all you're left with, but it's the one thing no one can take away from you." — **Seb**

Still, picking a direction and rowing wasn't good enough. Certainly not good enough for Seb. He wanted answers and he wanted to keep moving forward. But how?

The answer came in the form of two hired guns who, for a considerable amount of money, promised to find answers and get the project back onto greased rails.

Adam and Seb drove to downtown Ottawa to meet with the first consultant. Behind his grandiose carved Louis XVI–style desk, he confided that he'd recently persuaded Health Canada to approve a new flavour for a multinational beverage company he represented. Adam was impressed. After a few years in politics, he had a sense of the power this consultant could wield. Seb was less convinced. To him, the guy seemed like a lot of hot air and no action that would cost them more than they could afford. Because he and Adam had been so stressed, they'd implemented a daily 4 p.m. "Coors Light O'Clock" to briefly take their minds off the day. With their cash reserves draining, Seb knew this was a Hail Mary moment.

For $5,000 a month on a three-month contract, the consultant said, he'd find out where their application was and how it could be moved along.

"Anyway," he said offhandedly, "I play golf with a very senior official at Health Canada. Don't worry."

But $15,000? Seb and Adam held their noses, wrote the cheque, then crossed their fingers and toes.

They still had to deal with the issue of Gatineau, so they hired another consultant locally, one who knew the city and its councillors. He was just a young guy with no desk, no seniority, not even an office, but he wanted to be a lobbyist. Inexperienced as he was, he turned out to be one of the best investments Adam and Seb made.

Within a week, they had a meeting with Mayor Maxime Pedneaud-Jobin. The local consultant advised them to write, in advance of the discussion, a letter detailing everything they had gone through, how long it had taken, and what they wanted. Moreover, he added, if you make a good case to the mayor, he would listen.

The meeting was conducted entirely in French, much to Adam's disadvantage. But here, Seb was in his element. Over the course of an hour, Seb shared their vision: what the company was planning, the number of people they wanted to hire, the glowing future the industry would have in Quebec. He explained that there seemed to be a roadblock to getting permits, yet no one in the municipal office could clarify the situation. The mayor nodded and listened. He asked questions and listened some more. Eventually he'd heard enough. He switched over to English.

"This is unacceptable. You're trying to bring jobs to the region. You're bringing a business to the city. Let me see what I can do."

Leaving the building, Seb turned to Adam. Frustration and skepticism were written all over his face. "He'll do what he can? What the fuck does that mean?" He pulled open the car door and got in.

The next morning, he had a different look on his face. Just after 9 a.m., a Gatineau city clerk called to let them know that their business licence and zoning variation permit were both ready. It was their first major win, but the joy of it wasn't to last long. Late one night soon after, the pricey federal lobbyist emailed urgently from his golf vacation in Florida. Seb drove straight to Adam's house and together, they called him. There was a major issue, he said. He couldn't say what, but it appeared that their Health Canada application had either been halted or stalled. But that's all he knew.

"Gotta go," he said, then abruptly hung up. Adam and Seb looked at each other for a long moment. "I bet he's just after a contract extension," Seb scoffed.

But the call had spooked Adam. The consultant sounded confident in the information, even if there wasn't anything in the way of verification. As it turned out, the man was right.

The orange binder Seb had posted months earlier was collecting dust in the pile of rejected applications.

11 A.M., DECEMBER 2013
ADAM'S HOUSE, CENTRETOWN
OTTAWA, ONTARIO

The stress nearly brought them undone.

They had the start of a building. They were looking for employees. They had even lined up $20,000 in plants and seeds through a couple of people who had an MMAR licence to grow weed in the second bedroom of their apartment. But without a licence from Health Canada, they couldn't legally take possession of them. Plus, the legislated window to transfer plants from home growers to commercial operations was closing fast. After those three short months, on March 31, 2014, they could lose it all.

"For the first time, I was really getting a glimmer of the potential reality that we might be fucked," Adam recalls. "We were blowing through $1.1 million of our friends' and families' money. And we weren't taking a salary."

It was time to have a talk. They both knew it. For weeks, neither of them wanted to be the first to say what was on their mind. Seb drove over to Adam's place. He got in the door and sat down on the living-room chesterfield rather than heading to the basement office. The tension was palpable. So much was working against them, it felt like they were in the midst of a battering gale wearing cheap raincoats and holding a Mickey Mouse umbrella.

Under duress, humans have one of two reactions, triggered by cortisol and adrenalin. The body undergoes a series of lightning-fast responses that increase your heart rate and blood pressure, makes energy more available, and shuts down non-essential systems that would be detrimental in a fight, like digestion, reproduction, and growth. The bottom line: your body is primed and pumped to either turn tail and run, stand and hold your ground, or freeze into inaction.

Cortisol had already made itself felt in other ways. Adam and Seb were both gaining weight and weren't sleeping properly, if at all. Normally, stress levels drop after a threat subsides and stress hormones dissipate. But with sustained stress, the fight-flight-freeze tap stays on, resulting in insomnia, weight gain, and anxiety. In other words, the stress of the business was all-encompassing. And visible.

Seb cleared his throat. "So, things look bad. Something's not working." He remembered advice Michael Munzar had drilled into him: in an emergency, take your own pulse first.

Across the room, Adam nodded and tried to compose his face. Internally, he was deeply panicked and worried that the whole thing, every last penny they had, would be lost. He had a baby, a wife on maternity leave, and a mortgage. To lose it all now would be a failure of such proportions, he wasn't sure where it would end. The ramifications on both their lives, and the lives of every investor, would be massive. They were putting in 60-hour weeks with no guarantee of success, or even a suggestion that they were headed in the right direction.

He swallowed hard and looked at Seb.

Seb stared back. He could see the anxiety and fear, the question in Adam's eyes. "Oh crap," Seb thought. "He's going to walk. If he walks, we are done."

"I don't know what to tell you. I can't reassure you that we won't lose it all. But we're not out of options. We have options," Seb repeated, half to himself. He went on to outline a few more ideas and strategies, constantly assessing Adam's face for clues. He couldn't offer the kind of solid evidence that they were going to succeed that Adam wanted, and Adam wasn't able to assure Seb he wouldn't have to walk away in the interests of his family. But Seb needed Adam to be on board, now more than ever. Where Adam wanted to flee, Seb was determined to hold fast.

Seb's mind flew back to his first business, 3D1, which he'd formed with Will when the two friends were 17. They worked hard to make things happen for the business, and they did have some success. But with no follow-on deals, Will got a full-time job elsewhere, so he had no spare time for their joint business. Seb bought him out for $4,000, but nothing was the same afterward. Without Will, without a partner and a shared vision, Seb lost his motivation. It was the same with Adam: he needed Adam's skills and talents, but he also needed someone he could trust implicitly, no matter what.

Throughout the afternoon, they talked and bared their fears. In the end, they decided to stick it out, at least for a bit longer.

Billion Dollar Lesson

"CEO is a very lonely job. You've got a board of directors, but you have to manage them. You can't go whining about how you're not confident in a particular moment. Your spouse may be super supportive, but by the time you bring them up to speed on a situation and give them the appropriate background, you don't want to talk about it anymore. And you can't talk to your friends, because they're all shareholders. So the right partner is very important. You need that person to lean on. And your partner has to be 100 percent fully in. Otherwise, you go into a murky middle ground and risk losing both a friendship and a business." — **Seb**

Once more shoulder to shoulder, Seb and Adam faced their troubles head on. If only the troubles were just about the money or the licence. In their pitch to investors, they'd boldly asserted that they would be among the first 10 producers awarded a licence by Health Canada. They got their application in early, they pointed out, and nothing could stand in their way.

Sitting in the basement one afternoon shortly after that tough talk in the living room, Adam and Seb were doing what every other potential legal marijuana grower in Canada was doing: constantly hitting refresh on the Health Canada page that listed the successful applicants. Adam hit the button again and there it was.

A tenth company had been awarded a licence, and it wasn't Hydropothecary. He called Seb over, gestured to the screen, and said nothing.

"Damn it. Damn it." Seb brought his hand down hard on the desk.

They had heard of lawyers startling clients by showing up with bottles of champagne to celebrate, only to have the client admit they didn't know they'd been given a licence because they hadn't refreshed the page in the past hour. But that wasn't going to happen for Hydropothecary. Worse still, it was the first promise they had made to their shareholders that they couldn't keep. It was also the first lesson they learned about not over-promising.

"Well, fuck it. We have to own it."

And so together they composed an email to investors and family explaining that, while they were not in the top 10, they were on track. Things were happening. They had to believe it. And the more they wrote, the more they did believe it. This was a setback, they reassured each other. Nothing more than that.

Billion Dollar Lesson

"Return on failure is one of our core principles. It drives our decision making. To succeed, you have to fail and fail rapidly, then proceed. You want your team to take risks and fail. Under the Pareto Principle — the 80/20 rule — you'll never have 100 percent of the information you need to make a decision. Twenty percent of the causes will generate 80 percent of the results." **— Seb**

With the deadline for transferring plants looming and no word from Health Canada, things looked grim. But, as they had before, Adam and Seb settled into the elegant give-and-take business relationship that had propelled them this far. Every day, the whiteboard was covered with notes and plans. Every day, Adam wrote lists, updated spreadsheets, and made calls. Every day, Seb looked for ways to get their medical marijuana business on its feet. When the answer finally came, it wasn't from Health Canada at all but from a contact at the Gatineau municipal offices.

According to Seb's source, Hydropothecary wasn't the sole medical marijuana applicant in Gatineau. Did he know a guy named Louis Gagnon of Botanix, up in Masson-Angers? Seb didn't, but like anyone who'd ever shopped at the Rona hardware chain, he'd heard of Botanix, a Quebec-based company that supplied the hardware chain with ornamental bushes and exotic flowers. Louis Gagnon, it turned out, was a master grower who had a 7,000-square-foot greenhouse and a staging licence from Health Canada. That meant that he wasn't a full LP and therefore wasn't listed on the Health Canada website, but he did have a licence to grow medical marijuana plants. He just couldn't process or sell them.

Seb's mind raced ahead to the possibilities. He called Louis almost immediately to set up a meeting, then opened his laptop and checked a satellite map for the 68-acre Botanix farm on Chemin de la Rive. He made an approving noise in the back of his throat. It was just out of town, sandwiched between Lièvre River to the north and the Ottawa River to the south, near the Cumberland ferry landing. "Nice spot," he thought. "Very nice."

The question was, what did he want to know from this Louis guy? Obviously, he wanted to know what the hell he'd done to get a staging licence. Who had he dealt with? More importantly, could they do a deal that would hitch Hydropothecary to the staging licence Health Canada gave to Botanix while he and Adam waited for the industrial property at Rue Bombardier to come online?

Climbing into the Grand Am a few days later on their way to meet Louis, Adam and Seb looked like a pair of popinjays headed to a party. Seb eschewed his standard Under Armour in favour of a standard salesman's striped suit matched with a pink striped shirt. It was a lot of stripes. For his part, Adam had delved into his tie drawer and went straight to his most cherished items: two silk Zegnas. His hand hovered over the choices, one for summer and one for winter. Yes, the summer tie. It was a vibrant pink paisley number that was sure to impress.

A half hour later and they were driving slowly down the muddy, unpaved Chemin de la Rive. On the right, the banks of Lièvre River dropped precipitously to the water. To the left, past a massive stand of trees that acted as a buffer to a regional road leading to the Cumberland ferry, stood a charming, modest redbrick farmhouse, complete with gabled roof and decorative gingerbread trim. The rest of the site was a hodgepodge of seasonal outbuildings, retail, and storage facilities and garages, all bustling with spring activity.

Adam and Seb parked the car, walked up the wooden steps to the front door, and knocked. It almost immediately swung open. Louis Gagnon stood in the doorway.

"Bonjour, ça va? Vous-êtes Sébastien St-Louis? Et vous . . . vous-êtes . . . Adam? Bonjour. Entrez, s'il vous plait."

Offering them a coffee, along with a bemused "bon cravat" to Adam's splendid tie, they got down to business. Or rather, Seb and Louis talked, and Adam watched Louis. The man appeared to be genetically rumpled: everything from the deeply lined face from years of working outdoors to the sort-of-but-not-really-fitting work pants and nondescript green-grey windbreaker had the air of being pulled out of the dryer damp and thrown in a basket. But he was affable enough, curious, and definitely interested in why these two dandies were visiting a working farm in the middle of the day.

Adam watched Seb, too. In this environment, Seb was in a class on his own. He asked dozens of questions, and listened closely to the answers. Louis walked them through his facility with some pride, talked about the numbers of people he had working for him, and introduced them around.

It was clearly a working farm with plenty of things that needed replacing or upgrading, but as a future marijuana facility, they saw where it could end up with the right injection of money. There was already a vault in an underground bunker for dried product storage. By the end of the meeting, Louis agreed to rent them a corner of the greenhouse. He would tend to the plants with the Hydropothecary employees, and Hydropothecary would supply Louis with seeds to get his production started. The Rue Bombardier facility could remain part of the plan, maybe as something else, like a cannabis genetics lab. More exciting than all of that, however, was the licence itself.

Before they left, Louis showed them his Health Canada certificate. Adam held it for a few minutes, noting the weight of the paper, the smell of the ink. He memorized the number etched onto it and the exact shade of crimson of the seal. It felt like currency and looked like a key to the future. It also represented the closest he and Seb had come to realizing their dream and, although it belonged to someone else, it was a significant move forward for them. He handed it back reluctantly.

The next step was to involve their lawyer. He would paper up the deal immediately, and they could bring in the plants before the March 31 deadline, now only a few days away. As they drove back down Autoroute 50 to Ottawa, their smiles were more genuine than they had been in a very long time.

It was progress. But it wasn't quite enough progress for Seb.

Anyone who has seen a scent hound single-mindedly trailing its prey would be familiar with the laser focus Seb gave his next move. He had mused aloud to Adam on the trip home, wouldn't it be great if they could just buy out Louis, the farm, the licence, everything? Then they'd really be in business. They wouldn't be at the mercy of anyone. What did Adam think about that?

Adam chuckled. Good old Seb. Always charging up the next hill, sword out, voice in full howl.

"Let's just see how this plays out, Seb. We don't know this guy, but we've made real progress. I think we should just sit on it for the moment. But I like where you're headed."

The Merriam-Webster dictionary defines progress as "a forward or onward movement." Progress requires an onward propulsion and energy. But, as with any destination in business, it should always be a little bit out of reach, just over the crest of ideation. At least that's what

Seb was telling himself when he contacted Louis again to have a chat. A long chat.

A few days after their initial meeting, Seb burst into the basement office, eyes sparkling. He wasn't even trying to suppress his excitement. Nor did he give Adam a chance to ask why he was there.

"Look, I know you told me not to do it. I know! But I couldn't help myself, I did it! I called him back. I did a deal, a huge deal. We've got it all . . . the house, the buildings, the land, the licence! We've got a pot farm!"

Adam's eyes widened in astonishment.

"Are you fucking KIDDING ME?"

2 P.M., APRIL 2014
ADAM'S BASEMENT OFFICE, CENTRETOWN
OTTAWA, ONTARIO

Adam's basement office is not a place for board meetings. Cramped and chilly despite the space heaters, it has nevertheless been the scene of countless light bulb moments, daily grinds, and bitter disappointments.

Today, however, it was a lecture theatre, with Sébastien teaching Adam and their lawyer, Karl, a class in the courage to win.

The hustle of entrepreneurship, Seb has always felt, is the courage to win, where you have to force your will forward to succeed and where, when others lose hope, you do not. It's about recognizing your vulnerabilities and turning them into resilience. It's also about dreaming bigger than everyone else, then executing on the dream.

Standing at the whiteboard with a blue and a red marker in hand, Seb went through the details of the deal he'd put together with Louis a few weeks earlier. As soon as the company is profitable, he explained, Louis would be a full partner, plus he'd receive $800,000, with other tranches of cash tied to profit. In the meantime, he'd be paid what they were paid, and he'd get the same 650,000 shares that Adam and Seb both had. (At least that was the plan. It took much longer than anyone expected to close the deal with Louis.)

"Wait, what? Are you fucking crazy? The guy's a farmer growing ornamental shrubs! I'm not giving him a third of the company! We've worked way too much for this; we have too much sweat equity in it!"

Adam was incensed. He wanted this deal, but not like that. Not literally giving the farm away. He thought they had just bought it. Seb quietly capped his markers and placed them on the whiteboard ledge.

"Adam, listen to me. Do you want 20 percent of a $20 million company or 5 percent of a $1 billion company? Mmm? We have this shot. This one shot. You know what we're up against. And if you want to keep those odds, we have to make deals like this. Now, let me explain."

Until that moment, every decision made had been made by Adam and Seb together. This time, however, Seb had devised a robust, calculated plan on his own. He sat Adam down and went through it, line by line. He was seeking buy-in and approval, but it was clear to Adam that, when the titles were handed out, Seb's would be "chief executive officer."

"Seb was on a whole other level of enlightenment and understanding," Adam recalls. "He wasn't preaching, he was teaching. I was still uneasy with it, but I was convinced this was what we had to do at the end of the day. He wasn't just a salesman or negotiator, he was a thinker and planner. It was great leadership, and I remember thinking, 'Now we're really starting. This is it.'"

Billion Dollar Lesson

"Small entrepreneurs stay small because they don't want to share their pie. They're successful in their way, their pie is delicious, and they don't want to share it. They can't delegate and share with a partner to make the pie bigger. And they never get out. It's a constant mistake and a big reason small entrepreneurs are not able to become CEOs. One of my bosses was a visionary, very smart, a super hard worker who taught me tons about sales. I was working for him doing wholesale, and I wanted to take some files and do them my way. If he had let me, we could have made something pretty cool. But he didn't want to share the pie." — **Seb**

PART 2

WE
BOUGHT
THE
FARM

CHAPTER 4

Brick-and-mortar buildings. An actual honest-to-God licence to produce cannabis. A knowledgeable master grower in Louis Gagnon. And staff.

After months of uncertainty and sleepless nights, it looked like Hydropothecary was in business.

While it seemed like the company was starting to find success, the one thing Seb and Adam didn't have was the one thing they needed as much as they needed each other: money.

It was apparent their cash flow was more like a cash drought and would continue to be unless they could raise investment capital in an ongoing way. They had pretty much exhausted all private avenues for raising money, aside from selling their houses or raiding their piggy banks. They needed a bigger solution, something sustainable that would see them through to their first sales, whenever that might be.

By reputation, they knew about Bay Street. Who didn't? As Toronto's financial heart, it beat with the blood of a thousand investors, financiers, angel investors, and commission workers, all hungry for the big deal that would make them a name. Running from Queens Quay, by the lake, to Davenport Road to the north, its shiny shrines to capitalism have been home to law firms, investment houses, and banks nearly since it was named Bay Street in 1797. (Ironically, for a financial district that has survived the ups and downs of bear and bull markets, Bay Street was originally called Bear Street, after its original ursine inhabitants.)

Despite his experience in finance and commercial banking, Seb wasn't familiar with capital markets and how they worked. Sure, he'd studied the theory in university, but that's all it was to him — a theory. He was about to be introduced to its reality, through a tall, fit, and a little too-silky sales guy named Rene.*

Rene knew Bay Street and, according to him, he knew the upper echelon. This being their first excursion to Canada's financial heart, Adam and Seb had no reason to doubt it. True, Rene hadn't yet made that big deal — he drove nice cars that were always a little older than they should be — but he was thirsty for it.

9 A.M., DECEMBER 20, 2013
ADAM'S HOUSE, CENTRETOWN
OTTAWA, ONTARIO

By the time their first meeting was set with Rene, Seb was ready. He'd written, reworked, and refined an investor deck that outlined their immediate ask for a $1 million injection. It wasn't grandiose, but it was polished and concise.

Rene arrived on time and, after a few courtesies, they sat down at Adam's dining-room table.

"So, what do you have for me?"

This was the only cue Seb needed. He immediately went into pitch mode, shooting at Rene rapid-fire facts and numbers from memory as if from a semi-automatic, while Adam interjected where needed. In retrospect — several years and a billion-dollar company later — a million dollars is a laughably pitiful ask. But at that time, their hands in empty pockets, it was the magic number as far as they knew. Eventually Seb wound down.

"Sorry. Not interested."

Rene's words were like a bucket of ice water to the face. But he was just being honest. He threw the printed deck on the table. He paused to look at each of them in turn.

"What would you boys do with $20 million?"

The truth is, a $1 million raise wasn't juicy enough for him, nor would it be for anyone else on Bay Street for that matter. Between 7 and 8 percent of cash raised would go to brokers and, since Rene couldn't raise $20 million on his own, he needed the ask to be big enough to earn a decent chunk of change. On $20 million, $1.6 million would go to the brokers, and he would earn perhaps $100,000 of that.

Almost in unison, Seb and Adam swallowed. That was a much bigger deal than they envisioned. That kind of cash would mean . . . well, it would mean an accelerated and far wider-ranging plan. It would also mean that, if nothing else, they had room to breathe.

Rene rose to leave. "I'll tell you what. You think about it, and if you come up with a good plan, I'll bring you to Toronto to meet some bankers on Bay Street. When can you have it ready for me?"

Seb laughed out loud. "Give me 30 minutes."

As soon as Rene left, they got right to business. They were dealing with orders of magnitude this time: what they could do with $1 million was nothing like what they could achieve with 20 times that number. A few hours before dawn, Seb finally left for home. But not to sleep.

"I worked through the night. I had my spreadsheet in front of me and was going through thousands of data points," he recalls. "We had been working on financial models for a few months and it was a manic process to make it much bigger."

The next morning, he bolted up Adam's dilapidated stairs, leaping over the missing third step, half an hour before Rene was due to arrive. Barely saying hello at the front door, he ran downstairs to the office, shouting over his shoulder, "Come on, I've changed the plan again. I need to show you."

Back at their 4-by-3-foot whiteboard, Seb sketched out his strategy. It was all there — rapid expansion of the facilities, a much bigger 36,000-square-foot greenhouse, an army of salespeople working directly with doctors, aggressive growth, and an accelerated timeline. It was a hell of a proposition, and the first time they deviated from their plan to have a family-owned, $20 million company. The returns would be even more impressive, but would Rene be dazzled, too?

At the appointed time, their guest arrived and they ushered him downstairs. For the next half hour, Seb went through the game plan, stopping every now and then to answer a question or expand on a point.

"So, that's it. That's what we've come up with," he said finally to Rene.

Rene grinned. He liked what he saw. He could sell this. Hell yeah, he could.

"Let's go to Bay Street. You boys own suits?"

9 A.M., FEBRUARY 5, 2014
FINANCIAL DISTRICT
TORONTO, ONTARIO

About a month and a half after meeting Rene, Adam, and Seb's train pulled in at Union Station in the middle of one of Toronto's rare but wild blizzards.

To the rest of eastern Canada, accustomed to dealing with metre-high snow drifts and strategically tucking in behind a slow-moving salt truck, or shovelling the front step five times in an hour to make sure you can get to work, snowstorms are bad but not unusual. In Toronto, they're caused by cold air careering its way across the warmer water of Lake Ontario, picking up vapour, rising through the atmosphere, and freezing before landing like a runaway train on shore. In short, a lake-effect blizzard is a sight to behold. Not worth calling out the military, perhaps, but still something the average Canadian would consider a nasty bit of weather. And, when such things happen, Toronto has PATH, a 30-kilometre long underground pedestrian network linking the subway to shopping, banking, and entertainment. More than 200,000 Torontonians use it every day.

Seb, Adam, and Rene were not among them.

After trying to decipher the myriad turns and junctions on PATH, they opted for a more direct and infinitely more hellish route aboveground. On streets completely devoid of pedestrians, cabs, and other traffic, the wind whipping snow in vertical whirls along Bay Street and straight up their jackets, the three men trudged, heads bowed, from Union Station to King Street. It was slow going, but they were on a mission. As a start to their coming two days of meetings, it wasn't auspicious — but it was prescient.

Bay Street is Canada's Wall Street, populated by the same kind of people who inhabit New York's famed financial hub. Sitting at a long boardroom table throughout the first day, Seb and Adam pitched to men whose interest varied from "You have five minutes" to "I gotta take this call." One guy looked like Tom Cruise's combed-over douche canoe character in *Tropic Thunder*. At one point, a group of eight brokers trooped in, half of them on their phones, the other half verbally high-fiving each other for investing $20 million in a beach-footwear company marketing flip-flops with a bottle opener in the sole. Ignoring Seb and Adam altogether, some still carried on their conversations or walked back out of the room to attend to other business. And when they did pay attention, they couldn't understand that Hydropothecary would not only be the first to grow cannabis in a purpose-built greenhouse at a time when no one in their right mind was proposing that, but they would do it at a low cost while producing high-end products. The pitch was fulsome, layered, and far too complex. Seb fumed as he talked. Looking back, he admits the message should have been streamlined.

"We shouldn't even have said we want to be a marijuana company. We should have said, 'We're here because we need to raise $5 million. We've got one of the very limited licences in this country, and we grow in greenhouses. We're going to be a low-cost, high-quality producer.' But we didn't."

Billion Dollar Lesson

"When you are a start-up pitching to investors, know your audience. Who are you pitching to? A retail investor? A family member? An institution? If you're lucky, you've found a sophisticated retail investor. Then simplify. You've memorized all your numbers, and that's important. You need to know your numbers for the questions. But you probably have two minutes to grab their attention and say why you're there. If they don't know why you're there after two minutes, you've lost the pitch." — **Seb**

Inexperience was rearing its head. During drinks with potential backers, one mentioned that he did a lot of work on the retail investment side of things. Adam immediately perked up: as a brand guy, all this technical talk of money, fees, and granted equity was out of his wheelhouse. But retail? If it meant stores selling their product, it was something he could get his teeth into. Would it be possible to cross-promote between retail commerce and retail finance, he wondered aloud. After a moment's silence, during which the bankers sought to control their twitching smiles, they kindly explained that no, retail investment had nothing to do with stores. Adam squirmed at his blunder and looked over at Seb. Of all the emotions that can run across a person's face, Seb's was clearly "facepalm."

Still, Rene kept the meetings coming, even landing a face-to-face with the man dubbed "the Bulldog of Bay Street"* by the end of their first day in the Big Smoke. The Bulldog was a formidable financier with a reputation for being smart, asking tough questions, and nutting out favourable deals, at least for himself. It wouldn't be an easy meeting, Rene warned, but any time with the Bulldog was worth 10 times that with the guys glued to their phones.

Whatever else Rene had going on, whatever deals he was working, at least he got them in front of the Bulldog. Their faith — or was it curiosity — in Rene's connections had been piqued on the train from Ottawa. After showing them photos of his beautiful young girlfriend, he gestured to a large weekend duffle bag he'd refused to stow in the forward luggage compartment. Offhand insouciance on overdrive, he said, "I'll have to deposit the contents at a bank when we get to T.O." Seb and Adam nodded knowingly but privately wondered if he was telling the truth or setting them up. What was in that bag? How much money could fit in a bag like that? Was it even legal to carry that kind of cash? (Once in Toronto, Rene did stop at a bank on their way to their meetings; neither Seb nor Adam asked what he did nor discovered the bag's contents.)

The next day followed the same pattern: more pitching, lots of talking, a little listening, and not much interest. It was disheartening, but neither Seb nor Adam were put off. One thing they had learned from the experience so far was that Bay Street had plenty of money and some smart people behind it. They just had to find the right fit.

Billion Dollar Lesson

"Building a funnel matters. Build your funnel, because if you have only one opportunity, it's that much harder to land the deal. When you're a start-up, the mentality is all about chasing the dragon. You just have to get the deal, because that's the one thing you need to survive. You know you're not a start-up anymore when, with enough staff and resources, if you don't land that dragon, you have three more to chase and you just keep going." — **Seb**

The Bulldog was aptly named. A stocky 50-something weather-beaten Eastern European immigrant entrepreneur, the Bulldog was a man who clearly lived well, had large appetites, and pursued them with gusto. He was a lover of good white wine, skiing in the Alps, and the front row at Milan Fashion Week. If it was worth his attention, he pursued it with dogged focus until its natural conclusion, whatever that was.

Seb and Adam were ushered into the Bulldog's offices. After two days of ultra-monied boardrooms and pounding back beer in expensive bars populated by distracted and disinterested brokers, this meeting was nothing short of revelatory for them. The offices themselves weren't posh — they were okay but hardly top floor and top drawer — yet they spoke of a barometer that gauged just how much money should go into show and how much should be directed into weightier things. Maybe it was because the Bulldog and his two colleagues were older than the punks they'd met the day before, maybe it was the modest (for Bay Street) surroundings. Whatever the matrix, this was the meeting Seb and Adam were meant to have.

True to his reputation, the Bulldog asked all the tough questions. All. Of. Them. But, high on adrenalin after two days of endless pitching, Seb and Adam had the answers. And, for once, the answers were listened to and the content of them heard. More questions were asked. The brothers-in-law had been promised 20 minutes with the financiers. They had an hour, and not once did the Bulldog or his colleagues look at their phones. Watching Seb answer questions, exercise his knowledge and financial intellect, Adam was reminded of a man who kept his motorcycle in the garage all winter and was taking it out on the highway in the spring for the first time. He was in his element. At one point, the Bulldog's boss sidled into the room to listen. As the meeting drew to a close, the Bulldog stood up and extended his hand.

"I appreciate your time, gentlemen. Thank you for coming to see us. I'd like to review this and get some more information. It's very interesting, very interesting, yes."

Back at the Sheraton hotel on Queen Street West, Adam quickly changed out of his suit and left to relax in the pool. It had been a long and challenging day. While not despondent, Seb was not upbeat about the meeting they'd had with the Bulldog, and told Adam, "Well, fuck, that didn't work."

As it turned out, he was wrong. While Adam floated in the pool a few floors away, the Bulldog called Seb. He hit Seb with a few more questions, the last of which was "Can you come back to the office tomorrow? The boss wants a meeting with you and Adam."

The second meeting with the Bulldog and his boss went very well. They were straightforward, pragmatic people who asked the kind of questions Seb loved to answer. He knew there was a deal to be made, it was just a matter of how and when. There'd be another meeting, the Bulldog promised, but first he was headed to Europe for a holiday. He'd be in touch as soon as he returned.

Billion Dollar Lesson

"Start-ups will be allocated 15 or 20 minutes for the pitch, then you get questions. Cover your strategy. Cover the industry, your total addressable market, and how you're going to win that industry. You have to talk about what is going to prevent someone else with more money from beating you. Briefly talk about your team. But do not read to them. Bigger, more sophisticated institutions will read everything before the meeting, but not smaller investors.

They'll make an investment decision based on the feel and confidence you have." — **Seb**

Outside of Hollywood and its fascination with interminable youth, time does not stand still. It certainly didn't for Hydropothecary.

One week passed. Two. Still no bite from the Bulldog. But, as Rene pointed out, that was far from unusual. Pitches and ideas fly up and down Bay Street like leaves in a wind tunnel; if one doesn't land, the next one might. Such was the case with a broker named Dean.*

On their first night in Toronto, Adam and Seb had met with him and his colleague. He was smart, likeable, and curious in a way the other brokers were not. Maybe he wasn't playing at the same level, perhaps he was a bit unsophisticated, but Dean knew people, he understood the game, and he was removed enough to see cannabis for what it was: unexplored potential.

That first night in Toronto, Dean invited the guys out for dinner near their hotel on Queen Street West. As the group settled in and made small talk while perusing the menus, Seb took charge. Ever the stroppy alpha male, he ordered expensive Scotch and, fired up by a day of adrenalin-charged pitches, took the lead on ordering the food for everyone, no expense spared. Seb on a high is a juggernaut: unstoppable, impressive, and not to be denied. So Dean didn't. When the bill arrived, the waiter handed it to Seb without protest from Dean, likely assuming that the man who takes charge wants to pay. Every emotion played across Seb's face in a micro-moment as he examined the tab: shock (the $750 bill was just shy of 1 percent of Hydropothecary's entire $100,000 operating capital); annoyance, anger, and frustration.

Through the filter of several years, Adam and Seb recall the incident differently.

"Dean was appreciative of the meal but was abiding by basic social norms in letting Seb pay," says Adam. "I mean, he did end up offering us $2.5 million, so it was worth it. We were struggling to balance having no money and being frugal with being frugal when we should have spent money."

Seb? "He stiffed us for the bill. I go, 'What the fuck?' It was a lot for us, and all off my line of credit. Later he offered $2.5 million, and he had a bunch of rules around that, because he was going to his networks and trying to raise money. Now, in a phone call, I can raise $50 million. I've sat on my back deck and raised $2.1 million for a small start-up in an hour. Those guys? We've eclipsed their wildest dreams."

But that is now. Back then, as the clock wound down to the deadline for taking possession of the MMAR plants they'd purchased, landing a deal was all that mattered. February turned into March and as the snow disappeared, so, too, did their chances of getting the financing they desperately needed. No word from the Bulldog.

Then, on March 7, Dean and his colleague called back with the offer of $2.5 million. It seemed that the spring sun was starting to shine. It wasn't the big payday they'd hoped for, but it would get them out of a jam in the short term, offer some breathing room and a bit of space to think. There wasn't a big celebration, more a small sigh of relief. True, they hadn't heard back from the Bulldog, but that was business. They would take Dean's money and turn it into an even more attractive investment.

But sometimes, life zigs and you zag. You expect a smooth ride, but hit a bump in the road that sets you airborne. That's what happened a week later, on March 14.

The phone rang. It was the Bulldog. He was back from Europe, had had a great time in the Alps, and wondered if the guys wanted to meet to discuss a deal.

The deal was for $3 million. The brokers' fees were high, but still, it was money. Lots of money. And it aligned with the revised and rapid expansion vision Seb had outlined to Rene two months earlier. With this injection of cash, they could get started on breaking ground for their new 36,000-square-foot greenhouse known as B5 (or Building 5), budgeted to cost $2 million. Another $200,000 would pay off a debt, and Louis would get $800,000 for the property itself. Although they didn't have the money yet, it was already spent.

The offer posed a dilemma for Adam and Seb: they were days away from returning to Toronto to sign the deal with Dean and his colleague, and they would have to tell them they'd changed their minds. Their offer was good, but the Bulldog brought a seasoned and reputable Bay Street name with him, and they wanted to align with him and him alone. But they'd have to say all that, if not in person, then over the phone.

On a call a few days later, Seb spelled out the situation to Dean: they'd been offered a bigger cash flow and, to be honest, it was more the investment size they'd been looking for, but Dean's interest was really appreciated.

For a heartbeat, there was silence on Dean's end of the line. No one clicked a pen. No one breathed. Did these two punks from Ottawa really just say no to his offer? Dean was floored.

"They smoked us!" he spluttered to the other, unseen partner in the room. Back in Ottawa, as Adam squirmed in his seat, Seb beside him remained stone-faced until the call ended. It was a look Adam would come to know in future years, for a different reason.

A fan of the Mark Zuckerberg school of negotiations, in which you refuse to budge until the deal sweetens, Seb believed in fighting for the 1 percentage points, because eventually they add up. In later negotiations with other partners, Seb would flex that Zuckerberg muscle and maintain his position for hours until a deal improved. "And if it didn't, he'd keep trying," says Adam. Often, we'd eventually get a better deal by sheer virtue of the offeree fearing starvation or losing their mind. And Seb loved it. He could go 48 hours straight if need be, watching the other side of the table squirm."

Billion Dollar Lesson

"My approach to deal making from five years ago is nothing like my approach now. I used to grind every last possible detail. I've learned that's not always the right thing to do. I used to look at a deal and say, 'Oh, man, I wish I would've saved an extra 10 percent.' And you do need to grind it to within 20 percent reasonable. But you also have to look at a deal as a win-win. It's for everybody. You can leave some on the table, because that helps you get more deals done. The more deals flow, the more momentum you have. In a hyper-growth industry, it's very important to move deliberately, but quickly, as well." — **Seb**

6 A.M., MARCH 31, 2014
MASSON-ANGERS, QUEBEC

The day broke bright and clear, already 3°C at dawn, with the promise of at least seven degrees by mid-afternoon. It was, in fact, the kind of day that construction teams and outdoor workers relish: cool but not frigid air, and a bit of warmth from the sun to seep through their layers of jackets and sweaters.

It was a day to note for other reasons, too. Today was the Health Canada deadline for LPs to secure and transfer genetic material, or specific strains of cannabis plants, from MMAR-licensed home growers.

Like every other LP in Canada, Hydropothecary had six types of seeds, courtesy of Health Canada. But if everyone was growing the exact same thing, under the same government-mandated conditions, there was little competitive advantage aside from the growing facilities themselves. So Hydropothecary bought plants from people licensed to grow under the old MMAR regulations. Still, plants and seeds are just tools. Adam wanted to get to a place where there was instant recognition of what a product could do, without ever really spelling it out. Health Canada's restrictions on that point were vaudevillian in one sense, but Adam and Seb were also trying to build a landscape for a product that was entirely a hybrid: part medical, part recreational. Like the excise tax on cigarettes, alcohol, and gas-burning cars, marijuana would be penalized financially and through guidelines that cribbed from the rulebooks on tobacco, booze, and pharmaceuticals.

Months earlier, Adam and Seb had met with several growers willing to supply Hydropothecary. (Other, more established LPs could have supplied Hydropothecary, too. Not that they would have; before Hydropothecary focused on smoke-free innovations and consumer goods, a strain's genetic profile was often the only key differentiator in product development in the traditional smoked-cannabis market.)

Sébastien at the 2018 HEXO AGM.

Sébastien holding the MMPR application about to be sent to Health Canada.

Adam as a child.

Adam aged 12.

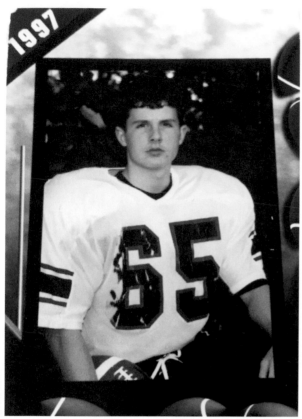

LEFT: Sébastien in 1997.

BELOW: Sébastien as a child.

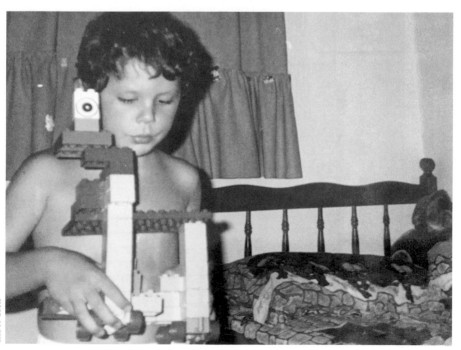

The farm house.

Justin Gagnon almost hidden in the 12' marijuana plants.

The first Hydropothecary office in Gatineau. November 2015.

Marijuana growing in Building 5. 2017.

The original Hydropothecary product lineup.

The first Hydropothecary boxes.

A vault (right) and a processing room (left) in Building 5.

The Hydropothecary team opening the Toronto Stock Exchange.

Sébastien giving a tour of Building 5.

Ground breaking of Building 6.

Armed with cannabis information — some accurate, some not so much — they'd visited homes and facilities. At one high-rise building in Ottawa's Carlington neighbourhood, Adam and Seb took the elevator up several floors and were greeted at the door by the potential seller. The two-bedroom apartment was nicely decorated; the only outward evidence of cannabis use was a lighter, a rolling tray, and a few papers on a coffee table.

The owner led Adam and Seb down the hall, past the bathroom, to the second bedroom. Taped to the door was a Health Canada MMAR licence. The owner opened the door and invited them in.

Adam wasn't sure what to expect from a home grow-op. Living in British Columbia, he'd seen TV footage of police busts. Some were massive illegal operations out in the forest, and some were black market grow-ops in nondescript houses made dank and dark by covered windows, hydroponics tables, and mildew creeping quietly through the drywall.

This was not that. Adam stepped forward into a massive black tent lined with silver reflective paper. On one side, the licensed grower had plants carefully drying in a controlled environment. On the other, sativa and indica shrubs burst with life and vigour. The entire operation was well-thought-out, fastidious, and obviously built to exacting standards. Adam nodded.

"We'd like to buy cuttings and plants."

Plants were in pots. Money was in the bank. The next issue was finding the right people to grow the former so they could be paid with the latter. Before then, however, Adam and Seb had already dealt with a few hires. The first was named Mary Lou.*

Mary Lou was a bright woman with all the right credentials to fulfill quality assurance requirements when the only thing on the cards was the Rue Bombardier facility in Gatineau. And she looked the part: a winsome, tie-dyed hippie with a vaguely distracted air. She was a paper employee who did not actually work but was hired through Kijiji to be a name on an application to Health Canada. The role, like an official agent for an election campaign, was a formality required by the Access to Cannabis for Medical Purposes Regulations (ACMPR) legislation that had replaced earlier guidelines — MMAR and MMPR — in 2016.

Then came Dante,* another Kijiji attempt, this time at finding an operations manager. At first blush, he seemed ideal. A soft-spoken and introverted cannabis enthusiast with a solid background in horticulture and farming, he was keen from the start. During the interview, Adam asked, "Is there anything you need to do this job?"

Dante didn't skip a beat. "In all seriousness, a cot at the building so I can work and sleep."

Yet, having been hired long before a licence was obtained, Dante didn't last long. Without financing, Hydropothecary couldn't put him on salary. At least not yet. Besides, Adam quickly realized after writing a few more Kijiji ads that his approach was not going to attract the kind of people he needed to be surrounded by. Prior to leaving for India the year before, Adam and Seb had hired a tiny human resources agency, not just to find the right people for the right money but to help define the company culture. While Adam and Seb were in India, the consultant had walked them through the exercises, drilled down to what they needed, and found them their first real employee. But when they returned, the consultant presented them with a bill for $2,500.

Given that the arrangement was for $1,200, Seb lost his cool. The scope creep in the final invoice was far beyond the contract. As Seb blasted the consultant and the consultant yelled back, Adam saw the balance of their relationship. Seb cared about the pennies and business; Adam, about the people and relationships. He could see more clearly how their interpersonal and business relationships would grow.

Billion Dollar Lesson

"As young entrepreneurs, an HR specialist seemed impractical. You're a gunslinger moving at the speed of light, and if people can't keep up, leave them. But if you get the right HR person, they can be an incredibly powerful and useful tool for building the culture and process. You have a strategy partner who oversees the people. This speaks to Seb's overall view of the industry, where talent is mapped over an XY graph of time and success, and the one thing that runs through it is a line, which is the people. Our first HR person was employee number 46. And she should have been number 6." — **Adam**

But one good thing did come out of the relationship with the human resources agency: a big, burly guy named Josh.* Before they parted ways in October 2013, the consultant had put him forward as a potential general manager. He seemed like a good fit. An operational engineer with an MMAR licence, he also held a Six Sigma Black Belt, a certification in business process improvement. Plus, he was a former World Wrestling Federation (WWF) fighter. For that alone, Adam was curious. And excited. As a kid, he followed WWF, most particularly Razor Ramon, a charismatic wrestler and multiple world champion. He was busting to ask Josh about his experiences.

For their first real on-the-books employee, an interview in the basement didn't set the right tone. Adam had long since relinquished his media offices, and the Rue Bombardier site was still under construction. Scrambling to find a meeting room, Adam found a small office rented out by the hour (which they rented for just one hour) and set up the date and time. Josh met them in the lobby, and for the next few minutes, followed Adam and Seb from office to office as they tried to locate the room. Josh said nothing. A blush crept up Adam's neck as he imagined this big man thinking, "Oh my God . . . and these two guys think they're going to grow weed in Quebec?"

Even so, the interview went well. At the time, Josh had two young sons and was walking 16 kilometres a day as a meter reader to make ends meet. He was looking for something a little more regular and in his wheelhouse that would allow him to be available to his family. By the end of the conversation, it was clear that Josh was the perfect fit. A big, calm presence, he would turn out to be the kind of employee who, no matter what was needed, could and would get it done.

The same could not be said of the next two employees, a pair of English-speaking-only MMAR growers hired for their experience in cannabis genetics and operations. Like almost every MMAR-licensed grower in the country, they'd accumulated a wealth of insight through trial and error and multi-generational knowledge transfer.

But there were problems from the outset. Unfamiliar with working in a corporate environment — or one hoping to become corporate — they viewed the 8 a.m. start time at the greenhouse as more of a suggestion than a hard-and-fast rule. But that wasn't what undid them. They also brought with them spiritual ideas about marijuana plants that did not mesh with Louis's practical, no-nonsense approach. He had no patience for their belief that cannabis plants have souls, nor that such a belief could dictate how they should be cultivated. In one instance, a heated argument developed over stakes being used to hold up the plants. The growers insisted that they were stressing the plants and diminishing their cannabinoid content but couldn't explain why. Louis dismissed their ideas with an impatient wave of his hand. To his credit, when they turned out to be right about the relationship between plant stress and cannabinoids, he immediately designed a potting cage that would rectify the issue and had them custom made.

Dissatisfied with the growers' performance and unable to adequately overcome the language barrier, Louis campaigned to have their employment terminated. In theory, he could have done it himself but instead inundated Adam and Seb with daily accounts of misconduct, tardiness, and unfinished projects. Team leadership, it soon became clear, meant listening to issues, then allowing managers to do their job. Eventually, the company would face several near catastrophes that would help them define roles, create trackable measures of job performance, and develop a system of controls and approvals. Fortunately, they didn't know what was coming.

Billion Dollar Lesson

"Fill the room with people smarter than you, then get the hell out of the way. We always meddled in team structure. That was a mistake. As if there wasn't enough to do, with not enough time, we effectively tied one hand behind the backs of many on our leadership team. It took us a long time to overcome this." — **Adam**

Firing the two growers was unpleasant but necessary. The men were called in to Karl's office in downtown Ottawa on a Monday morning in late May 2014. Adam, Seb, and Karl were present. If the decision to let them go was hard, their reaction made it that much worse. One stared, bewildered at the news and, after a moment of digesting it, burst into tears and sobbed uncontrollably. The second responded with anger, at first insisting that the decision be reversed before throwing out expletives like verbal hand grenades.

Shaken after the meeting, Adam walked to a coffee shop to get cold drinks. The whole experience was horrifying, not just because of the mens' reactions but because he had caused two people to lose their livelihoods. There were grounds for dismissal, of course, but it was still an uncomfortable feeling. Nearing the coffee shop, he noticed a car driving aggressively toward him. Was it? Oh, shit, it *was* one of the two former employees. Adam stopped in his tracks, his skin instantly prickling with a flood of adrenalin. The man abruptly hit the brakes and rolled down his window. Adam took a step back. He had no idea what the man was going to say, but given the angry scowl on his face, it wasn't going to be a cheery hello.

"Hey, I forgot to return this," he said, tossing a piece of equipment at Adam. As he hit the gas pedal to drive away, Adam heard him yell over his shoulder, "And go fuck yourself!"

JUNE 2014

THE FARM, CHEMIN DE LA RIVE

MASSON-ANGERS, QUEBEC

Even without problematic employees, life on the farm did not run in a straight-plowed furrow. Front and centre of the operation was Louis's farmhouse, where he lived with his common-law wife. Built to resemble a Victorian gabled home, it was small but welcoming. The next biggest structure was the 7,000-square-foot greenhouse, but other parts of the operation were a hodgepodge of make-do buildings that had seen better days. Loose plastic sheets draped over the skeleton of a disused greenhouse flapped disconsolately in the wind. A few sheds that once housed flowers and perennials now stood vacant, their signs faded in the sunlight. Some housed farm equipment, others the remnants of growing tables. Attached to the disused greenhouse at the entrance of the property was a machine shed, over which was a staff kitchen and toilet, the pipes of which froze every winter. Every interior wall was inscribed with effusive love notes written by Louis or his partner to each other, scribbled in marker or pencil. At the centre of the farmyard was the uninsulated former retail area, a wooden structure with a verandah and peaked roof. During the summer months, it became a makeshift office for Adam, Seb, and whoever else needed its folding chairs and wobbly card table. Investors visiting the property required a leap of faith and a vivid imagination if they wanted to sleep at night.

What the farm lacked in finesse, it made up for in the willingness of everyone there to get their hands dirty with any task that arose. "Farm job" became common parlance for getting as much of a task done yourself or with help for as cheaply as possible. After a pipe burst outside the main storage shed and flooded the driveway, Seb grabbed a shovel and joined Louis, already exhausted and burned out by the pace of cannabis life, in a trench he'd been digging for two days to get to the bottom of the disaster. For multi-person farm jobs, Adam would hit the phone to call in as many favours as possible. The prevailing attitude was that of scarcity: if anyone saved a buck by doing a job themselves rather than hiring a professional or tradesperson, it was rewarded with great praise. When Louis engaged a local man to grate the ground for the foundation of B5, the guys mentally back-slapped each other for saving $15,000. The smiles disappeared when it was time to install joists. The levelling was off by a quarter of an inch, a catastrophe that cost an additional $50,000 to fix. Then, Louis ordered and installed steel posts — backwards. Intended to slope down the roof line, they had to be trimmed by almost 0.5 metre to correct the error.

Billion Dollar Lesson

"Hire people who are good at what they do. A lot of people think they are better than everybody else at what they do. They underestimate how complex someone's expertise is. Look at a successful food truck operator. You think, how hard is it to run a food truck and make tacos? No. That guy probably has 20 years in the kitchen, has this awesome recipe his mom taught him a long time ago, and has knowledge you can't ever replicate." — **Seb**

As B5 began to take shape, the company's thriftiness continued. Two vaults were needed, similar to the one in the bunker that was being used to store dried product. They had to be big enough to store millions of dollars in weed, cheap enough to fit the budget, and impenetrable enough to keep out the bad guys.

Security, or rather the criminal element engaged in the illicit cannabis market, was very much on Adam and Seb's minds. That year, Statistics Canada estimated that Canadians were consuming almost 700 tons of cannabis a year, worth about $3.4 billion. If legal cannabis companies were going to scoop up the lion's share of that illegal trade through medical marijuana, surely that would put the owners at risk?

They'd spoken to enough career criminals running large grow-ops to know that organized crime was involved. Besides, rumours were already flying about intimidation by biker gangs, each version more threatening than the next. Seb recounted how he'd heard bikers roll up at one facility in a show of force. The story strained credibility when the owner allegedly convinced the hardened criminals to go home by piously citing government oversight and camera surveillance as the reason he couldn't just hand over his product. Adam countered with an even more apocryphal version in which bikers paid a midnight visit to an owner's house, left two "soldiers" with the family, and took the owner away.

Whatever the truth — and there was no guarantee it landed between either tale — it rattled them enough that they hired a former RCMP officer who worked for Interpol to assess the risk. Did they need to replace their front doors at home with triple barricades? Did he think personal security was necessary? Adam was particularly shaken, as his first thought was for the safety of Meena and his family. Seb had a different attitude. As he listened to the stories, his blood boiled, and he recalled the one time in high school when an older student with a background in petty crime threatened him. Seb, then 16 and a football player, picked up the thug and threw him to the ground, saying, "I don't give a shit who you know, and if they want to talk to me, send them over. So shut the fuck up and don't be an asshole." To him, the potential threat from a biker gang sounded the perfect Rambo fantasy. "I was dumb enough to be totally like, 'Yeah! Fight to the death and here we go,'" he now says, laughing.

The consultant downgraded their fears, but it was Louis's homespun common sense that dispatched them altogether. Security wasn't meant to keep people out, he said, but rather to delay their getting in. Besides, what was the scenario they were panicking about? Do the thieves come in a truck? Five trucks? Twenty trucks? Do they crash through the fence? Whoever they were, it's not like they'd have an hour to make the haul by grabbing as many plants as they could, because the police response time in Masson-Angers was 3 minutes. And even if the police took 15 minutes, he added, there is only one way in and out of the farm, on the deeply rutted and bumpy Chemin de la Rive. A quick getaway? He started laughing.

Fears assuaged, Seb and Adam pressed on with finding vaults. Miraculously, a grocery chain had just bought a new property and wanted to unload two vaults it contained. They were free to anyone who could dismantle them and take them away.

If it sounds too good to be true, as they say . . . but dollar signs were ka-chinging at the thought of getting two $30,000 vaults for nothing more than the cost of labour and vehicles. Local workers were hired, and someone loaned them a truck. It seemed like a win. Not so much. None of the workers had ever dismantled or installed a vault before, much less two of them, which meant more hours on the clock as they struggled to figure it out without instructions. The borrowed truck was brought in — surely this would work?! — only to be deemed too small. A bigger truck was rented. Ultimately it cost the same, if not more, than if they had just ordered new vaults and had them professionally installed. All in all, those early penny-pinching decisions proved to be false economy that cost the company far more than it ever saved.

It was a dire lesson to learn, but it also spoke to the gunslinger mindset rampant not only at Hydropothecary but in other areas of the nascent cannabis industry. Faced with a daily frenetic pace, an uncertain landscape that seemed to shift by the minute, and a deep-seated sense of urgency to turn a profit and make good on promises to family and friends who supported them, Adam and Seb were shooting from the hip. Decisions were made quickly, instinctively, and without a backwards glance. Sometimes it worked, sometimes it didn't. As it had been in the basement office, it felt like constantly moving forward was more important than having a set destination.

Billion Dollar Lesson

"Take the time to breathe and think a project all the way through before jumping in at full speed. We had to learn the hard way the value of presenting plans that speak specifically to a problem, while undergoing extensive internal stakeholder consultations with everyone from finance and operations to IT and marketing. As the company grew, in terms of both the complexity and number of decisions being made, it became harder to know what was being decided and even harder to properly communicate to the rest of the management team. The two-hour weekly show-and-tell with standing room only was often the only time department heads heard from one another and got a glimpse into the hundred things going on that week." — **Adam**

That month, the deal with the Bulldog's company finally closed.

"It was huge. More money than we'd ever seen in our lives, and we were feeling pretty good about that. It was a ton of equity and capital. It was $3 million for half a second, but the greenhouse budget was now $3 million, plus we had to pay out Louis, so we were broke again," Seb recalls.

Fortunately, another $1 million in the form of a convertible debenture appeared through talented and well-connected financiers from Toronto, Chris Kaufman and Jay Ewart. Jay had first met Adam and Seb when he was running Fountain Assets Corp. and the duo pitched their pot company to him.

"Adam was always buttoned down," Jay recalls. "He had everything but the smoking pipe. If he walked into a room with a pocket watch and a monocle, I'd have said, 'Yup.' Seb was a little more upscale casual. They came in, and I was convinced they would be successful leaders in the space. They practically finished each other's sentences."

That relationship came to fruition when the money from Jay and the others came through, though the deal attached to it carried some fairly predatory terms. Had the loan been called in, for example, it would have sunk Hydropothecary altogether. Seb was determined to get out from underneath the debt. One weekend, Adam, Seb, and Jay gathered for a meeting at the cottage of their investor and board member Dr. Michael Munzar. Once that was over, it was down to the dock on the lake for a campfire and beers. The topic of the convertible debenture came up, with Seb insisting the debt be converted into stock to get it off the books.

"I had to present it to my company's board, but Seb was adamant he would get this done or he'd drown me," recalls Jay. "We were yelling at each other, though he was doing what any CEO would do — pointing out that the company was doing amazing things, that he wanted out of the debt, and that we would do well on the conversion. Eventually we wound down and went to bed."

The next morning, no one said much amid the tense atmosphere. Ultimately, the debt was converted, to everyone's satisfaction. "And I didn't have to go to the bottom of the lake for it," says Jay, laughing.

8 A.M., OCTOBER 11, 2014
THE FARM, CHEMIN DE LA RIVE
MASSON-ANGERS, QUEBEC

The Facebook post was made with the best of intentions. But it nearly blew up in Adam's face.

A few days earlier, Louis had announced it was time for their first harvest. Every plant burst with life; flowers were visibly covered in the tiny, terpene-rich hairs called trichomes. Louis and his eldest son had walked Seb and Adam through, proudly pointing out the biggest and bounciest buds. The sativa plants were enormous. A staggering 14 feet tall, they had grown unfettered in the greenhouse next to their shorter, stouter indica cousins. Louis's son, who had grown up on the farm and was then the company's facility and security manager, posed for a photo among the plants, with their 20-gram buds. They dwarfed him by 2.5 metres.

Adam was excited. After everything they'd been through — all the money worries, near misses, and full-on calamities — this at least was visible, tangible progress. Their first harvest! Not only were they paddling with the tide, but for once it seemed like they knew where they were going. Plus, the weather forecast for Thanksgiving was fabulous: sunny, a few clouds, and around 14°C.

There was just one issue. They weren't ready. Not even close, largely because, in all their planning, they didn't anticipate when the crop would be ready. Although Louis had spent years as a master grower renowned for cultivating thousands of exotic plants, he'd never had to oversee a harvest. What he grew had never needed picking. So when he decided it was time to start trimming the plants, it had to be done immediately, especially since some were beginning to look like they could develop mould. But even with the existing crew, plus Seb's mother, Lise, they didn't have nearly enough hands to do the job. Nor did they have enough equipment, much less the right equipment.

Adam went into overdrive, hitting every dry cleaner he could find to buy two thousand metal coat hangers, intended to be used as drying racks. Then, he called every possible person he knew who had a week off, a current and clear criminal record check, and a pair of scissors. Still, he needed more bodies, at least 10 more. A contact at Invest Ottawa offered to post something on its Facebook page, if Adam cared to draft it. Up it went and immediately the fur flew. A competitor start-up sent the ad to Health Canada. And Health Canada was not happy.

"We really didn't do anything wrong," says Adam, "but they didn't like it. One of the lines said, 'Bring your own scissors.' What Health

Canada heard was 'Hey, anyone come on by to what is supposed to be a secure licensed facility (which it very much was) and have a go at snipping some plants' — like a pick-your-own strawberry farm. That was the first time we came up against the regulator like that."

It was a near miss, but in the end, the harvest came in. The question was where would they dry it? As the crew worked around the clock to trim the buds, Seb and Louis talked over the problem. The underground vault was licensed to store marijuana, but it was in no way big enough to do the job. They had to think of something, and quickly. Seb looked up at the ceiling for inspiration. There was an idea, vaguely formed in his mind. No licensed space to dry in . . . but they did have a licensed space! "Louis!" he shouted, startling his partner. "We dry it right here, in the greenhouse! It's big enough, we have the space. There's nowhere else."

Louis laughed and slapped Seb on the shoulder, then immediately began giving instructions. "Grab the truck," he said quickly in French. "Head over to Russell — I'll give you the address — we'll need several rolls of gardening cloth. Take two guys with you. And hurry!"

Jumping into the cab of a beat-up blue Dodge truck with a noisy exhaust and a propensity to gas whoever was in the cab, Seb set off down Chemin de la Quai to the Cumberland ferry for the two-hour round trip to the supply centre in rural Ontario. By the time he returned with a pounding carbon monoxide–induced headache and the rolls of fabric, Louis and his son were already building drying racks. Seb clambered up a ladder to start putting things in place just as Adam showed up with Meena and Aruna's Rajan Uncle.

"Hey, Seb!" Adam shouted up. Seb glanced down and continued his work. Two minutes. Three minutes of awkward silence passed. Adam half smiled at Rajan, who was visiting from India and was privately impressed at how hard everyone was working to get things done. Eventually Seb climbed down the ladder, exchanged a warm, brief greeting, and then was off again to work. There was no time to lose.

Meena and Aruna hadn't been seeing much of their husbands, so Meena brought Iyla and one-month-old Nalina to the farm for a quick visit with Adam. (Meena had been shocked to learn she was pregnant in January, when Iyla was just 11 months old. Sharing the surprising news, Aruna had waggishly quipped, "Why are you surprised? We used to watch *Teen Mom* together. That's what happens when you have unprotected sex.")

The hard work was over. There was definitely a sense of accomplishment in the air, together with the distinctive skunky odour of cannabis. As the crew packed up, amid jokes and laughter, someone asked, "I wonder who our first clients will be? Who's going to admit to the government that they smoke weed?"

The answer came the next day, which was Thanksgiving Sunday. And it was devastating.

At age 52, Adam's father, Gaston, was a man in his prime, raising three girls aged 7, 9, and 12 with his second wife, Kim, at their home outside Edmonton. He hiked in the hills, sometimes taking Adam with him. He loved getting out on his mountain bike or in his kayak. He ate well and lived clean. He seemed invincible.

And he believed he was, too. When a persistent cough didn't clear up, he was initially diagnosed with pneumonia and given antibiotics by his GP. They didn't work and, as the days passed, he became dizzy and was struggling to breathe. At the local hospital, a young ER doctor looked him over.

"You're having trouble breathing because your lung is filled with liquid," he said. "This isn't pneumonia. Everything you've been told is wrong. There's something happening in your body that's causing all this liquid to seep into your lungs. I have to drain it."

When the doctor explained that he'd have to push a thin metal tube into the chest cavity to drain the liquid, Gaston point-blank refused the treatment and marched out. He didn't believe the doctor. But the following week, when he saw his own GP again, she had revised her opinion. An X-ray had showed that Gaston had lung cancer.

He was shocked. Bilateral stage-four lung cancer in a non-smoker? Inconceivable. Impossible. How was this even a thing? It was small comfort when his specialist later pointed out that non-smokers account for 20 percent of lung cancer cases, the disease mostly caused by exposure to things like radon gas, asbestos, or second-hand smoke, or due to genetic mutations.

When his phone rang that Sunday, Adam was still bubbling from the satisfaction not only of seeing the cannabis company taking shape with its first harvest but of working with his hands. There was something so elemental about the repetitive nature of harvesting, being surrounded by these towering plants and feeling muscle stiffness at the end of the day. It felt good.

But that evaporated the minute he heard the tone of Gaston's voice, audible despite what sounded in the background like three hundred kids going ballistic. Gaston had brought his daughters out to a fun park, as a distraction. But as he tried to share the news with Adam, he couldn't seem to form the words.

"Sorry, Dad, I can't make out what you just said. What are you saying?"

A break in the noise coincided with Gaston's next words. "It's cancer. I have cancer."

In fact, it was so far advanced, the most anyone could do was reduce the tumour size and maybe buy him some time.

"But what does it mean, Dad?" Adam asked, his voice rising over the noise coming down the line. "Tell me. What are they doing to fix this?"

At the other end of the line, Gaston gasped for another breath. "We don't know. We don't know anything, but there is water in my lungs." His oncologist was recommending chemotherapy, he added, as well as clinical trials. Gaston wasn't going to give up that easily.

Long after the call, Adam sat on his porch step, staring at the phone. He had a million questions, but first he needed to digest the news. His heart was beating double time and his mouth was dry, but around him, all distractions fell away. He tamped down the panic and resorted to his default position of planning around problems: What am I going to do without my dad? What can I do to help?

He'd think it through. And then form a plan. It's what he did, how he operated. He'd go see his dad immediately with Meena and the girls, for sure. Talk to his sister, Ashley. Talk to Aruna. And Seb. If only they had their sales licence, he could get his dad signed up and using cannabis to manage pain and nausea from the chemo.

But they had time. They had to have time. After his parents split when he was 16, Adam's relationship with his father had deteriorated, and only in recent years had they reconnected in a truly meaningful way. Gaston had rarely visited Ottawa, but when he did, they continued to build a new level of connection. That his hero, his father, was terminally ill was hard to fathom.

Adam had barely time to share the news with Seb before the next landmine went off under them. They were being sued.

It wasn't working, the Rue Bombardier location. Yes, there was a signed offer to lease. And yes, the intention had been to establish some of Hydropothecary's activities there, such as a cannabis genetics lab. But in the contract were several stipulations outlining points that had to be fulfilled before the lease would no longer be conditional, like obtaining a sales licence for medical cannabis from Health Canada.

As the dealmaker in the partnership, telling the building owner that they would have to cancel their plans fell on Seb's shoulders. Besides, Seb and the owner got along well; Seb liked the guy — and Seb doesn't like just anyone. The meeting started out well. After a few pleasantries, Seb smiled and said, "I have good news for you. We aren't taking the lease, but we've found a buyer for you. You don't have to worry about that aspect at least."

Good news? The owner was furious. From his point of view, it seemed that the Hydro boys had just found a better deal at the farm. And now they were going to stiff him. He came out swinging, throwing accusations at Seb and threatening to sue Hydropothecary for half of the entire term of the $1.5 million lease. After a few minutes of arguing, it was clear to Seb that there was no point in wasting any more oxygen.

Over the next few weeks, through lawyers, a settlement offer was made and rejected. The building owner, convinced there was a conspiracy, was determined to have things play out in court. And that's what happened. For three and a half years, the only people happy with the turn of events were the guys with law degrees.

A lawsuit hanging over them added incredibly to Adam and Seb's stress about raising financing, hiring staff, and the multiple unknowns in the cannabis space. At least, it stressed them out for the first year. By the time Seb stood up as a witness in court years later, the issue was more of an annoyance. Hydropothecary had moved on and had much bigger problems.

But the building owner wasn't the only person realizing the potential financial power of the cannabis industry. Investors were starting to come forward, together with true believers. Even if banks and mom-and-pop investors were skittish, and would remain that way for several more years, it was beginning to dawn on outliers that cannabis could well become bigger than the wine industry in Canada. They could envision it, but Louis could not.

Despite witnessing Seb's almost religious zeal for business and the success of the harvest, Louis didn't fully believe in Adam and Seb, at least not then. Compounding that was the complete inertia around obtaining a sales licence. Sure, if he sold his property, he would get stocks and officially be a third partner, but partner of what? Talking it over with his lawyer, Louis decided he wanted more out of the deal he had made for his farm. So he pushed for cash to be paid out at the close of the transaction, rather than out of future profits. And rather than $800,000, he first asked for $850,000, then $1.2 million, in addition to 650,000 shares and a full partnership. Seb fumed. This was just like Darth Vader in *Star Wars Episode V: The Empire Strikes Back* when Lando Calrissian objects to Vader taking Chewbacca and Leia rather than leaving them with him. "That wasn't part of the deal!" Lando says. Vader is unmoved. "I'm altering the deal. Pray I don't alter it any further."

"We had a good relationship," recalls Seb, "but he had never done a transaction like that before. His offer was based on us failing. He didn't think we would pull it off or get the money we needed to succeed. He had his lawyer in his ear saying, 'You've put your whole life into this place, that's worth more than $800,000.' When I saw the deal, I said no way. So, I sent it back. Boy was his lawyer pissed."

Like so many other small business owners, Louis could see only the potential for failure and wanted to ensure his immediate tomorrow was covered.

"He wanted a bigger piece of the pie. I get that," says Seb. "But what the fuck? Never mind the bigger piece of the pie. Let's just make sure there's enough fucking pie for everyone. Do you want a big piece of a small pie or a small piece of a really big pie?"

By the time Adam returned from visiting his ailing father out west, Seb was clearly on edge over the stalled negotiations with Louis. It had already been months since they started talks, and until they had ownership of the land, buildings, and a Health Canada production licence in hand, raising more capital would be a challenge.

Over lunch at McDonald's soon after Adam arrived in Ottawa, Seb explained. They still had a million dollars in the bank thanks to the recent injection of $3 million from the Bulldog, but if they paid it out to Louis, they couldn't finish the much-needed B5 expansion. And without that, they couldn't raise more capital either. Rock, meet hard place.

Adam chewed his fries thoughtfully. There was only one way forward. They needed the land and the licence. Without them, they risked losing everything. "We have to pay him, Seb. We have no choice. We have to pay him right now, like within 48 hours, but he has to sign the bloody agreement in the same time frame."

On November 5, Seb, Louis, and Louis's lawyer sat down to finalize arrangements that would make Louis a partner with shares and a fat cheque upfront. Seb wrote the cheque — wiping out half of the company's financial footing in the process — and handed it to Louis. Seb stood up.

"Let's go. We're depositing that now." Louis started to object — "I have too much to do around here," he spluttered — but Seb was firm. "It's dated today. We deposit it today."

If at any time Louis changed his mind and ripped up the cheque, the deal would evaporate, so Seb escorted Louis out to his car and drove directly to the Scotiabank in Hull, about 30 minutes from the farm. Walking up to a teller, Seb slipped the cheque across the counter. "We need to deposit this into his account. And we both need receipts."

With a stroke of the pen, Louis became cash rich and his roles as master grower and partner were established. Two weeks later, they all met at the lawyer's office and, for most of the day, worked through several binders containing the partnership deal. The partnership had been a reality for a while, but now it was down on paper.

Adam and Seb finally owned their own medical cannabis farm.

Billion Dollar Lesson

"One of the mistakes I made early, because I could shape a deal fairly quickly and I was adept at negotiating, was selling the deal to the other party. I'm a salesman, so the person would think it was a great deal, but later as they digested it and talked to advisers, they found out the deal wasn't as good as what they'd agreed to and they'd slowly walk it back. So, it's really important not to sell a deal to your partner. You want to be very transparent that it's a win-win. Be transparent about how you think they're going to win and how you're going to win. Write everything down on one page with the partner, and you both sign off before the lawyers paper it up. Don't be greedy. A bigger pie and smaller slice is always better than a bigger slice of a small pie." — **Seb**

CHAPTER 5

While Seb's focus throughout 2014 was financing and deals, Adam faced a less tangible but infinitely more challenging and — to his way of thinking — far more entertaining issue: How could he sell the idea of Hydropothecary products without actually having a sales licence?

It was one thing to sell pot — any street dealer with grade 9 math and flexible morality could do that. But long before Health Canada handed them their golden ticket, they needed to sell the *idea* of high-end, high-quality products to Canadians. And to do that, they had to make cannabis accessible to the non-stoner crowd. That meant product development in a market already crowded with every other LP out there using the same well-known strains everyone recognized, like OG Kush, Northern Lights, CBD Remedy, and Maui Wowie.

But if everyone else was using variations of those names, how would Adam set Hydropothecary apart? He recalled his experience in Amsterdam and his vow to keep one foot out of the cannabis culture. Anything else would be inauthentic. They wanted to sell marijuana to people like them. That would be their differentiator. That kind of thinking would years later form the foundation of their adult-use brand, HEXO.

Armed with his whiteboard markers, Adam ruminated. Did weed need to be like aspirin, where the medicinal piece was at the forefront? Or should it be aligned with lifestyle, like condoms and cola? He took note of Health Canada's list of illnesses that cannabis could be prescribed for, then did some digging of his own. The whiteboard soon filled up: fibromyalgia, arthritis, Crohn's disease, epilepsy, glaucoma, HIV/AIDs, sclerosis, cachexia, seizures, post-traumatic stress disorder. Then he looked at the statistics to get a sense of market share for each disorder or symptom. Where was the sweet spot? The list got longer and longer, but he got no closer to a solution.

The answer came in the form of Dr. Michael Munzar, who had proven to be a stalwart financial and psychological support. Michael was soon to be named chairman of the newly formed Hydropothecary board, with Adam, Seb, and Jay Ewart. He had published in peer-reviewed journals, designed clinical trials, and was the medical director of both Nymox Pharmaceutical and owner of Statcare medical clinic, which treats fifty thousand patients annually in Pointe-Claire, Quebec. In short, when he offered his advice, Seb and Adam listened.

And he wanted to help. Two weeks into Adam's reclusive navel gazing about how to brand, Michael was in town from Montreal. Adam wasn't sure what Michael knew about marketing, but he knew that he brought a special and specific insight into the marijuana industry. Whatever he had to offer would be better than the void Adam was working in, anyway.

For the first half hour, Adam went through his approach. If they could look at certain symptoms that were common, perhaps they could brand their product accordingly? He itemized the illnesses he'd researched and listed the symptoms medical marijuana had been used to treat. Nearly everything, aside from some very well done and ongoing gold standard studies in Israel, was pretty much anecdotal. Still, it was evidence, of a sort.

Michael sat back in his chair and pondered the whiteboard. Sure, there were common symptoms to these illnesses, but they were universal, too. He had an idea.

"Well, you know, Adam, it doesn't matter what condition you have. At certain times of the day, everyone feels the same. In the morning, you need a Prozac and a coffee. At lunch, you need something to pick you up and get you through the rest of the day. After work, you need to switch gears when you realize you have to cook supper and get the kids to hockey practice. Your second job has begun. And that's hard for anyone. You need that shot of energy, transitioning to the evening. Then, bedtime is hard for anyone with pain, depression, anxiety. It doesn't matter what your illness is, and you can point to all the stats you want, but bedtime represents an issue for many people. All of those experiences are things we all have, whether we have an illness or not."

Adam swung around from the whiteboard and looked at Michael. "Fuck, that's genius. You're right. Four times of day, four strains of marijuana to suit them."

Adam started pacing around the office, or what there was of it. Sativa, indica, and hybrids in between. They could be the basis to develop an entire line around four times of day, like morning, midday, after dinner, and bedtime, each with its own THC and CBD percentages. It was a simple, elegant solution for anyone dealing with garden-variety symptoms of modern life. Anxiety. Panic. Depression. Chronic pain. Tension headaches. Jeez . . . just Too Much To-Doism.

Of course, it would have to be put past Health Canada — another nightmare — but it was the perfect jumping-off point. Adam nodded with satisfaction.

"Michael, I do believe we have a product line."

FEBRUARY 13, 2014
ADAM'S HOUSE, CENTRETOWN
OTTAWA, ONTARIO

They had a gorgeous brand. They had a signature product line, thanks to their basement brainstorming about Time of Day. They even had a stunning ad campaign, reminiscent of the glamorous and chic 1961 hit film, *Breakfast at Tiffany's*.

It was time to hit the ground running and roll out a price that would reflect the high-end quality of the brand. They still didn't have a sales licence, and had no idea when they would, so they'd use the time to prepare the market. Adam was excited, but a bit nervous. Talking through his strategy for the price per gram with friends, there were some raised eyebrows, not to mention gasps of surprise. Publicly, he was confident about the course of action, but having seen initial reactions, he had to admit to a flutter of concern.

Turns out, he was right to be nervous. Adam was about to launch one of the most vilified pricing strategies in the short history of Canadian cannabis.

In positioning Hydropothecary as a premium brand for connoisseur tastes, Adam was convinced they would access a market sector that no one else had tapped into: the well-heeled soccer moms, over-achieving professionals, and people to whom the traditional stigma of cannabis consumption was abhorrent. If they weren't already secretly using cannabis to medicate, those on the fence would hopefully be reassured by a medical cannabis brand that aligned with their self-image. Hence, Hydropothecary's products were to be packaged in a thick white and black cardboard box, stamped with the signature H, interwoven with a stylized cannabis bud.

Each box was adorned with a wide black satin bow, specifically tied to undo with a gentle pull. It was based on a thoughtful analogy typical of Adam's way of thinking: once a client decided to overcome the seemingly restrictive and binding notions around medical cannabis, it was as surprisingly simple and easy to obtain and consume responsibly as it was to pull open the ribbon. Once the box was opened, there was yet another barrier — as easy to overcome — watermarked tissue paper sealed with a gold sticker embossed with the Hydropothecary "H." Inside were glass jars of dried bud. (As any canna-seur would know, cannabis should be stored in glass jars. Only after the Cannabis Act forced LPs to use environmentally unfriendly plastic containers did the company change this approach.) From the masked return address to the entirely gratifying and pleasurable experience of unpacking Hydropothecary boxes, Adam wanted to align the company with elegance and to give clients a product and experience that would make them feel better. Everything would affirm the good decision they had made in purchasing from Hydropothecary.

That's what should have happened. Instead, with just one press release announcing the Time of Day line and the prices that would go along with the elegant experience, Hydropothecary became infamous among cannabis purists. At a time when most black market street weed went for $4 a gram (with the 2018 marketplace tipping point at just over $8 a gram), Hydropothecary determined that its products would range from a staggering $26 to $32 a gram, once awarded a sales licence.

The prices were astronomical. Daring. Outrageous.

Not surprisingly, the backlash was harsh and immediate. Both Adam's phone number (he was listed as the company contact) and the Twittersphere lit up in a blinding flurry of outrage. "Fuck you, you greedy fucks!" roared one furious tweet. "I hope you burn in hell!" added another. For days, Adam weathered a hurricane of reproachful and angry tweets, texts, and emails. To each, he offered to have a real conversation rather than a keyboard war. Most refused and renewed their online derision, though a few accepted. If he and Seb were going to stick to their guns on price, Adam thought, they were going to have to engage and educate their target market. Not everyone would be ready to pay six to eight times the cost — but they weren't marketing to everyone.

"We knew we had to completely change the mindset of soccer moms, professionals, and non-smokers if we were actually going to make cannabis socially acceptable beyond the current hardcore community," he says, recalling the hostile conversations he had. Late one evening his phone rang as he was shopping at a Home Depot (most of his errands occurred late at night, to balance work hours and family time). It was a very angry medical cannabis consumer in Alberta. The man was beyond furious and let Adam feel the heat. How could you assholes take a plant that should be accessible to everyone and put it beyond the reach of 90 percent of the population through astronomical prices?

Adam let the man speak, then wind down. In one way, Adam and the Albertan believed in the same thing, which was that cannabis should be accessible to all medical patients who needed it. Perhaps $32 a gram was out of reach of most people, Adam admitted to the man, then noting that the shadiness of purchasing street weed also made cannabis inaccessible to people who didn't want to buy a plastic baggie of weed called Green Crack or Alaskan Thunderfuck from a guy named Doogs. By calling their product After Dinner, wrapping it in a bow, and shipping it for free on evenings and weekends, Hydropothecary was also trying to make cannabis accessible. In the end, the Albertan relented. He still hated the prices, but he agreed that they shared the common goal of creating stigma-free access to cannabis for Canadians.

Although it had seriously alienated the existing traditional cannabis community, Hydropothecary's strategy did intrigue its new market and captured the attention of Toronto once again.

> ### Billion Dollar Lesson
> "Blue-sky thinking and brainstorming are important in reaching for a dream. But you have to be able to come back to the idea in a reasonable amount of time, test your assumptions, put a basic financial model together, look at the market size, and figure out if you can reasonably do what you want to do. You need a sober second thought and financial expertise. As an entrepreneur, you're always challenged and butting your head against the wall, and there will be a lot of people telling you no. But you have to look for the wisdom in that. Why are they saying no? What's the real objection? Look at their assumption and really test that against yours." — **Seb**

MAY 2014

TRUMP INTERNATIONAL HOTEL, FINANCIAL DISTRICT

TORONTO, ONTARIO

They were headed back to Bay Street.

Hydropothecary had been invited to present at a financial conference being held at the Trump International Hotel (later renamed the Adelaide Hotel). Seb and Adam were thrilled. As with their previous trip to pitch to Toronto's money men, they'd be front and centre in a room full of bankers, brokers, and investors. Unlike that time, there'd be no blizzard. At least, that was the hope.

For weeks, Seb had written and rewritten the deck, then memorized it and practised it until he could say it in his sleep. On the drive down

Highway 401 in the Grand Am, he and Adam went over every word, the tone, the content. It had to be right. It had to grab the attention of decision makers in a way they hadn't been able to in the past. And, despite sharing a bedroom in the cheapest hotel they could find in downtown Toronto, they were confident and as ready as they ever could be.

Adam and Seb walked into the hotel's plush conference room, with its deep, tall windows reaching up to the vaulted and intricately plastered ceiling. The space was buzzing. The bored middle-level brokers with their trendy haircuts and phone addictions were replaced with those who were increasingly aware of and interested in these young canna-preneurs, who would be the innovators and outliers of a brand-new industry. No one knew exactly where this new industry would end up, but between media reports and the impressive financial news coming from already legal states like Washington and Colorado, Bay Street was interested. A lot more interested than during the two's first venture to Bay Street.

Seb awaited his opportunity to speak, silently reviewing his notes, unobtrusively observing the faces in the crowd and listening to the current speaker. Jeeeesus, he thought. This guy's putting them to sleep. Between his slow, uninspiring delivery and thickly accented English, he was losing his listeners. Seb grinned at Adam and leaned over to whisper. "This is perfect. I'm going to kill it."

Maybe their PowerPoint presentation didn't have all the bells and whistles. Maybe they weren't as teched out as one competitor's deck, with its drone footage of empty greenhouses and dramatic music. But Hydropothecary had something the others didn't: Sébastien St-Louis.

Seb bounded up on stage, grinned at the crowd, and launched into his spiel. The complete opposite of the previous speaker, Seb commanded the stage like a seasoned veteran — or someone who'd spent hours preparing. (One of the quickest learners around, Seb overcame any hesitancy in doing live broadcast media interviews by polishing his skills for hours in his bathroom, unbeknownst to Adam. One day, Seb showed up at an interview and, according to Adam, "he was better than I was — the guy who was a spokesperson for the leader of the Liberal Party of Canada! He was damn good at it.")

Today was no different, just better. "He grabbed that microphone like it was the last cold beer on the planet on a hot day," recalls Adam.

"He took a breath and let 'em have it. Everyone fell silent as Seb started to talk. He was strong, confident and, holy shit, he knew what he was talking about. I knew then he would be the CEO of a billion-dollar company. I just hoped it would be this one."

As Adam mouthed the memorized words of the presentation from the audience, Seb gave him a shout-out, concluded his talk, and left the stage. Ever confident in his abilities, he knew he'd crushed it. Another LP's CEO stood up to talk, in the process giving a shout-out to the seven or eight staff he'd brought along with him, all of whom were staying at the hotel. The CEO even mentioned that they'd be taking meetings in a private suite they'd rented. Once again, Seb and Adam couldn't believe how much money the competition was spending on things they thought were frivolous at best. Seb mentally shook his head. What a load of bullshit.

Or was it?

"This was the second time we made this mistake, underestimating the value of our competition's aggressive spending," notes Adam. "You can't be afraid to spend money right away." If you want to make money, as they say, you have to look like money. By 2018, two of those companies were respectively worth eight times and five times as much as us."

But for right now, Seb's dynamic personality and the content of their presentation had worked. They'd been invited to meet a Calgary banker who seemed interested in talking about financing them. The guys were buoyant, positively bouncing on their toes. This had gone so much better than the last financial trip just over a year ago.

In the elevator on the way to the banker's suite later that day, the doors opened and a woman walked in. Pushing the button for her floor, she turned around and looked levelly at Seb. "Mr. St-Louis?" Adam watched Seb nod and smile at the woman, then caught his eye. There was a gleam in it. Seb had liked being recognized and admired. On the stage, in the boardroom, or in public. He liked it a lot.

The elevator ride down the Trump Hotel was another matter altogether. Like a newly single guy who'd just discovered the buffet of online dating, the Calgary banker wouldn't commit. He couldn't get his head around

Hydropothecary's high-end approach, price, or product line compared with other LPs. Plus, they had no sales licence.

But, like particles in CERN's Large Hadron Collider, Adam's frustration and overconfidence slammed into each other with terrific force. If no one believes in our product or prices, Adam reasoned, why not prove them wrong? He'd suddenly remembered a story he'd heard about how a well-known figure in Ottawa's high-tech industry once sold $2 million worth of some mobile device that hadn't even made it to the prototype stage. Adam remembered how impressed he was with the strategy and, despite being unsure if it were even true, vowed to implement something like it.

Thus was born Hydropothecary's Premier Access Program. At the time, some LPs awaiting sales licences were toying with the idea of preselling their cannabis to medical patients worried that they wouldn't have consistent access once the anticipated deluge of new patients rushed to sign up after the company did receive a sales licence. The Premier Access Program would be open to just five hundred customers, each paying $500 for guaranteed access and attractive perks. If he could sell all five hundred spots, Adam figured, it would be the kind of proof of concept, market validation, and revenue that would show the doubting investors they were mistaken. Hydropothecary would prove them all wrong.

Within the 30-floor elevator ride, Adam had a sketched-out plan and a new direction. The minute they returned to Ottawa, he made some calls, first to a former colleague at *iPolitics*, a masterful content strategist. He also briefly contracted a creative project manager and a graphic designer. A staff member would handle the digital and social media end of things. Their friend Max, now Hydropothecary's compliance officer, also bought in to the idea.

Then, Adam flinched.

They still had no sales licence. They were six months late on their promise to shareholders that they'd be selling cannabis. As such, Adam had to wonder: Why would anyone sign up to the Premier Access Program, only to cool their heels waiting for Hydropothecary to obtain its sales licence?

So he listened to his gut and dropped Premier Access. And his gut was spot on. Hydropothecary wouldn't get a sales licence for another year.

Yet, it wasn't the only stumble that spring. Adam also had to shelve the *Breakfast at Tiffany's* ads after he realized that not one publication would run them and risk the wrath of Health Canada. The same was also true of a series of five beautiful, heart-wrenching videos envisioned as a way to establish the company brand as beautiful but relatable through real cannabis healing stories told by real people. There was a teenager whose fibromyalgia and complex regional pain syndrome were so crippling, she hadn't been able to get out of bed until she discovered medical cannabis. A 27-year-old who managed pain and nausea during cancer treatments with cannabis, and eventually became a competitive runner. A wife who used cannabis to contain her husband's violent and involuntary spasms after he was partially paralyzed by a stroke. Each story was devastating yet enlightening.

But in the few months it took to produce them, regulations had evolved. Health Canada would never approve of testimonials about the benefits of cannabis, even if they were true. Licensed producers existed to grow cannabis and sell cannabis, but not to tell Canadians why or how they should use cannabis.

Billion Dollar Lesson

"It's very easy to get caught up in your ideas and run with them when the pressure is on. And it's very easy to turn them into false starts. Think them through, create a strategy, and understand where they'll take you. When you're young and eager, it's easy to spend 80 hours a week 'doing,' when with a bit more planning and thinking, you could spend 60 hours a week being effective." — **Adam**

JULY 2014
OTTAWA, ONTARIO

As Seb travelled back and forth to Toronto seeking financing deals, and Louis grew cannabis and managed a thousand details at the farm, getting the company name out there was proving to be a challenge for Adam. It was time to find a publicist. A few months after their presentation in Toronto, Hydropothecary had been present at a women's networking event on the rooftop of the National Arts Centre. It was a sweaty summer afternoon luncheon, even under the tents. As one of the few men present, Adam stood out. Never mind that he was roasting in his neat sport jacket and open-necked shirt as he stood next to the basket of dozens of white roses he was giving away, together with an elegant matte black card with simply the company's name embossed in silver. Amid raucous conversations, inspiring speeches, and cocktails, a woman with a slick, swept-back pompadour walked over and introduced herself as Julie Beun.

"She was fierce, sharp, and sunk her teeth into me in a way that confirmed my belief she had prepped for this conversation," says Adam. "We said hello, nice to meet you, and after a subtle side-shuffle for a moment of privacy, she jumped right in. 'You guys need help and I can help you.' Since then, she's been part of the story and had a front-row seat to the magic."

That summer and into autumn, Adam and Julie worked on a communications strategy, hired a media-monitoring company, pulled together contact lists, and generally prepared to engage with the Canadian media.

Julie rang around to colleagues at Postmedia, CTV, Rogers, Transcontinental Media, CBC, *Vice*, and the now-defunct *Metro* to pitch the Hydropothecary story. She'd worked in Canada and Australia as a journalist, columnist, broadcaster, and national magazine editor for decades, and had spent many of those years as a writer and editor for magazines, including *People*, *Family Circle*, and *Canadian Living*. As a publicist, writer, and content strategist, she'd hustled for music festivals, performers, fashion designers, the pharmaceutical industry, government agencies, and anyone else who had great ideas and energy. She was a social animal who seemed to know everyone. To her mind, the Hydro story was pretty cool, as start-ups go: Two conservative brothers-in-law, from marketing and real estate respectively, getting into cannabis. One was a dashing Franco-Ontarian who preferred athleisure wear over suits, the other was a snappy dresser with a flair for natty vests and cravats. Through sheer hustle, they were creating a cannabis company with little money and a lot of balls. Before long, they were "Ascots and Flip-flops" in her list of story ideas.

Three months later, in the autumn of 2014, Julie would be able to add the story arc of Ed Chaplin, who would join in October: Here was an unusual, brilliant chartered professional accountant who had brought Corel public before becoming chief financial officer at a start-up pot farm. He was a straight shooter who'd taken on the job of bringing Hydropothecary public as a side project, which quickly turned into a hundred-hour-a-week job. Ed delighted in recounting the reaction when he told his kids, then 10 and 12, that he was leaving high tech for marijuana. "My daughter got really pensive and said, 'So, you're going to sell drugs?' I was like, 'Nooooo, and please don't say that at school. The last thing we want is child services showing up!'"

For Quebec media, Julie had the Louis Gagnon pitch about a well-respected horticulturalist who'd won provincial awards and was now pivoting from ornamental to medicinal shrubs. Really, she thought, these stories wrote themselves.

Even so, it was apparent that, without something spectacular like a well-known rapper as spokesperson, or a waterfall of millions pouring in from highly regarded and secure investment firms, there wasn't much interest in doing a story on a small cannabis farm somewhere up the Ottawa River in Quebec. However, the press releases and badgering phone calls slowly started to work, with *National Post* and *Financial Post* articles mentioning the company in the same breath as Bedrocan and Tweed. Locally, the *Ottawa Citizen*, Radio-Canada, and *Ottawa Business Journal* started to notice them, too. But for every story pitched, there were plenty of wisecracks about working on a pot farm . . . and would she send samples?

Part of the problem was that the cannabis business was still so new, so nascent, it was barely an industry. And most people simply didn't understand, and still don't get, what the federal government was trying to do. The social stigma around cannabis use was locked in the pre-legal 4/20 mentality, in which thousands of pot smokers would congregate in public places like Ottawa's Parliament Hill and openly defy authorities by lighting up spliffs and bongs as a protest to what they saw as the egregious and overly harsh penalties for carrying cannabis. An opinion piece published years later in a national newspaper would note that any law that the population routinely disregards is not good for the rule of law. By making medical cannabis legal, it argued, the government was moving toward overall cannabis legalization and a legislative environment more in step with Canadian society. Even so, early adopters in the new industry found themselves struggling not just with financial conservatism among banks and investors but also with a fearful general public convinced that legal weed would lead to the downfall of Canada.

If Bay Street investors were elusive, perhaps Montrealers would prove more accepting. Adam and Seb had hired a consultant to help them set up a meet-and-greet evening to introduce the Hydropothecary brand. Hundreds of invitations were sent out, an art gallery was booked as the venue, and the best sushi in the city was ordered for 80 people. On the night, a massive winter storm levelled Montreal. Few people could get from the Metro to home, much less an art gallery. In the end, eight non-Hydropothecary people showed up. It was intimate, informative, and a total disaster.

Then there was the utter lack of anything resembling good news from Health Canada regarding a sales licence. As the two men discovered, one of the reasons was that Hydropothecary didn't yet have seed-to-sale tracking software. By default, it became Adam's chief task. He'd connected in early 2014 with a software developer in Bulgaria who'd turned the static Hydro website into something a little more dynamic and interactive, so they could announce they were ready to take patient registrations. (In a press release, Adam noted that "although our 2017 target is to support 4,500 Canadians, we are initially offering just 150 customers a chance to experience the Hydropothecary difference." By 2017, patient registrations had happily blown the doors off his predictions.) Adam contacted his Bulgarian again, this time for help in building a program that would meet Health Canada's requirements.

But what were the requirements? What were the guidelines? What was the tracking process for a pharmaceutical-grade product from planting to packaging?

It was relentlessly depressing and challenging work, made worse by the achingly cold winter of 2014. Awake before his kids stirred when it was still dark, Adam would fire up his beater Mazda 3, purchased several years earlier for the princely sum of $7,000. It was a noisy, peppy set of wheels not designed for the bone-rattling drive to the farm up Autoroute 50 and through Masson-Angers, then down Chemin de la Rive, which was little more than a series of interconnected potholes. (At the time of writing, with constant expansion underway and heavy trucks rumbling down the dirt road, absolutely nothing had changed.) Once, he lost his back shock, resulting in a cacophony that sounded like a bucket of wrenches tumbling downstairs. A month later, the same thing happened, on the other side. It was a bit of a theme for that entire period: working hard, having a major setback and trying again, only to be faced with another set of issues. After all, even without a sales licence and the hoped-for revenue, they still needed to act and plan as if it were all imminent. Everything, from packaging and product names to cleaning regimens and tracking software, had to be created and prepped, ready for action the minute the call came from Health Canada. Locked in the windowless, jail-like environment of the security bunker, Adam would spend long days going back and forth with the Bulgarian, trying to figure out what information or component was missing and how to get it.

Adam's negative frame of mind was compounded by Seb's absence. His brother-in-law was frequently on the road, like pot's version of a third-party politician, drumming up funding and interest. On one of his rare visits to Gatineau, he asked Adam for an update. Before long, they were settled into a tangled conversation about the obscure logistics required for a variable factor to do with weight and packaging. Seb asked a few key questions and, within minutes, came up with a solution. It was good to have him back.

Billion Dollar Lesson

"I'd love to be able to say exactly how Seb approaches problem solving, but I can't. He simply has a different computer chip in his brain. He looks at problems and comes at them in a way that not only solves that issue, but two others at the same time. In this case, the main takeaway was 'Don't recreate the wheel.' We could have used existing software to do what needed to be done." — **Adam**

9 P.M., DECEMBER 20, 2014
ICE-FISHING CABIN
MASSON-ANGERS, QUEBEC

Flames flickered in the wood stove. The succulent tourtières Meena had bought for the Christmas party were a long-digested and savoury memory. Beer bottles were starting to litter every available surface.

How they managed to fit 12 people into the ice-fishing cabin for the party was a mystery. The rugged and basic building owned by a neighbour was perched on a peninsula near the farm, right on the Ottawa River. It felt as remote as Kapuskasing, but it was right next to their land.

Their land.

Adam rolled the two words around in his head. It had been a right bastard of a year, all things considered: being perpetually broke, raising money that disappeared like mist, hirings and firings, the crazy harvest, his dad's illness, and the stressful lawsuit that promised to sit like a cannonball in his and Seb's guts for the foreseeable future.

Still, spirits were high.

If they weren't quite operational from a sales perspective, at least they had a facility, plants, and a production licence. That in itself was a hallelujah moment. It seemed like a decade since Max had first pitched the idea of medical marijuana to Seb, around a campfire not unlike this one. Not for the first time, Adam marvelled at how far they'd come in an extremely short time. If dogs live seven human years in one of their own, the cannabis industry mustn't be far behind. What other industries did in 20 years, the cannabis industry's early adopters were doing in two. There was no question that the pace was going to pick up. And it did.

But for now, Adam pulled his toque further around his ears against the cold and leaned back in his chair. Sure, there was a pile of things to do, but for right now he was content. He looked over at Ines,* one of the handful of Louis's staff present at the gathering. She worked hard, swore like a trucker, laughed often, and was one of the most diligent and reliable people working for Hydropothecary. If she wasn't chuckling at a joke, she was making one. And she had a heart of gold. All night, she'd cradled his three-month-old daughter, Nalina, who was now asleep, her long eyelashes dusting her downy little cheeks. It felt great to belong to this tight-knit team. They were down to earth and had accepted Seb and Adam like family.

Except they weren't.

For the first time, Adam and Seb had to draw a line between themselves, as bosses, and the people who had put equal measures of sweat equity and faith into the venture. Adam caught Seb's eye from across the room, raised his eyebrows, and looked at the door. Seb nodded. Before everyone really started partying, they'd agreed to leave. They didn't want to, but there had to be a bit of separation between decision makers and those enacting decisions. They needed their staff's trust, faith, and loyalty. And that meant behaving like bosses.

The past year had kicked their asses to the curb and back again. They'd had to learn to be bosses or fail. Money, or a lack of it, was part of the problem. And then there was the rest of the shitshow.

MARCH 2015

MJBIZCON, HILTON HOTEL, MAGNIFICENT MILE

CHICAGO, ILLINOIS

As winter of 2014 melted into the spring of 2015, Adam and Seb walked through the lobby of the Hilton hotel in Chicago. It was a historic spot, at least for Adam. As a political junkie, he knew this was the site of the disastrous 1968 Democratic National Convention. The US had been in the grips of the Vietnam War controversy. The Dems had a presumptive heir to the hugely unpopular Lyndon B. Johnson in the form of Vice-President Hubert Humphrey. Humphrey was just as loathed, at least by hippies, black militants, antiwar protesters, and Jerry Rubin's infamous Youth International Party, with its Yippies. As Jerry later wrote in his book *Do It: Scenarios of the Revolution*, the protesters were "dirty, smelly, foul, loud, dope-crazed, hell-bent, and leather-jacketed. We were a public display of filth and shabbiness, living in-the-flesh rejects of middle-class standards." (The publication was also prefaced with the instructions "Read This Book Stoned!")

Whether or not the conference organizers realized it, the location was deeply ironic. Forty-seven years after the dope-smoking protesters and their cannabis counterculture made headlines at the hotel for the violent clashes with police, Adam and Seb were attending an MJBiz Conference entirely devoted to the legal business of cannabis. And Jerry Rubin? The man was born to make noise and, ever the outlier, ended up as a successful Wall Street stockbroker, after all.

Dumping their bags in their room, Seb and Adam immediately hit the convention floor. Working from opposite ends, they walked up to anyone who caught their eye, told them who they were, what they were about, why they were there, and what kind of investment Hydropothecary could represent to anyone smart enough to back them. Meals were split into three sessions: they'd each get a small plate of food, find a table, and pitch to it. Once done, they'd get another small plate, find more subjects, and pitch again. And so it went, netting them three times the exposure, uncomfortably full stomachs, and a couple of hoarse voices. On a break, they headed to the men's bathroom and stood one urinal apart. A man walked in and took the spot between them. Adam broke the unspoken rule of urinal etiquette and glanced over at Seb. No . . . he's not. He won't. Oh, my fuck, he thought. Seb is going in for the kill. Sure enough, Seb caught the man's eye. "Can I tell you about an interesting opportunity in Canada?"

Eventually, after 72 hours of pitching, sleeping, pitching, eating, and sleeping, during which Seb even pitched to a startled woman in an elevator, they decided to go for dinner and a movie. Within 20 minutes of the screen flickering to life, Adam was asleep.

Like the Trump Hotel experience in Toronto, Chicago didn't result in investment capital. But it did prove the value of business-to-business conferences in another way. Over the course of three days, Adam and Seb saw that their struggling cannabis farm was part of something much, much bigger. Everyone in the Canadian cannabis space seemed to be there: MedReleaf, Aphria, Tweed, and two guys from Tilray. In many ways, it was a seminal conference that lifted the curtain on how powerful the Canadian cannabis industry would soon become.

9 A.M., MAY 26, 2015
THE FARM, CHEMIN DE LA RIVE
MASSON-ANGERS, QUEBEC

It was the kind of spring day that made you think of summer. In the space of a week, the faint blush of pale green on the trees had burst into a lush frenzy of leaves and buds. Although the Ottawa River and Lièvre River were still hosting occasional barges of ice floating down from the north, the air was a summer-like 28°C.

Around the farm, people who'd spent the winter crouched behind desks in the two sterile ModSpaces or in the secure bunker were now spending more time outdoors, madly jumping between mud puddles on their way from one building to the next.

In the small reception area tucked into one of the old greenhouses, a weekly management meeting was underway. It was an uncomfortable gathering to be in. Everyone present was dreading the next day, when a board meeting was scheduled. Despite Seb's best efforts, investment capital was not forthcoming. No one would finance them, and they'd run out of options in bridge loans. Despite the buzz from being in Chicago and Toronto, the needle hadn't moved at all. It seemed to everyone that doomsday was upon them.

A week earlier, Seb, Ed, and Adam had met in a small three-season office attached to an old greenhouse. There was one topic on the agenda: making payroll and keeping vendors happy. Ed went through their current status, which amounted to being just this side of broke. Adam grabbed a pad of sticky notes and stood up. He may have had the fewest number of academic degrees of anyone present — none, in fact — but his natural flair as a facilitator and leader was particularly valuable in difficult times like these.

"Right, Ed, let's list every asset we have. Everything. Let's not leave anything out," he said, penned poised. There was a 20-year-old blue Dodge truck they'd inherited in the purchase, and a tractor of the same vintage. There was the house, if they could subdivide the land quickly. One by one, the notes went up on the wall, then were moved around based on the value of the item and how quickly it could be liquidated. It wasn't long before the men realized that even if they could sell everything, it still wouldn't solve their money woes.

And so, in the next day's regular Tuesday management meeting, the mood was glum. They were going to have to answer to an unhappy board of directors and nervous shareholders, including family and friends. Adam kept up the energy, and they'd managed to get through a few agenda items when Seb's phone rang. It was one of the board members. He stepped into the adjoining storage room to take the call.

As he left by that door, Louis walked in through the other. He grinned and pointed at his cell phone. "I just got an email from Health Canada," he said. "We've got our sales licence!"

The room erupted in wild cheers and shouts. Everyone leapt to their feet, talking over each other, and demanding to know the details of the email. Was it true? This wasn't an interim or progressive licence? They were really licensed to start selling cannabis? It seemed incredible, but Louis just kept nodding and beaming. "Oui! C'est vrai! C'est vrai!"

Someone threw open the door to tell Seb, who was still engrossed in his call. He mouthed "Shut up!" before using a kickboxing backspin to slam the door closed. By the time he was done his call, the exuberant group had moved outside to the driveway. Seeing Seb's quizzical look when he finally emerged, Adam shouted, "We got it! The sales licence!" and pounced on Seb, in the process tearing open the seat of his baby blue Brooks Brothers pants.

By 10.45 a. m., a celebration was in full swing. Louis had raced over to the liquor store in nearby Buckingham for cases of champagne and beer, then dug up caviar from somewhere. Adam called their lawyer, Karl, who stopped by Adam's house for his humidor of cigars and some takeaway pizzas. Someone set up stereo speakers and started pumping out the tunes. From every building, staff emerged, happy and ready to party.

When a car pulled up and tall, nuggety redhead emerged from it, no one noticed at first. Finally, the man — Jay McMillan — caught Adam's eye. With the party raging around them, Adam grabbed a beer and handed it over. "Thanks for coming up, Jay," Adam said, shaking his hand and motioning to Seb to join them at the picnic table next to a shed. "Sorry about this . . . bit of a celebration going on. We just got word this morning! We have a sales licence!"

Jay chuckled at Adam's exuberance. This was good news indeed. He was on site for a job interview as VP of business development. A sales licence? Handy thing to have in his line of work. He pulled on his beer and relaxed a bit. Odd place and time to have a job interview, but the next hour and a half was more of a friendly, if directed, conversation between men who clearly understood each other. If Jay was nonplussed by the chaos around him, he didn't show it. A strong but steady personality, he had come from a diverse background in sales, having worked in everything from communications and emerging technologies to energy management. His ability to roll with whatever opportunities presented themselves, then find a clear and strategic way forward, would later prove invaluable to the company.

That night, Adam, Meena, Seb, and Aruna celebrated quietly but in style, with 80-day aged beef. The next day, the sparkle still hadn't worn off their news and naturally was the topic of conversation at the board meeting. With a sales licence, Hydropothecary would seem much more attractive to financiers and investors alike. Obtaining it was a major hurdle, and with it in hand, they could really begin the business of building a significant medical cannabis company. Later that day, back in Centretown, Adam, Seb, and Ed ordered takeout from a few places, opened a bottle of wine, and let loose. The last thing Adam recalled as he drifted off to sleep on the couch, nestled against Seb like an infant, was Ed studiously looking at numbers on his bulky 4-by-6-inch calculator and punching them into his laptop.

Getting the sales licence was one thing. Implementing the rest of the plan was another.

It was beginning to dawn on them that the development was about to trigger significant financial and operational issues. Waiting for it, they'd burned through all of their cash. There were no reserves, yet a sales licence also meant they had to double down on packaging, labels, courier contracts, and clinic outreach, with utmost dispatch. They had to hire customer experience staff for the 24-hour bilingual hotline. Having Jay on the road for sales was great, but there were a thousand tiny details to be buttoned down before they even signed up one customer.

It was funny, getting that sales licence. Adam and Seb used to think that if only they had it, everything would fall into place. They were wrong. It just meant more work, higher costs, and longer hours.

Billion Dollar Lesson

"We used to say, 'If only this happened, we will be set.' We said it a dozen times over the years before we realized 'this one thing' would never make other things right. We fooled ourselves with 'if only' magical thinking. There's always going to be something else. You have to change your thinking from the ground up. In business, you have to remember this is a game that never ends." — **Adam**

But getting that sales licence did mean that Adam could finally help Gaston. Shortly after his father's diagnosis months earlier, Adam and Meena had flown out west to see first-hand what was being done and, if he was being honest, to make it happen if things weren't being done.

Adam walked into his father's house in Spring Lake and involuntarily gasped. His father looked nothing like the wiry, muscled, and capable man he'd always known. Gaston's face was sunken, together with his chest and belly. His skin was the colour of putty. His energy and vitality seemed to have drained away, like a slow leak in a car tire. After his initial shock, Adam recovered enough to fall back on his own coping method. He'd help. He'd plan. He'd ask questions. Was there a plan to sell the house and get something easier to maintain? Were his dad's taxes in order? Adam wanted to help — needed to help — but Gaston brushed him aside, assuring his son that he planned to beat the cancer. He had too much to live for.

A few days later, as Adam hunted through the West Edmonton Mall H&M for Meena, a family friend called. He was a doctor in Edmonton. He wasn't Gaston's specialist, but he was familiar with the case. Adam wanted to get straight answers about what to expect, because Gaston was resolutely sticking to his firm belief that he would beat the disease.

As Adam walked back into the mall, the oncologist went through the update, point by point. It was a lot for Adam to take in, and where was Meena? I need someone else to hear this, he thought.

"So, okay. What are you saying? What does this all mean?"

The doctor drew in a sharp breath. These conversations never were easy, no matter how often he had them.

"It means he's dying, Adam."

Adam's stomach turned to acid and an involuntary blush of sweat appeared on his forehead.

"So it's terminal?"

"Yes. Has no one told you that yet? He might have 12 months."

The sweat spread to the palms of his hands. He thanked their friend and hung up. If he was the first to hear the news, that meant he was the only one in his family who knew, aside from Gaston. And he'd have to be the one to share it, too.

The minute Adam spotted Meena walking out of the store, he hurried her over to the glass railing overlooking the indoor skating rink. His voice cracked and his eyes filled with tears as he struggled to share the news. He took a moment to watch the skaters below. If it was this hard telling her, how would he handle confronting the finality of it all with his father?

On the way back to his father's house in Spring Lake, they discussed the best way to approach the conversation with Gaston and Kim. Knowing his father's resistance to accepting the inevitable and understanding Gaston's DNA-deep scrappy spirit made it all the more challenging.

Once at the house and seated in the living room, Adam took a deep breath.

"Dad, we need to talk. I had a conversation with a friend who's a doctor," he began, before sharing the news. The words came out surprisingly clearly, considering the effort it was taking. He looked from his Dad to Kim and back again. There was a flicker of anger on Kim's face that Adam interpreted to mean she wondered if Gaston knew and if he did, why hadn't he told her?

"No, it's not true," Gaston responded, calmly. "It's not gonna happen. It's not going to take me away."

Adam's gut burned with swallowed frustration. He wanted to shout, to cite facts, to convince and cajole. But none of it would have made a dent in his father's faith. The next day, as Adam was helping him replace a piece of broken house siding, he tried to reason again.

"Dad, you have to sell this house. This is nuts. You can't do this."

Gaston removed his work gloves and looked at his son with a serious expression. "Adam, in order for me to do this, I need you to believe, just like I believe, that I'm not going to die. I need your support. I need to count on you. I need you to believe it, so I can believe it."

Adam was floored by what he was hearing. And he told his father so, too. "This is bullshit. Irresponsible. You have a family to take care of, to prepare for. You are being selfish!"

He caught himself. Slow down, he thought.

"Okay, Dad. That's what you think. But I need some time to process."

He turned and walked into the house, told Meena he was going for a drive, and hit the road to Spruce Grove in search of his go-to stress beverage, an A&W root beer milkshake. In the parking lot, sucking the thick sugar bomb up the straw, he phoned the most rational person he knew, Sébastien. From the other side of the country, Sébastien listened, then asked three questions.

"What are you there for? Are you there to fix the problem? Or are you there to be with your dad?"

It was all Adam needed to hear. Turning his rental back toward his dad's house, he reviewed his thoughts as he pulled in. He walked back in the front door and took Gaston aside.

"Dad, I honestly don't think this is the right way to handle things — I need to say that. But I also get what you're trying to do. I think my job is to be here for you. I'll go along with what you want me to do."

Now, months later and with a Health Canada sales licence firmly in hand, Adam could help his dad in a very real way. For some time, Gaston had been asking Adam about cannabis. He had been taking oral chemotherapy in an attempt to shrink the tumour, but the side effects were debilitating headaches, lethargy, loss of appetite, and nausea. Did Adam think cannabis could ease his symptoms? It had taken a few days to find someone to prescribe it, but in the end, Gaston Miron became Hydropothecary's first registered client.

"We talked about it often. Or rather, he talked, and I listened," Adam recalls. "There are few things that make a 'doer' — and a son — feel more helpless than facing his father's imminent death. This medical marijuana industry wasn't just a business for me anymore. It had become an achingly personal and practical way to do something, take action, make it mean something."

Having couriered Gaston his medicine, Adam flew to Edmonton, rented a car, and drove the familiar highway to his father's house. Gaston had wasted away considerably and was clearly suffering. Although not a cannabis consumer himself, Adam had got a demo on how to use the equipment and now gently passed on the knowledge to Gaston. By the end of the trip, his father's nausea had diminished, along with the head-aches. His discomfort was far more manageable.

Client number two was very different. A well-known cannabis industry figure from Montreal, that person's order had come in late on a Friday, some time after Adam had returned from Edmonton, just as the customer service team was packing up for the weekend. Thrilled that things were finally moving, Adam drove down to Ottawa for the ritual Coors Light O'Clock he and Seb had initiated a few years earlier. Adam shared the news of the second client with Seb and speculated that the person was well known enough to possibly get buzz if this customer took to social media, saying that they were a Hydro customer. Seb was pumped. He immediately wanted to know how long it had taken for the order to be prepped and shipped with their new system.

"Oh. We haven't sent it yet. It goes out on Monday," Adam said, sipping his beer. At any rate, he added, the only guy who really knew the new program had left for the weekend to a remote cottage with no cell phone reception.

Seb's eyebrows shot up. Multiple expressions rumbled across his face, the final one being "What the fuck?!" Within minutes, the pair was on the phone to a manager who more or less understood the system, before hopping into Seb's car and heading back to the farm. Together they packed the order and located a bonded motorcycle courier who could deliver it to Montreal by 11 p.m. The customer was elated and, for Adam and Seb, it underscored the importance of putting the customer first. If Hydropothecary was to become known for outstanding customer service, they'd have to roll up their sleeves, no matter the situation.

With the sales licence, Hydropothecary became the first licensed producer in Quebec to have real skin in the game. And the press took notice. Julie had been busy: *La Presse*, *Le Droit*, the *Ottawa Citizen*, and *National Post* all ran stories, along with Radio-Canada and TVA Gatineau-Ottawa. She'd also arranged for Adam to be interviewed by his hometown papers. The *Valley Sentinel* in McBride, British Columbia, proudly described Adam as a former local student with "great entrepreneurial drive," while *Kamloops This Week* screamed "Kamloops Cannabis King," a headline it would later resurrect in 2017 when Kamloopsian and former BC health minister Dr. Terry Lake joined Hydropothecary as vice-president of corporate social responsibility and communications.

"Adam Miron doesn't look like your average pot grower," gushed the Kamloops journalist. "In cufflinks and a sport coat, sipping coffee, and checking his smartphone, the former Thompson Rivers University student looks more like the political operative he once was."

Even the now-defunct *PRESS The Fashion* magazine did a profile on Julie's "ascot and flip-flops" angle, describing Seb as a "numbers man" and breathlessly reporting on the glamorous world of Canada's "first luxury marijuana brand" by mentioning that, during the reporter's tour, a rich investor's helicopter landed on the lawn of the farmhouse. The writer also asked Adam and Seb their advice for the next generation of entrepreneurs — even though they had only just turned 31.

"St-Louis is quick to answer first," the story continued. "'Keep swinging . . . keep rolling the dice and give yourself as many opportunities as you can.' Miron smiles wryly and insists, 'Two feet in. Backup plans and safety nets don't work. If you want it to work, you will make it work.'"

And so it went. They were featured more than once on the cover of the *Ottawa Business Journal* and got a mention in the *Financial Post*, which referred to Hydropothecary as the "Grey Goose of marijuana." But it wasn't until *Maclean's* magazine ran a one-pager in July 2015 that Adam felt vindicated.

Headlined "The Apple Store of Medical Marijuana?" the article dropped the company neatly into its market. Hydropothecary, writer Martin Patriquin noted, aimed "to sell grass to the moneyed classes. The pitch: assuming you have a prescription and the means to spend $15 a gram, nearly double the Canadian average, you can have the same shopping experience for medical marijuana as for, say, an iPhone — that is to say, swanky presentation, smart design, and free shipping. Plus brown paper bag discretion."

Adam was delighted by the media coverage and that the brand's messaging was finally beginning to stick. There was just one problem: the attention wasn't translating into sales. Once again, he had to wonder if they should be listening to the Bay Street naysayers who repeatedly told them, "Just sell weed at $8 a gram like the other LPs and call it by a street name. It's not rocket science!"

FEDERAL ELECTION NIGHT
OCTOBER 19, 2015
ADAM'S HOUSE, CENTRETOWN
OTTAWA, ONTARIO

There are few things political junkies in Ottawa love more than a federal election, especially a tightly won election. Adam and Seb were no different. That mid-October day was hardly out of the ordinary — meetings, business development, phone calls — and they powered through it with the sole aim of gathering later at Adam's house for an election party. Other friend groups in other cities might have hockey parties, but Ottawa loves an election get-together. (Don't judge.)

Adam was in fine form. He'd printed off 8-by-10-inch colour images of 12 Conservative and six NDP MPs he hoped would lose, then taped them to the walls of his living room, like political dartboards. It wasn't done out of malice. It was entirely hopeful thinking, based on the hope that a Liberal win would advance the cause of legalization in the cannabis industry. True, the Conservatives had ushered in the era of medical marijuana, albeit grudgingly and with such tight regulations that it was hard to breathe. But it was a start. Justin Trudeau had campaigned hard on the legalization platform, and if he could kick Stephen Harper's Tories to the curb, the Liberals would be entirely responsible for making Canada the first G8 country to legalize cannabis and ignite a new industry.

But first, they had to win.

From across the room, Seb watched Adam happily putting big, colourful "X"s through the faces of his victims. One by one, they fell. As the results rolled in, and more and more of the national electoral map turned from blue and orange to red, Seb's mind started to churn. It was happening. But not until the CBC called it. Seb had to laugh. Adam looked poleaxed. Having been a practically moribund political party after their defeat years earlier, the Liberals had swept the country. Cannabis would be legal. They could not, would not, squander this opportunity.

As the party raged on, Liberal candidates delivered delighted and sometimes ridiculously incoherent TV interviews. (Still a working journalist, Julie was across the city with a Rogers TV camera crew, reporting live from newly elected Liberal MP Karen McCrimmon's raucous campaign headquarters.) Seb caught Adam's wide-eyed delight. It wasn't just the election tonight. It was the news they were putting out tomorrow. Hydropothecary was making an announcement that would fix all their money problems.

Sometimes, life zigs when you expect it to zag.

7 A.M., OCTOBER 20, 2015
CANADIAN CANNABIS CORP.
OAKVILLE, ONTARIO

Canadian Cannabis Corp. to Acquire Hydropothecary for $21.3 Million

OAKVILLE, ON — (Marketwired — Oct 20, 2015) — **Canadian Cannabis Corp. (CCC)** (OTC PINK:CCAN) plans to acquire Hydropothecary Corporation, a licensed producer of cannabis and cannabis oils and licensed distributor of Medicinal Marijuana under the Marijuana for Medical Purposes Regulations.

The parties have agreed to general terms, where CCC will pay a total consideration of $21.3 million in cash and stock ($28 million CAD) for 100% ownership in Hydropothecary. CCC has paid an initial $500,000 as a deposit, with the transaction expected to close on November 17, 2015.

Hydropothecary is the largest MMPR licensed landowner which operates a grow facility located on 65 acres in Gatineau, Quebec. The facility's flowering production area currently totals 7,500 sf. A 35,000 sf. structural expansion of the facility has been recently completed, with production in the expanded space planned to begin in the first quarter of 2016.

"This acquisition of Hydropothecary represents one of the most important milestones in our development," said Benjamin Ward, CEO of CCC. "In addition to allowing us to produce and distribute medical marijuana in Canada, the addition of an industry leader like Hydropothecary will allow us to deliver unparalleled products, service, and customer convenience."

At 7:05 a.m., soon after the press release crossed the wire, Adam's phone started lighting up.

Family, friends, and even acquaintances from elementary school all reached out with congratulations both for the cannabis-friendly election results and for the spectacular takeover deal. Everyone who'd invested would be bought out at a very attractive premium that would net them a huge return. There was a lot of over-the-phone backslapping.

Moreover, Seb, Ed, and Adam would all walk into executive roles, with none of the drama of a start-up.

In addition to valuable physical assets and customers, the Hydropothecary acquisition will bring to CCC about 17 employees, including three seasoned executives who will be appointed to CCC senior leadership positions:

- Sébastien St-Louis, co-founder and CEO of Hydropothecary, will be appointed president
- Ed Chaplin, CFO of Hydropothecary, will be appointed CFO
- Adam Miron, Hydropothecary's co-founder and chief brand officer, will be appointed chief marketing officer

St-Louis commented: "Together with the talented CCC team, we believe we can grow the company into the world's largest comprehensive medical marijuana provider, while continuing to provide our customers with the highest standards of quality and service."

For some time, Seb had been quietly working on the deal with a group of wealthy Toronto-based businessmen behind the Canadian Cannabis Corp. (CCC). The men saw the possibilities the cannabis industry represented and wanted in. Adam and Seb had been sitting on the deal ever since September 22, when they'd met the Torontonians in person at Soif, the Gatineau wine bar owned by celebrity sommelier Véronique Rivest, renowned internationally since 2013, when she was named second-best sommelier in the world, the first woman to hold this title.

For CDN$25 million ($6 million in cash and $15.3 million in Class A common stock), Seb and Adam could walk away from the constraints of regular jobs and be free to create another company, if they wanted to. They believed, once again, that "if only" they had the money, everything would be fine.

Besides, the timing was pretty much perfect. In November, the company broke the one-hundred-client mark. Word was getting out, and they could see a solid future. The CCC deal was an anchor to their valuation, too. As a private company, they were worth whatever price they could sell their stock for, putting their value at anything between $10 million and $25 million. It was a surprisingly subjective exercise. Adam's grandmother would point out, when a young Adam would rummage through his uncle's discarded comic books, looking for a rare gem he could resell for a pot of gold, "It's only worth what someone is willing to pay for it." But, with CCC, their value was firmly and unarguably established. Secretly, Adam and Seb were a bit disappointed that they couldn't have pushed it higher. But it was still a chunky number. The transaction was to close on November 17.

Billion Dollar Lesson

"When you're a start-up, if there's cash on the table, take the cash. You need to grow your business. Until you're profitable, access that capital every time. Not having enough money forces you to make really bad decisions in terms of where and how to allocate capital. First step in accepting capital is to figure out the market conditions and if you're in the ballpark. Make sure your capital structure is in good shape. You don't want to overly dilute, but you don't want to take up a bunch of debt you can't pay. Until you generate cash, I'm a big believer that debt makes no sense." — **Seb**

Until November 17, then, it was business as usual. Adam and Seb continued to rise at dawn in order to be the first at the farm. The cannabis plants still needed to be cultivated. Deals still need to be finalized.

On a deeply personal note, Adam and Seb were also experiencing a bit of a mind shift. In the three months since Gaston had first signed up as a medical client, his quality of life had improved. Really improved.

"We were capitalists in starting this business and, like most Canadians, we knew someone who knew someone who was using medical cannabis to treat a chronic or terminal illness," notes Adam. "Now we were capitalists who believed in their product so damn much."

Although Adam was increasingly filled with anger and fear about soon losing his father, he realized he had been able to make a difference in his life. And for that, he was thankful to Rona Ambrose, the Conservative health minister who'd rolled out the medical cannabis legislation. They were natural political enemies. He was a staunch Lib and a pot farmer, so to speak, but as the member of Parliament in his father's riding, Rona deserved Adam's thanks for creating the circumstances under which he could help his dad. He decided he needed to put his thoughts to paper. He called Julie and asked her to pen a note. Letter written, she sent it off. He had said his piece. A short time later, Adam spotted the minister on a flight to Ottawa, and for a nanosecond considered thanking her in person.

"I was almost certain I would break down and cry. I just caught her eye, smiled, walked past her in business class, and took my seat in economy at the back of the plane."

News of the $25 million buyout ricocheted across Canada. By November, Hydropothecary was making headlines and everyone in the industry, from activists to other LPs, figured the two young guys running the show were ordering gold-plated toilet seats for their bathrooms. At an industry conference in Vancouver that month, Adam went for dinner with a group of people who ran a cannabis prescription clinic, the very people who could make recommendations as to which cannabis company a client should enrol with. By the time the meal was over, it was clear they expected Adam to pay. And, of course, he had no issue with it. But the perception of Adam as Mr. Moneybucks was in full force later when everyone retired to the bar. Every single additional person who gathered post-dinner, all the activists, enthusiasts, software providers, and clinicians, looked to Adam and another LP's representative to foot the bill. After all, didn't he sleep on a bed made of $100 bills?

Nothing could have been further from the truth. On a shoestring budget for his personal expenses alone, Adam was hardly in a position to cover the bar bill. The money from the CCC deal hadn't even been deposited into escrow. Holy shit, Adam thought, as he looked at the happy, expectant faces. "Ed Chaplin will kill me."

Financial realities and concern for Gaston aside, 2015 didn't end as badly as it could have. Apart from Seb having to step in to let one of their VPs go, they had happy employees. Their name was starting to get traction. And they were worth $25 million.

What could possibly go wrong?

CHAPTER 6

Gaston was dead.

A few days earlier, he had lapsed into a coma, at the Cross Cancer Institute in Edmonton. As he was exiting this world, his wife, Kim, had lay down beside him as a moment of solace, her head on his chest. He took one last breath and his heart stopped.

It was a merciful end. Over the final months, as Adam flew back and forth between Edmonton and Ottawa, he'd seen the precipitous pace of Gaston's decline and his resolute spirit refusing to admit it was happening. On one trip, Gaston had to be admitted to the cancer centre to drain his lungs. "I just need three or four days, five at the most," he said, almost apologetic that Adam had arrived just as he was leaving for the centre. As Kim packed his bag, it was clear Gaston would not be returning home again, yet he never once admitted it to himself.

On another trip — by this time, it was clear Gaston was not coming home — Adam had met with the oncologist. The cancer had spread; Gaston's brain was filled with a thousand tiny tumours. And those tumours were going to change Gaston's personality. Before Adam left to go back to Ottawa, he set up a video call with some 20 family members back east who were not able to say farewell in person. Within two minutes, however, Gaston ended the call; he wasn't ready to go, wasn't yet able to accept that the end was near. He even railed against other terminal patients, grumpily surmising that they were going to die because they had given up. If he went, his thinking went, it would be his own damn fault for not trying hard enough. Even so, he told Adam on a visit, "I don't have much else in the tank."

After his final trip to Edmonton, Adam sent a letter for his father to Kim, asking her to read it to Gaston after he left. It felt selfish, saying goodbye in this way, but Adam wasn't ready to lose his father.

"I hugged him and of course, I said, 'I'll see you soon' as I left. It's what he wanted to hear, but we both knew that I wouldn't."

The knowing of what was coming, the grim and relentless wait that put a grey fog over everyone, had finally ended. Adam flew into action. In the face of chaos, uncertainty, and deep grief, making plans at least meant creating some kind of order. To use his old analogy in the early days of business, he picked a direction and started rowing. In this case, it meant flying out to Edmonton with Meena and his sister, Ashley. Seb had offered to go as well, but he was more needed in Ottawa. Once at their father's house in Spring Lake, Adam wrote the obituary, designed an event rundown, and worked through the details of the service with his family.

JANUARY 5, 2016
AIRBNB RENTAL HOUSE
SPRUCE GROVE, ALBERTA

Spruce Grove, 11 kilometres west of Edmonton, population 34,000, is Alberta's ninth largest city. It's got a leisure centre, local theatre, and performing arts centre. Its two best-known exports are both female Olympians: freestyle skier Jennifer Heil, the 2006 Winter Olympic gold medallist, and Carla MacLeod, who helped snag a silver medal for the Canadian women's hockey team at the 2010 Winter Olympics. But a tourist town it is not. And that was posing a problem for the extended Miron family, who were flying in for Gaston's funeral.

With few hotels and budget-friendly accommodations to be had, Adam and Meena rented an Airbnb. But it wasn't your typical Airbnb: this was the kind of multi-million-dollar, 10,000-square-foot dream home that Adam privately fantasized about owning in the not-too-distant future, if all went well. It was so spacious that Adam and Meena could offer beds to a number of Mirons. It was a house built to host family.

And it was where Adam's dream of living in a house like that was put on hold.

In the midst of planning Gaston's funeral, Hydropothecary had a scheduled board meeting. Under the circumstances, it was a conference call, with Adam, Seb, Michael Munzar, and Jay Ewart calling in from around the country. Adam and Seb relished these meetings as an opportunity to seek guidance in a meaningful way. Even so, this wasn't a happy call. For the third time since inking the agreement to sell Hydropothecary, CCC failed to deposit the money into escrow. Hydropothecary had been running on fumes, and the CCC deal represented a much-needed cash injection. Ed and Seb had been working on alternatives for a while, but the upshot was clear.

"We very carefully weighed what this all meant. We wanted to make sure that they had not performed, that we were right to cancel this deal," recalls Seb. "It was a very significant decision. It seemed like a good deal at the time. But, if we canned this deal, we would be back to the grind, looking for the next source of funding."

Back in Gatineau, sitting in a wooden shed that served as his office at the time, Seb explained the details to the board. Talking it over for more than an hour, they reviewed the situation, and toyed with different scenarios and possible solutions. Michael had from the start been an outspoken critic of the deal. He had tried to find out everything he could about the company when the deal was first tabled, but he couldn't get a proper picture. For him, there was nothing surprising about this deal going pear-shaped. In the end, they all came to the same conclusion: it was time to dump CCC.

It was utterly devastating, not just because the choice signalled yet another return to nickels and dimes but because of the circumstances under which it was made. "As the shock started setting in about the decision we unanimously made," says Adam about the moments after he hung up the phone, "I suddenly remembered it was my dad's funeral the next day."

Adam's organizational skills meant the funeral went off without a hitch, despite everything churning through his mind. An old friend of Gaston's who worked at CTV had interviewed him before he passed, and was on hand to be master of ceremony for the service. There was a slideshow, then friends and family stood up to recall their relationship or their favourite moments with Gaston. Adam could not: there was a lot he could do, but speak publicly about his father so soon after his death was not one of them.

JANUARY 2016
OTTAWA, ONTARIO

A few days later, Adam and Meena arrived at Ottawa's Macdonald-Cartier International Airport, grabbed their bags from the carousel, and headed into the bracing minus 15°C weather. After the relatively warmer 1°C in Spruce Grove, Ottawa's chilly embrace reflected Adam's frame of mind. Winters in Ottawa are a study in extremes: bitingly cold weeks of minus 25°C that never seem to end; snow storms that follow, one after the other, until you forget there ever were things like grass and flowers; rare and welcome days where minus 5°C is a cause to leave the toque at home for a goddamn change.

There was little to smile about. True, the company could announce it'd made $100,000 in revenue and now had more than a hundred registered customers. But the CCC offer was dead, even though they still had a million dollars as a deposit on the deal. (CCC's lawyers tried to insist it should be returned, but the letter of intent signed at the outset meant CCC could have stock, not cash, if the deal went south.) They were back to square one. Again.

As long as CCC was in the pipeline, Seb and Adam had hired and spent on the B5 greenhouse construction. All that came to an abrupt halt when, without the deal, they burned through what cash they had left in just one month. Seb gave his brother-in-law the news over the phone, in his usual blunt way. Adam was in Banff for The Gathering conference, a marketing lovefest dubbed "an exclusive union of the world's bravest brands." For creatives and entrepreneurs in that space, The Gathering is Comicon, every best Christmas ever, and a $20 million lottery win, all rolled into one.

"Adam. We're fucked," Seb announced abruptly. "We're completely out of money. We can't make payroll. Nothing."

Adam swallowed and breathed deeply. This winter could literally not get any worse. It was beginning to feel like they were walking through a dark canyon, feeling their way blindfolded, and bumping into walls at every turn. It had only been a month since Gaston's death, but it felt like a decade. A grim, goddamn decade.

Adam glanced over at his guest at the hotel bar and gave an apologetic smile. "I'll call Rajan Uncle, Seb. Leave it with me."

Rajan Govindarajan had always backed Seb and Adam, even before the moment they'd unveiled their cannabis plans during the visit to Coimbatore, India, for the family wedding, back in 2013. As the family patriarch and Meena and Aruna's uncle, he viewed the young Canadians as he did his own sons. He had considerable success with his India-based international oil-valve manufacturing company and so, the first time they asked for an injection of cash, he invested $100,000. If his boys needed anything from him, he gave it willingly, having been through his own entrepreneurial setbacks. In other words, he was a living definition of his name: in Hindi, Rajan means king. (And he was kingly in more ways than one: throughout his highly successful business career, says Seb, Rajan always focused on security, fencing, and toilets. "He's always about making sure employees have a nice place to eat, clean toilets, and they're safe. That focus on people is part of what we've brought through our own corporate culture.")

Hanging up from Seb, Adam looked at his phone. It was 8 p.m. in Alberta, almost 8 a.m. in India. No time like the present, he thought, and dialled Rajan Uncle's number. Like most wealthy Indian businessmen, Rajan had a driver, partly for security, partly so he could work on his phone during the hour-long commute through Coimbatore's crowded streets.

Upon answering the phone in his usual rushed "Hello!" Rajan heard the hesitancy in Adam's voice, even above the hawkers and honking in the streets around him. "Rajan Uncle," Adam started, "we need help . . ." They needed to make payroll but couldn't, he explained. They'd made progress, but without the deal, they were broke. They had prospects, and no doubt things would turn around, but for right now, they were in a bind. That day, Rajan offered them $100,000, doubling his investment in the company.

That kind of money was welcome and gave Adam and Seb breathing room, as did another cash injection from Michael Munzar. On a golf holiday in Florida at the time, Michael dropped everything and immediately reached out to friends and colleagues to put together a sizable investment. It meant Hydropothecary could keep the lights on for a while, but they needed another miracle. Or a million-dollar idea.

As it turned out, they'd been sitting on a winner for at least six months. Jay, then vice-president of business development, had been pushing an idea he had. Returned soldiers and veterans were a growing medical cannabis demographic, allowed 10 grams per day per person funded by the federal government. They were signing up to Hydropothecary, thanks to Jay's efforts, but some were grumbling about the Chanel-esque look and feel of the Hydropothecary packaging. It was just too . . . pretty. "Every time I go through this goddamn tissue paper, I feel like there's going to be lingerie inside," grumbled one vet in an email. But the guys had put Jay's idea on the back burner and instead focused on building Hydropothecary as a premium luxury brand. Now, with the CCC deal extinct, it was time to take Jay's suggestion seriously.

Adam immediately got to work with a graphic designer in Italy who he'd contacted online. He needed something that would reflect the values and reality of Canadian veterans and soldiers, a brand that would speak to them but still have exceptional design value. Doing much of the design work himself on his laptop, Adam developed a new look and feel, including a box printed to look like a wooden crate and with a fire-stamped logo, using an iconic military-style font. He'd loved doing design work ever since he'd built his first Flash website for a customer when he was a 16-year-old. In university, Adam designed student council posters and, when Photoshop appeared on the horizon, he taught himself how to use that, too. (An atypical student but robust intellectual, Adam eschewed classroom learning for hands-on knowledge. His creativity touched every aspect of Hydropothecary branding and is still present in HEXO. In other words, he says, laughing, "I meddled in everything. I couldn't help it.") Keeping to the military theme, they called the diffusion line

CannaForce. It would prove to be such a success, it sometimes accounted for 70 percent of Hydropothecary's early revenue.

Do one thing well and the temptation to replicate it elsewhere rears its head. Sometimes that works — consider the entire *Star Wars* franchise — sometimes it does not. Delighted by how well received the private labelling of CannaForce went, Adam dug out his Photoshop software and got back to work creating private brands for other demographics. In discussing brand development one day, Julie had explained to Adam that, in the fashion industry, parent labels often create sub-labels bearing the same look and feel but different price points and styles — for example, Michael Kors and MICHAEL By Michael Kors. And so, before long, there was a western Canada–themed label and one about Canadian bears. As with CannaForce, clinic partners would carry the inventory as a sort of house brand. But the more labels Hydropothecary came up with, the more complicated things got. At one point, they were stretching resources with 150 different products.

> ### Billion Dollar Lesson
>
> "Just because you have great success with one product doesn't automatically mean you can or should endlessly replicate it. We did one thing well and went too far, too fast, and it really bit us on the ass. The idea of replicating the success was seductive, but we didn't take responsibility for managing it all. We didn't increase staff, IT, or other resources. We took one idea and turned it into a monster." — **Adam**

MAY 2016
THE FARM, CHEMIN DE LA RIVE
MASSON-ANGERS, QUEBEC

Insulated in the Hydropothecary bubble, with all its struggles and turmoil, it wasn't difficult to forget what else was happening in the world of Canadian cannabis.

A month earlier, then federal justice minister Jody Wilson-Raybould introduced Bill C-45 to the House of Commons, formally following through on the Liberal Party's election promise to legalize marijuana.

A few days later, on April 20 — the 4/20 date is infamously associated with cannabis ever since four high school students in San Rafael, California, used that time to meet and smoke up after school in the 1970s — federal health minister Jane Philpott announced the news to the world at a special session of the UN General Assembly. "We will introduce legislation in spring 2017 that ensures we keep marijuana out of the hands of children and profits out of the hands of criminals," she said. "We know it is impossible to arrest our way out of the problem."

(The date would prove to be too ambitious by half. The Cannabis Act would go through months of debate and more than 40 amendments before it was passed in June 2018, with legalization waiting until October 17, 2018.)

Ironically, the news that Canada intended to become the first G8 country to legalize marijuana saw an immediate spike in the number of illegal dispensaries, with municipalities complaining about a lack of clarity from the provinces and feds on how to police them. The Toronto Police Service figured out a solution. On May 26, 2016, it raided 43 dispensaries, arresting 90 people and laying 257 charges. (The majority of charges would never see the inside of a courtroom, having been settled, withdrawn, or stayed.) In the meantime, on the other side of the country, Vancouver was the location of a 4/20 celebration on April 20 for twenty-five thousand people at Sunset Beach, the biggest ever held; all the while the City was filing injunctions against a raft of illegal dispensaries.

The crew at Hydropothecary should have been celebrating — and indeed, plans were being laid — but behind closed doors, they were about to have a very difficult conversation with many of the people who'd joined the team at the beginning. To stretch Rajan's money as far as possible, they asked a number of staff and contractors to go on half pay. Every person immediately agreed. It wasn't a hard decision to make: Adam and Seb had been leading by example for some time, paying themselves a tiny amount, more of a stipend than a salary.

"It was not an easy thing," recalls Seb. "We hadn't paid ourselves anything. I'd pulled out $35,000 in two years and invested $260,000, so working for Hydropothecary cost me a quarter million in after-tax dollars. But we knew we had to stretch every dime, so we asked a bunch of people and contractors to go on half pay."

"We really had the confidence of our team," adds Adam. "Even if we were broke, they believed in us. It was a nice boost."

AUGUST 15, 2016
BEERBISTRO, KING STREET EAST
TORONTO, ONTARIO

Adam was standing in front of the Beerbistro's TV screen, on a break between meetings. His eyes flickered upward, then down to his phone. Always multitasking, he looked at emails, texts, social media, and then back up to the breaking news. Beerbistro was just down the street from the Canadian Press office, was close to the action of Bay Street, and had the added attraction of 22 beers on tap. Adam took a sip of his lager and went back to his phone — at least until he heard the news anchor say something about the pot industry. Yet another licensed producer was facing a Health Canada recall. Oh shitty, he thought. That can never be us. Never.

Later that day, the news came in from the regulators. Hydropothecary had to pull its products.

Unlike black market weed, which frequently tests positive for human fecal bacteria, illegal carcinogenic pesticides, mould, and mildew because there is no oversight, the regulated cannabis industry couldn't sneeze sideways without reporting it to Health Canada. As Seb would later say at a government oversight committee hearing, "Yes, recalls happen in this industry, just like other industries. This is evidence that regulations work. We should be worried if there aren't any recalls."

In this instance, it was innocent enough. In error, a team member had purchased an organic rather than synthetic type of elemental sulphur. Once known as "brimstone" because it stinks of effluence, burns with an almost invisible flame, and melts into a blood-red liquid, elemental sulphur is also helpful for cannabis growth during the vegetative stage. It supports roots, stems, and leaves, is critical to the production of cannabis oil and terpenes in the flowering stage, and helps plants utilize nitrogen.

But in a strictly regulated environment, any new product — organic or not — had to be submitted to Health Canada for approval before being used. This one had not.

AUGUST 18, 2016
THE FARM, CHEMIN DE LA RIVE
MASSON-ANGERS, QUEBEC

Like meerkats suddenly alerted to threat, employees responded silently but immediately to the arrival of Health Canada inspectors. Today was doubly stressful given the recall, and everyone rushed to be in place, including Seb. It was all hands to the pump, with everyone running around, anticipating and answering questions, pulling up files, and ushering the government people through the system.

After Health Canada left, Adam took charge. Pulling together everyone into the marketing ModSpace, which consisted of seven IKEA desks and a square table, he set up a precise approach to the crisis. Truth is, he loved a bit of chaos and a good war-room situation, having been involved in more than 20 political campaigns. Adam could feel his mind sharpening and his blood racing. This felt good, even though it was bad. He came up with a plan, centred on reaching out to clients personally to deliver a well-crafted set of messages to explain the situation. Over and over, he reviewed the wording, with every team member interjecting and adding to the volume of conversation.

And it worked. In the end, the recall was well received at the consumer end and created an emotional determination to add "honest" to the list of adjectives people would associate with Hydropothecary.

Billion Dollar Lesson

"Even in the early days we were able to divide and conquer. If there was a problem, it was always clear who was going to tackle it and that there would be support from the other. Often, after a quick briefing on the issue and planned response, either Seb or I would stand up, offer our usual fist bump, then say something like, 'You got this' and simply walk out of the room. As the company grew, we kept this same approach with our leaders and problems in their departments, but there were still plenty that we continued to tackle on our own." — **Adam**

The downside to any recall is the recall itself. Product was pulled by Health Canada and held by the government. The current growing crop had also come into contact with the organic sulphur, but if Health Canada quickly approved it, the crop could be saved. It was a long shot, given that approvals typically took 12 months from go to whoa. Facing a supply crunch, Adam, Seb, and Jay began searching for cannabis produced by other LPs. But this, too, would take time. Although the purchase and paperwork could be turned around in a few days, the Health Canada paper trail was a solid 10 business-day process. Third-party testing of the purchased cannabis would take at least another fortnight.

They needed a miracle. And that's exactly what they got.

Within traditional cannabis counterculture, the skunky, terpene-rich smoke associated with lighting up is part of the process. It signals the moment before the journey, a gate opened, and a thought released. It's been immortalized in poem, film, novels, and song, most famously by Bob Marley and later, Ben Harper, in "Burn One Down."

But for those who don't or can't smoke cannabis, the options had been few. Until now. Cannabis contains at least 113 known cannabinoids, of which tetrahydrocannabinol (THC) and cannabidiol (CBD) are the most widely known and studied. In a dried marijuana bud, THC is THC-A, an acid molecule that has to be broken off through heating before it can be metabolized. Cannabis enthusiasts who dislike smoking turn to activating THC through cooking, incorporating ground or milled cannabis buds into gummies, brownies, and chocolates. That was a fine solution for some, but not for a growing marijuana company with a serious supply issue.

And so, one Saturday, Jay, Seb, Adam, and the then VP of quality assurance and scientific affairs, locked themselves in the bunker for the weekend. The question was simple: What could they do with trim, those iconic fan leaves and stems that were typically discarded in favour of buds and their higher cannabinoid content? There was no point in trying to sell it, because it was worth so little. But it wasn't affected by the recall.

What else could they do with it? For people who preferred vaping cannabis over smoking it, a fine-milled product could work. Would anyone also use it as a baking ingredient . . . or better still, what if they could pre-activate the cannabinoids using heat? People baking brownies were activating the THC and CBD but losing up to 70 percent of the active compounds through overheating. What would happen, for instance, if Hydropothecary offered an activated cannabis powder that could be taken in capsule form? Or sprinkled on food?

They got to work. On the floor of the bunker, they packed a standard kitchen mill with dried trim and milled it finer than any bud grinder could. It was fiddly as hell to shove it into tiny capsules, but eventually, they did it. But activating the powder itself would require a fair bit more effort and technology than a kitchen mill. It would mean slowly and steadily heating the powder through a process called decarboxylation and keeping it there until 99 percent of cannabinoids were bioavailable to the human system. Thus was born Decarb, the Canadian cannabis industry's first commercially manufactured decarboxylated powder and Hydropothecary's first revolutionary smoke-free product innovation, entirely born out of desperation and ingenuity.

Throughout that summer, Seb scrambled to find investors, even looking south to the United States. Conservative and cautious, Canadian banks were still skeptical about the future of the cannabis industry in 2016, despite the federal government's promises to legalize it. They didn't (and still don't) like the pot-smoking stigma attached to the industry, and few wanted to pull the tail of the anti-cannabis American government. In fact, most LPs like Hydropothecary and Tweed had turned to credit unions like Desjardins Caisse Populaire and Alterna Savings and Credit Union for their banking. And so, Seb and Ed set off to New York to meet with a bigger, richer investment firm than they could land in Canada.

"It was a challenge in the United States," says Ed. "You're dealing with the stigma, the legalities; you have extra hurdles to overcome. If they took a meeting, they were open to it, but there were a lot of corny jokes about pot. Pockets of the US investment community got it, pockets didn't. It was about finding the right group of people willing to hear the story."

To stretch a dollar — and what else can you do when you're travelling with your CFO — the two men flew economy and booked a single room to share in a grubby downtown Manhattan hostel. It was functional and at least somewhat clean. But it did have one bonus: a Ping-Pong table. That night, Seb discovered his CFO wasn't only a brilliant financial tactician; he was the Ping-Pong King of Lower Manhattan.

(During an interview on October 16, 2018 — the day before Canadian legalization — Seb reflected on how far the company had come. "Back then, no banker would meet with us. You couldn't finance anything," he recalled. Yet, that week of legalization, he'd attended a capital conference with $60 billion American funds wooing Canadian cannabis companies. Three weeks before that, he flew to London, England, to meet with a trillion-dollar private fund. He laughed and shook his head. "I didn't even know trillion-dollar funds existed.")

On a cold and rainy evening, Ed asked the guys to meet him at their favourite watering hole, Pubwells. A place for high-level strategy meetings it wasn't, but the open-concept atmosphere, friendly bar staff, and interesting beers on tap had made it their go-to when they needed to talk things out, especially in the early basement-dwelling days. It had the added advantage of being a block from Adam's house. For Ed to formally request a sit-down at their "remote office" was alarming in itself. But when Adam and Seb walked in to find Ed and his wife parked at a table, alarm bells sounded.

Was Ed about to walk? Certainly, there'd been enough chaos over the past few months to warrant it, and Ed had worked non-stop since joining Hydropothecary, with no staff, few resources, and hardly even a regular desk to call his own. Hundred-hour weeks had been the norm for years, and it wouldn't have been unreasonable if Ed had decided he'd had enough. Then Adam noticed they'd ordered their usual heart-attack-inducing deep-fried zucchini sticks and beer. Maybe it wasn't all that bad, after all.

"Hey, guys. What's up?" Adam didn't have the patience for niceties.

"Well," Ed said slowly. "We have some news we want to share." Ed is a deliberate and thorough thinker who doesn't rush his sentences; when he speaks, people tend to listen. And if they're freaked out enough, they assume all sorts of things as they wait for him to elucidate. Adam and Seb stared at Ed. Please God, don't let this be when their CFO jumps ship. In Pubwells of all places. Adam's mouth parched.

"We remortgaged the cottage and the house. We want to make a real investment in the company."

Seb's heart nearly burst. Once again, at a pivotal point, a lifeline presented itself. Ask and you shall receive. Visualize and manifest. However you wanted to put it, Ed had offered a major show of support, with a six-figure dollar amount. If small acts of meanness in relationships are a death by a thousand cuts, major leaps of faith are a pillar upon which outliers can build their dreams. At a time when the cannabis industry was still forming, still populated with rule breakers and remnants of those with a disdain for the law, Ed's gesture was visionary.

"This was a pivotal point for the company," recalls Ed. "We were at the point where I had to make a decision to be all in or get out. So we decided to go all in, because I believe that a significant investment by the CFO does have an impact on financing. It sends a signal to the market that helps provide credence to future investors."

It also meant that, no matter what, it was his duty to make the company succeed.

He was a good man to have in the company, for all sorts of reasons, including his history of navigating equity and debt financing, mergers and acquisitions, and regulatory compliance for several private and public high-growth companies in Canada and the US. He would also prove invaluable as they started to contemplate the company's next strategic move.

Billion Dollar Lesson

"Should you hire a CFO? It depends on your business, your industry, and your size. Strategic finance is critical to any organization for financial controls, accounting, and strategy. Besides, a good CFO costs nothing, because they'll raise more investment money than they'll cost." — **Seb**

NOVEMBER 1, 2016
ADAM'S HOUSE, CENTRETOWN
OTTAWA, ONTARIO

Growth must have been in the air on Adam's 33rd birthday. For one thing — or rather two — Aruna and Meena were both pregnant and, to their delight, both having girls. There was talk of company expansion and, with it, a great deal of debate about the pros and cons of going public.

Adam and Seb had debated the wisdom of being a publicly traded entity. On the upside, it drew capital, publicity, market share, and eventually an exit strategy for the company founders. The downside was far more onerous. It meant extensive disclosures, submitting to stringent financial reporting regulations, and answering to pressure from investors who, no longer just family and friends, can and do complain about a company's performance.

Drawbacks? Sure. And Seb considered them.

But the truth was the company needed to go public or perish. And the latter was not an option, not for him. For months, Seb and Ed had met, talked to investors and securities companies, drumming up investment capital and interest. Seb had been busy throughout that summer, and not just with the Americans in New York, who were promising $3.275 million. A broker friend had told him about a former real estate and corporate lawyer named Vincent Chiara. Now president and sole owner of Groupe Mach in Quebec, Vincent was looking to diversify investments from real estate. So Seb cold-called him in Montreal, told him their cannabis story, and asked for a meeting.

The first thing you notice about Vincent is his presence. Like the art in his office, it's huge. From his perfectly tailored suits to the sharp gleam in his eyes, he immediately struck Seb as a man he wanted to do business with. Michael Munzar wasn't so sure. From the outset, Vincent's lawyer grilled the two men about Hydropothecary, its structure, its funding model, who was involved, and how much debt they had. It was the kind of conversation where Seb would shine. Although he had yet to develop a truly global scope for the company, the idea of becoming a hub-and-spoke business with multiple joint ventures that would create vertical and horizontal ownership of everything from distribution to consumer products was already bubbling away in the back of his mind. Still, the questions were fired at them, from every angle. Michael was becoming annoyed and impatient. Just do the deal already, he seemed to be signalling. It wasn't the tack Seb wanted to take, not on this first meeting when initial impressions were critical. Plus, it was clear that Vincent and Michael were not seeing eye to eye, so Seb took control of the conversation again. And it went well . . . well enough to garner a second meeting with Vincent. By then, it was time to talk specifics.

"We were looking for money at $4.50 a share at that point, and we had a warrant attached to it. Then Vincent looked me straight in the eye and said, 'I'll do $3.50 a share.' And I knew not to negotiate," says Seb. "I took the deal, and I'm glad I did. It was a hard discount to take, but we ended up with $5 million in two tranches. And we have a very solid relationship."

In the meantime, trying to work with American capital and the US investment scene was fraught with issues, not the least of which was their puritan approach to cannabis itself. Just four states had legalized it, and it didn't look like others would follow anytime soon. It was getting easier for Seb to get the bankers excited about Canadian cannabis, but significantly less so to close a deal that would be compliant with federal law on both sides of the border. Still, he and Ed had put a lot of sweat equity into the American focus. So, when Peter Kirby from Canadian investment firm Canaccord approached them with an offer, Seb felt he didn't need to pursue it. The market was about to open up, Peter told Seb, and Canaccord wanted to invest. Seb heard him out. And turned him down. Canaccord went on to back Aurora, making it instantly one of the leaders in Canadian cannabis. In retrospect, Seb admits he should have taken Peter's offer — they did do business, much later — and dropped the Americans. "But they got behind Aurora, and that created another great competitor in the game," Seb says.

Overall, there was a lot of energy in the air. Money was starting to come to them. It seemed like the tide was finally beginning to turn. Becoming a publicly traded company started to be a point of discussion.

To list on the TSX Venture Exchange, they needed a securities firm. It didn't take long to find a Toronto-based company that promised them a shower of investment money. In total, Seb and Ed had orchestrated three different deals, each with its own benefits and drawbacks. Each wasn't enough on its own, but they had to pick one and make it work. But, Seb being Seb, he figured they could somehow stitch all three together, now that the company had its feet under it. For a year that had started with death and despair, things were starting to look up.

What better place to celebrate the possibilities presented than at Adam's birthday dinner with their growing families?

Amid the family chatter and laughter, Seb's phone rang. He looked at the screen, mouthed to Adam "Tim and Tom,"* referring to a pair of investors, and went to sit on the stairs to the basement office, the door closed behind him to block out the noise of the celebration. A few minutes later, Adam peeked down the steps. Seb wasn't saying much. A quarter of an hour passed. Adam looked again, and this time distinctly heard both Tim and Tom raising their voices down the line. They were vigorously discussing the idea of going public.

Seb listened to their arguments. Tim seemed somewhat open to the idea; Tom was more concerned with the downside. Adam liked Tim and Tom. He appreciated that they had been early investors. And, shit, were they ever like him and Seb, in their relationship. Tim was a numbers guy for whom strategy and execution was everything. Tom was more like Adam, a people person. Respectively, Tim and Tom were in construction and finance, and were very successful, very knowledgeable. But this wasn't their company, and as helpful, smart, and available as they always had been, it wasn't their future on the line. In the end, Seb made his point.

"Guys, if I'm not going public, are you writing the cheque? Because if not, this is what we're doing."

And so, three days later, on November 4, Vincent's first tranche of $2.5 million hit the bank account and Vincent joined the Hydropothecary board. Ten days later, the American financiers invested $3.275 million. On November 17, Hydropothecary announced its intention to list on the TSX Venture Exchange. With money in the bank, on December 1, Adam and Seb were able to buy the small, rundown house and land next door to Louis's farm and begin planning their first mammoth capital works, in the form of a 250,000-square-foot greenhouse expansion.

Overall, 2016 was ending much differently from how it began. The grief of losing his father was still fresh, but with a third daughter on the way, Adam felt some small measure of comfort in witnessing the cycle of life. For his part, Seb had achieved two years' worth of work in one. They were freshly financed, sales were strong, more and more employees were coming on board, and, if everything panned out, they'd be publicly traded in the spring. They had a few more hoops and hurdles to get through before that happened, but they knew what they were up against and were excited by the challenge. Plus, they had their securities firm on board, which would take them to the Venture Exchange and beyond.

DECEMBER 18, 2016
SEB'S HOUSE, CENTRETOWN
OTTAWA, ONTARIO

Across the open-concept living room and kitchen, Seb could see his cell phone light up from where he'd left it on the L-shaped kitchen counter. The house was small — smaller even than Adam's house, and that was saying something. Once a turn-of-the-century worker's row house in a less than salubrious part of downtown, it had been updated and renovated on a budget, which included knocking down walls to create one airy space. He pulled himself up off the couch and ambled the five steps it took to cross the room. Seb scanned the email and swore under his breath.

The securities firm taking Hydropothecary public had just shut down. They'd have to find another.

Billion Dollar Lesson

"Everyone fantasizes about the start-up in the basement. It's fun and exciting, but out of the basement, life really sucks. Most people will not sacrifice their lifestyle for the start-up. That's the tipping point between a $100 start-up and a billion-dollar start-up. These days, we say 'Easy come, easy go.' But that's not how it used to be." **— Seb**

PART 3

HITTING

A

BILLION

CHAPTER 7

Oh, the irony.

Three years earlier, Seb and Adam had eschewed Toronto's famous PATH in favour of trudging through a massive blizzard on their way to meet with investors . . . who'd ignored them.

Today, Seb and Adam had the whip in their hands. They had backers and securities lawyers. They had smart and skilled employees. They had a great future, because today, Hydropothecary was becoming a publicly traded company on the TSX Venture Exchange.

But they had to get there first.

Just after breakfast, the troops gathered in the lobby of the upscale One King West Hotel, where they were staying. Everyone who should be there was there: Seb and Aruna (with newborn Chala), Adam and Meena, as well as key investors. The company was well represented, too, with a handful of people having made the trek to Toronto. Adam, Seb, and the Rajulu sisters left in a cab for the Toronto Stock Exchange and, after an excited debate on whether to walk three blocks outside in the late March Arctic blasts or hit Toronto's underground pedestrian system, the rest of the crew chose the latter.

Down the marble lobby stairs to the hotel's famous former bank vault they went, around a few corners, and into the PATH. The team was buzzing; with the exception of Ed (who wisely chose a taxi), none had been at a public listing before. Energy on high, they laughed and chatted as they marched through the labyrinth. Down through Commerce Court they went, wrong footing it, then backtracking, turning around, and eventually making it to the Toronto-Dominion Centre. By the time they reached First Canadian Place — was it left or right from there? — they'd abandoned the PATH and popped up at the Exchange Tower. On the ground level, the wind was bitingly cold and brisk as they huddled against it and scurried to 100 Adelaide Street. By the time they arrived, teeth chattering from the cold, Seb and Aruna, Adam and Meena, plus Ed, were waiting and wondering where the hell they'd been.

Never mind about getting lost, or about the traffic, or that wind, or running late. This was the Toronto Stock Exchange! More accurately, it was the Venture Exchange. If the Toronto Stock Exchange is where Fortune 500 companies play, the TMX is where young, emerging private companies strap on their training wheels to become publicly listed entities on a junior exchange. It's where great ideas get skin in the game and grow into global corporations. Or not. (Between 2000 and 2018, TMX incubated 563 companies that graduated to the TSX, where the average market cap is $1.4 million, compared with the average market capitalization of $17.8 million on TMX. As Kevan Cowan, president of TSX Markets, once remarked about venture companies, "Lots succeed, and lots don't. Most companies that thrive in the public market have a very good growth story. It's about their ability to execute on growth." That would soon become a major strength for Hydropothecary.)

For Seb and Adam, public listing represented a poke in the eye to Canadian banks and investors who'd shied away from the risky business of cannabis. But it was more than that. It was a validation of belief, hard work, sweat equity, and the bull-headed determination that, of all the crazy-assed business ideas Seb and Adam ever had, this one was the winner.

It was time.

Along with staff and supporters, there were other familiar faces in the crowd: Rajan Uncle, Jay Ewart, Michael Munzar, Tim and Tom, among others. The TMX staff and TV producers had done this hundreds of times, herding in massively excited groups representing their nascent public companies, getting them to stand around the blue desk against the stock wall with the big red button so that, at exactly 9:30 a.m., they could open the market for trading.

This group of 25 eager beavers from Gatineau was no different from any of the others, with two exceptions: they were a pot company and they'd brought a baby.

The countdown was on: 10 ... 9 ... 8 ... 7 ... the TMX folks instructed everyone to clap for at least 60 seconds after the market opened, so they could get good video footage ... 6 ... 5 ... 4 ... 3 ... 2 ... Seb lifted Chala into the air like Simba in *The Lion King* and pressed the button with her little diapered bottom. A ripple of laughter ran through the crowd, anticipation written on every face. This was a moment to relish, something for the books. No one needed to be told to keep clapping.

Afterward, there was an excited hubbub as everyone filed into an adjacent glass-walled room for an underwhelming continental breakfast, accompanied by mediocre mimosas. None of that mattered, not a jot. Someone pointed out that, overhead, a digital ticker was running the words "The TMX Group welcomes The Hydropothecary Corporation to open the TSX Venture Exchange." It was real. Really real.

They'd done it.

And then it was game on. Julie ushered Seb upstairs for a post-market opening TV interview, at which he explained that "the main driver of patient flow [were] coming from specialized medical marijuana clinics" as a result of pain management and the opioid crisis.

Behind the camera, Julie watched him. Incredible. At the biggest moment in his career to date, he was commanding. He flowed. His high school years spent as a theatre geek, doing musicals and public speaking, were being dusted off and put into play. She didn't need to stand there, monitoring and interjecting if a question was offside. She took a few photos, to feel useful. There was no need for any more media training, with all the explanations and coffee-table discussions about what journos want and how to stay on point during 12-second sound bites. Not anymore. Seb fully understood what he was about in front of the camera. And in a candid interview, no less. She caught Seb's eye and gave him a thumbs-up. Bloody fucking brilliant, she thought.

Ten minutes later, everyone was on the move again. Seb, Ed, Adam, and their board members headed to Hydropothecary's securities lawyers' offices for a board meeting; everyone else either went to a post-opening celebration or headed back to work, organizing media interviews, touching base at the farm, or responding to emails. Journalists from CTV, BNN, Radio-Canada, Rogers, *La Presse*, the *Financial Post*, and online weed media were all eager to be part of the moment.

"Quebec's Hydropothecary Corp became the latest medical marijuana company Tuesday to open its business to investors eager to cash in on the burgeoning marijuana sector," noted the *Financial Post*, before pointing out that "nearly 3.6 million shares changed hands as many investors seek opportunities to pour into the hot marijuana market ahead of an expected recreational legalization announcement by the federal government this spring."

Like so many moments in the cannabis industry, achieving one major milestone meant catapulting into a whole series of other tasks, at double time. As one observer would recall years later, "The semiconductor industry is pretty fast paced, where every three months there are new gadgets. It was exciting. But the cannabis industry . . . it blows that out of the water. In two years, cannabis achieved what would be reasonable for other industries to do in 20."

A few blocks away, Seb and Adam were on a mental high as they headed into the board meeting. Their hearts and minds were expanding at a rate of knots, because this day — this achievement — was incredible. And it helped that they had brought on a team of true believers who, although not all cannabis consumers, were invested in the vast potential that lay ahead.

Yet, for some, it had taken a lot of convincing.

Despite buying into the Hydropothecary dream, board member and investor Vincent Chiara had resisted the notion of it becoming a public company. He and others felt that staying private, keeping things at a casual and reasonable pace, built slowly over time, was the right way to handle a mostly unknown industry like medical marijuana. But the public market was exploding. All of a sudden, despite the hurdles of compliance and financing, cannabis was getting so big, so fast, that going public was the only way to maintain the velocity needed for expansion. Some competitors who were visionary enough to establish cannabis companies 20 years earlier had waited too long to go public and, at a time when they should have been market leaders, were now being gobbled up outright by hungry cannabis corporations.

But whatever, right? They'd done it, they were publicly traded. (THCX shares that day opened at $1.82 and closed at $1.55.) Best of all, their lawyers' boardroom had their name on the door. It was a vastly different scene from three years earlier, when the disinterested brokers barely glanced up from texting to acknowledge them. Seb, ever Mr. Casual, was decked out in tidy new jeans and a button-down shirt embroidered with THCX.COM over his heart and the stylized Hydropothecary "H" on his right cuff. Adam had gone all out. He was sporting a brand-new blue three-piece suit in the smallest size he'd worn in years (he'd lost 22kg that year), and despite bringing several ties with him from Ottawa, had followed his personal traditional routine and risen early to buy another "bon cravat" to mark the occasion. In this case, a pink Brooks Brothers silk tie.

The atmosphere in the lawyers' boardroom was one of delighted caution. Yes, they'd just listed publicly, but what about this agenda of items to get through? After the obligatory handshakes and congrats, they got down to business. And, with the exception of Ed, who understood perfectly the amount of work that lay ahead, the board meeting, as light-hearted as it was, drove home to Seb and Adam just how much they didn't know. They were under-resourced. At that time, they had 58 employees, with another 35 positions to fill. And despite having raised over $35 million in financing, much thanks to Canaccord's Peter Kirby, they needed more money. And they needed to think much, much bigger. Immediately. Plus, despite knowing precisely what going public meant, they had now committed to a level of transparency like they'd never dreamed of. They had access to capital — theoretically — but they were now subject to the vagaries of the markets. They'd have to lift their skirts and show their knickers to any investor who needed to know. There was also the intimidating spectre of shareholders demanding and deserving constant, perpetual, unbroken, stable, and uninterrupted growth.

"It was 'Holy crap, we have the licence,' and we had financing, but that's when we realized that growth would be the next big challenge," Adam notes of that momentous day. "Every time you think you're on the other side, passing that next video-game level, you realize how big the next level will be."

Even so, it was gratifying. Their lawyers were hosting them in their boardroom. Their staff were all heaving away at the next big task that lay ahead, whatever that was, and wherever they were. There was a task (or several) for every person, but not enough people for every task. At least, they weren't doing "farm jobs" anymore. Or not as often.

That evening, at Katana restaurant on Bay Street, family, friends, investors, and staff continued to celebrate. Adam was beaming as he chatted with a group seated near the window. They were friends of Meena's from her university days, all highly successful financiers, consultants, doctors, lawyers, or physicians. Having them there at that moment was one of the most gratifying things in Adam's life. The other was being cornered by the Bulldog of Bay Street, who took him aside to tell him, "Buddy, you should run for prime minister. You really should!"

The celebrations continued into the early hours back at the One King West Hotel, with the crew shutting down the lobby bar as they passed around a $1,500 bottle of Moët & Chandon champagne someone had gifted Adam as if it were an Oscar. They didn't drink it — it went back to Gatineau for the marketing team members who weren't at the opening — but they did send Jay out for a late-night snack of two dozen "poor man's Big Macs": double cheeseburgers with special sauce, which were half the cost of the iconic sandwich but tasted exactly the same.

Back on the farm, life returned to normal. Or as normal as the cannabis industry could ever be. With the public listing, everything had to change, from the involvement of investor relations and who was hired, to what went into press releases and how they went out. Equally pressing was the matter of finding someone to be Seb's extra set of hands. For ages, he'd resisted having an assistant, muttering, "What would they do all day?" and complaining that there'd be nowhere for them to sit. But Adam and their human resources manager pressed on with interviews. They were looking for someone who could anticipate Seb's needs, even if he didn't know what they were at the time. What Seb needed was an assistant they eventually dubbed "the CEO's secret weapon."

Adam was thinking about the future in other ways, too. He recalled sitting on the plaza steps at Simon Fraser University as a young dreamer years earlier, staring up at the clouds after he'd been on a phone call for a job interview as the Young Liberals' national director. If he got the job, he had thought, he'd write a book about how he came from nothing and was now in charge of a national political organization. (He did get the job, and it was nothing like how he'd imagined it would be — he didn't write the book.)

It was a pivotal moment, a time when he started to understand the value of self-actualization, of visualizing something and feeling it so deeply it becomes a part of your DNA. Maybe now was the time to make it happen. Adam called Julie to see what she thought about writing a book about their business story. She was in. They immediately fell into their usual creative hyper-language, riffing and pushing each other to dream bigger. Two days later, she sent him a two-page draft outline. It was good — for a hot minute. Within six months, the cannabis industry changed, then changed again, and Hydropothecary with it. If the cannabis story was to be written, it'd have to be written as it happened, just as in journalism. It was a novel approach; then again, everything about cannabis was.

As the company grew in employees and footprint, so too did the number of clients. But it didn't seem to be translating to sales. Although the privately run Natural Health Services cannabis clinics in Alberta were bringing in the lion's share of new clients, something wasn't right. It was time to find out what.

As it turned out, grey market dispensaries were downloading Hydropothecary's online prescription applications, giving them to clients, and sending them to clinics that would put them through the system. After registering as a Hydropothecary client and perhaps placing an order, they would return to the dispensary for the "deal of the week" cannabis. In many other cases, clinics were incentivized by competing licensed producers that offered clinic staff perks like big-screen TVs if they netted an LP the greatest number of sales. It was a common enough practice for companies whose strategy was to sign up as many new clients as possible. But that wasn't Seb's approach. From the outset, he was focused on making the company attractive to investors by lowering the production cost per gram of growing the best-quality product possible. This wasn't just about selling weed but selling and creating a company with longevity and scope. Even so, something had to be done to create more energy around clients and sales. So, with almost military precision, Adam, Jay, and the sales team, hit every clinic and spoke to every salesperson about Hydropothecary products. Eventually, they were showing up at a newly opened clinic before any other LP's sales rep. At one point, Hydropothecary had more than a hundred clinics on side.

Billion Dollar Lesson

"Although short-term gain can be alluring and valuable in terms of revenue, establishing and sticking to core values nets long-term benefits. In the case of HEXO, the focus on cost per gram and ROI over the entire ecosystem has meant that the company has a well-earned reputation among investing bodies for solid management." — **Adam**

But working with clinics wasn't the only thing the sales team were doing. For months, they and some of the marketing squad had been attending business-to-business cannabis conferences, which were popping up like dandelions across Canada. They were making multiple fact-finding trips to the legalized states of Washington, California, and Oregon. There, the industry was far more advanced in terms of access, product innovations, and edibles. There were massage therapists using THC oil, and women's cannabis conferences advocating cannabis oil for everything from sexual pleasure to managing endometriosis pain. Everywhere they went, the team would buy products, then take them apart back at their hotel. Some products came in straightforward bottle-and-dropper packaging. Others had more inventive packaging. One company had used a system that cleverly atomized cannabis oil rather than putting it into a vape. It was a great piece of engineering, but it was also awkward and odd-looking. The upshot of the brothers-in-law's research was that cannabis oil was going to be a key product, but what delivery system would they use? And more importantly, how would they get around the funky flavour universally associated with cannabis oil?

Those two questions would form the basis of Hydropothecary's second major product innovation, Elixir, which would go on to win Product of the Year and Innovation of the Year at the Lift Canadian Cannabis Awards in 2018. The company wanted to make a high-THC and a high-CBD cannabis-oil product, but what was the best and easiest way to use it? Adam was adamant that, after all their product research, any new innovation had to be easy to use, easy to understand, smoke-free, and convenient. No gimmicks. No potential for mess. Something a business-person could carry in a jacket pocket, for example.

The product development team tested multiple containers, slowly narrowing down the options to a small and discrete childproof spray bottle. But what about the taste? Granted, some people didn't mind the flavour of marijuana oil, but most people did. And that's where the team got creative. Like many cannabis producers making oil, the pure product had to be mixed with a carrier oil, most commonly a medium-chain triglyceride (MCT) oil that was a by-product of coconut oil. It was flavourless and neutral. But if Hydropothecary could add another flavour, like peppermint, perhaps that would make Elixir a pleasant experience.

It was a great idea, but for months after the full marketing plan was developed and ready to go, weekly marketing and communications meetings invariably began with an update on whether Health Canada had approved it, and if not, did they know when it might?

(There was, of course, the underlying fear that Elixir would never be approved for production or sale, because no one else had been able to get a cannabis oil with a peppermint taste past the regulators. It was commonly believed in the cannabis community that it was simply never going to happen. When Elixir was eventually approved and launched on July 31, 2017, it sent shockwaves throughout the industry. One Hydropothecary executive reported how a contact at another LP had insisted to his CEO that Health Canada would never pass a flavoured cannabis oil. When news broke that Hydropothecary had somehow made it happen, within the regulations, the colleague was raked over the coals and nearly lost his job.)

As it turned out, the delay on getting Elixir into production would prove to be only a minor irritation compared with what was about to happen.

9 A.M., MAY 1, 2017
GATINEAU COURTHOUSE
GATINEAU, QUEBEC

In cannabis years, the events of 2014 felt like they'd occurred 20 years earlier, but the past was about to become the present and not in a good way. The spat over Hydropothecary declining the lease on the Rue Bombardier property had moseyed its way through the court system and was now on the docket in Gatineau. When the court date arrived, it gave Seb an opportunity to have his say and win the day. Which he did — handily.

As the judge listened to both sides of the story, the relationship between Seb and the property owner came under discussion. At one point, Seb had invited the owner to join him for an event in Toronto.

"I intended to pay, Your Honour," Seb clarified.

The judge looked down at his notes. "Well, that's what it means if you invite someone."

Seb smirked. "That's not my experience with my past girlfriends, Your Honour."

In the end, it was the contract itself that was the proving ground to drop the lawsuit. Seb had handwritten a clause into the lease in front of a notary public that a condition was the acquisition of a sales licence from Health Canada; without it, there would be no need for the Rue Bombardier space. Whatever else the owner thought or believed, the clause was in black and white. In the end, the judge ruled that the document was an offer of lease and that, without all conditions fulfilled, there was no deal. The owner had spent $150,000 on lawyers to lose.

On day one of the hearing, Seb and Adam were fairly confident they would win and could return their attention to running their business and growing weed. Unfortunately, the next morning brought news that nearly stopped them from doing either.

MAY 2, 2017
THE FARM, CHEMIN DE LA RIVE
MASSON-ANGERS, QUEBEC

Health Canada had scheduled a conference call for that morning. The agent hadn't said what it was, but it sounded serious. As Seb, Adam, and others sat around the conference call on the table, the Health Canada employee opened the conversation with, "Hey, so we've discovered pesticides in your products . . ."

The effect was galvanizing.

Hydropothecary didn't use pesticides, and in fact, the staff relished telling anyone who would listen that it used biological controls, like ladybugs and damselflies. How did something like micro . . . what did she call it? Myclobutanil. Where did that even come from? Myclobutanil, the Health Canada agent explained, was a commonly used fungicide pesticide, registered for use on a wide range of food crops but banned for use on marijuana. Health Canada had taken five samples and found exceptionally low levels of it, representing low or zero health risks. But finding any level of pesticides on medical marijuana was unacceptable. While Health Canada was going further into the investigation, the writing on the wall was clear. They'd have to destroy all their plants. Listening to the agent, Seb felt time slow and a deep sense of calm come over him.

"I remember thinking clearly, 'So, this is how the journey ends.' I thought the company was finished. It was very clear, very serene, kind of like accepting death at that point. That lasted for about four seconds and then it was back to 'Okay, let's figure this out. What can we do, what's the path, and how is thing going to roll out?' And we got down to business."

Billion Dollar Lesson

"When you're growing a company, it's important to understand everyone's strengths and weaknesses but also realize that you're not in this alone. I would not have carried this company on my own in the first three years. In the rare moments where it was difficult to carry on, Adam would push through. When he had moments of doubt, I pushed him. It's like climbing a mountain tethered to each other. Whenever one person falls, the other guy is still holding on." — **Seb**

Adam immediately prepped a war-room meeting. Although politics and business don't always align, Adam had uniquely been able to pull lessons from political war rooms he'd been part of to take charge when the cannabis shit hit the fan. And as always, it was a sight to behold.

"For all Adam's gifts," notes Seb, "one of his most powerful is the ability to be given any situation and solve it. It might not be the prettiest solution, and it might not be the most elegant, but he's going to get people around the room, and he's not going to come out until it's solved. It's a beautiful thing to see."

The company's phone was set to voicemail. ("We were the one company that would answer even on Christmas morning, but until we knew what was going on, we weren't risking anything," recalls Adam.) Adam handpicked a team from legal, compliance, quality assurance, communications, and investor relations. Everyone was reassured and given their assignments. Should they have to issue a recall, they had to be ready. After a few minutes of addressing the assembled employees in English — one of the many times his lack of French was apparent — Adam started handing out tasks. They would retest everything, from greenhouse walls to rubber gloves. It wasn't required, but they'd built their reputation on trust and transparency, so it had to be done. They had to develop a client communication plan and scripts to ensure everyone who was registered heard directly from a Hydropothecary employee. A press release and strategy had to be created, together with emails and social media. And then they had to set up a call centre and get volunteers on the phones. They got to work putting together a press release announcing a voluntary stop-sale and stop-shipment, until they could get a bead on where the myclobutanil came from. And they decided to do daily updates on the company website, to keep clients fully informed with evolving news. They worked around the clock, eating fast food, sleeping when they could, rotating shifts, and hitting the phones all over again.

"A number of recalls had already happened in the industry, and each was a 'what not to do' from a communications perspective," says Adam. "We got in the *Globe and Mail*, we wrote to clients and called them, shared it with the cannabis community news and product site, Lift.co, and did daily updates. The only way to maintain trust was to be very transparent, honest, and communicative. So that's what we did."

Marketwired
May 02, 2017, 12:53 ET
The Hydropothecary Corporation Announces Precautionary Voluntary Stop-Sale of Cannabis
GATINEAU, QC — (Marketwired — May 02, 2017) — The Hydropothecary Corporation (TSX VENTURE: THCX) ("THCX" or the "Company") today announced a voluntary stop-sale and stop-shipment on all products.

This action was taken as a precautionary measure immediately following a Health Canada notification at 6:07 p.m. (EDT) on May 1, 2017, that test results of cannabis leaf samples taken on March 8, 2017, indicated the presence of myclobutanil, a general use fungicide registered for use on a wide range of food crops but which is not approved for use on cannabis. The results indicate levels of 0.023 parts per million (ppm) and 0.012 ppm. Hydropothecary notes that it has been conducting voluntary pesticide testing on all lotted products since February 2, 2017, through a certified third-party laboratory. All such pesticide test results have been negative for pesticides at a level of 0.05 ppm. THCX's testing program was developed on industry advice from Health Canada and industry norms. The source of the myclobutanil is unknown and the Company is conducting a review to determine the source of the pesticide. The Company has not received any serious adverse reaction reports related to its products.

The response from the media was immediate, with the *Globe and Mail* reporting that the banned substance was found on trimmings from mother plants, which are used to create genetic clones. Previously, the report noted, Health Canada hadn't tested for banned chemicals and was imposing acceptable limits on LPs with little forewarning. The problem wasn't limited to Hydropothecary either.

Though harmful chemicals are a known problem in the black market, this is the fourth time in less than six months that the government-regulated sector has been hit with a tainted cannabis problem. Mettrum Ltd., Organigram Inc., and Aurora Cannabis Inc. each announced recalls in December.

For 11 days, staff poached from across the company hunkered down in the makeshift war room on the first floor of the farmhouse, making thousands of calls and repeating the same script over and over.

"Hello, may I please speak with Mrs. X? This is the Hydropothecary calling. We have an important update to share with you; have I caught you in the middle of anything?"

Billion Dollar Lesson

"A political war room's purpose is to get someone elected. In a corporate environment, the lessons from a political war room can be very effective in convincing people your idea is the right one. During the recall, we had to know exactly where we were and where we wanted to be. There are plenty of romanticized notions about the long nights and camaraderie, but after four days of eating takeout and not showering, you need structure to keep going. The three key elements are these. First, handpick representatives from key departments for their input. The last thing you need is outside counsel. Next, define your objective. In cannabis, a precedent had already been set for stonewalling the public about recalls, and we wanted to define a new standard for how an industry would take a leadership role in communicating and respecting our customers and the media. Finally, communicate with your team. We had daily 8:30 a.m. operational calls and a 5 p.m. board call every afternoon. Explain to people what's happening, reassure them, and the company stays strong." — **Adam**

By the time it was over, the team was exhausted but knew they'd done everything they could to mitigate fallout. That day — May 16 — the company announced resumption of sales but introduced a voluntary recall of three lots of dried bud sold between February 14 and May 1 of that year. With Health Canada moving the goalposts on testing pesticides, Adam, Seb, and the scientific team decided to go completely over the top with their own testing to ensure the products not only met the standards but exceeded them. "In the interests of our clients, we are responding with twice-over rigorous testing at 0.005 ppm of our products to ensure we exceed whatever regulatory standards are set," Seb said in a press release. (On June 5, the company expanded the voluntary recall, laid out new preventive measures to standard operating procedures and policies, and announced the results of the investigation. "As a result of the investigation, the Company has determined that the voluntary pesticide management systems implemented in September 2016 have proven effective and that the contamination occurred during an earlier period," read the press release.)

The company was mulling over other options to change the conversation, too. Optically, the recall wasn't just terrible for business and their reputation; it was bad for the industry as a whole. After trying so hard to change the stigmas around cannabis by moving away from the black market and stoner culture, a recall would only cement the public's view of cannabis as a sketchy industry. Maybe they could embed journalists. In doing so, they could witness first-hand the oversights, processes, and transparency that Hydropothecary had been built upon. There was only one hurdle. With newsrooms shrinking and freelance budgets disappearing, such investigative features were not really a possibility.

Meanwhile, Adam was about to become a Hydropothecary client himself. Despite talking up the benefits of CBD and THC for myriad complaints and health issues, he'd never had to use any of the company's products himself. That all changed on the Mother's Day before the resumption of sales, when he and his daughter Iyla left Meena to rest at home, as she was three weeks overdue with their third daughter, Sohana, and were blindsided by a speeding car as they were on their way to deliver a gift to their nanny. The impact shoved Adam's Mazda a half-car width over. In the back baby seat, Iyla bawled. Her head had hit the side of the car seat so hard, the back of her earring pierced the skin. Adam immediately comforted her and went into crisis management, arranging a tow and calling police. It wasn't until a few days later that the muscle stiffness and headaches become a major concern. The whiplash left him with persistent pain and, together with visits to a chiropractor and physiotherapist, he signed up as a client for Decarb CBD. "It's not a curative; it's a tool," he notes.

An old friend of Adam's, Dr. Terry Lake, had also turned to CBD. Before he'd made national headlines for his leadership during the opioid crisis as British Columbia's health minister, Terry had been mayor of Kamloops. As an eager young political neophyte, Adam had worked on his 2005 campaign and admired Terry's abilities as a strategist and long-term thinker. The two remained friends from that time onward. When medical marijuana first became a headline, Adam called Terry in British Columbia to ask if it had a future.

"I was very honest. I knew nothing about it; it was a federal program," says Terry, who returned to politics when he ran in the 2019 federal election. "The provinces had nothing to do with it back in 2013 and didn't want to take responsibility for it. I had precious little to offer him, but in typical Adam fashion, he didn't let that deter him. The next thing I knew, I was reading an article in *Maclean's* about Hydropothecary. I had a mini heart attack when I read his name. That's when I realized he'd gone through with it."

With Terry declining to run again in British Columbia's tumultuous 2017 elections, Adam called him up and invited him to meet the board in Ottawa.

"I'd had my interest piqued by the Liberal win in 2015 and, as health minister, of course I was asked by the media about it. I said it was a good thing, as Canadians were among the most frequent users of cannabis, so regulating safe access while shifting profits from the black market to legitimate taxpaying businesses made sense. Plus, my daughter Stephanie had just presented a paper in New York on cannabis as part of her graduate studies, and I was fascinated by the science. I realized prohibition ending was a better idea than I had thought. There would be a policy shift. So I agreed to come out and see what Adam was thinking."

The meeting was set for May 24, their second board gathering after the post-listing meeting in Toronto. Now it was time to get down to work. As a publicly traded entity, the board was subject to an enormous number of charters. Without anyone to write them, Adam cut and paste them from previously drawn-up legal documents, revised them, printed them out, and presented the four-inch-thick pile to the board for review. That day, Hydropothecary also offered Terry a position on the board.

Two weeks later, during an East Coast holiday with his wife, where he was presented the Canadian Public Health Association Health Hero Award for his work in handling British Columbia's fentanyl crisis, Terry called Adam and declined the board position.

"My heart sank," says Adam. "Then he said, 'Offer me a full-time job.' I had to think of something on the spot, so I said, 'VP of corporate social responsibility' without really thinking what that meant. I painted a picture of him carrying a big stick and ensuring there were no deviations from the overall plan in terms of CSR, that the company stayed on mandate and didn't go off into the weeds. He accepted, thank God, but soon after he started, there was almost an uprising in the cultivation department. They wanted to know exactly how big the sheriff's badge was. Terry wanted to halt the use of a specific soil from India because there were no guarantees that child labour hadn't been involved."

(For his part, the transition from being a high-ranking politician with an $18 billion budget to working in a small company establishing itself in a rapidly evolving, make-it-up-as-we-go industry was a massive shift. "It was quite refreshing; it forced me to think differently and be more creative. All of a sudden, I had to figure out how to do a purchase order while working in a ModSpace office with no plumbing and an outdoor toilet. I must have complained about it too often, because Ed wrote 'Dr. Terry Lake's Executive Washroom' on an old white bucket and put it in my office.")

At that time, Terry was the highest-ranking Canadian politician to join the cannabis industry, and bringing him into the mix proved to be a wise decision. With the announcement he'd been appointed, the company's stock gained $20 million in value in a day. It sent a signal to the industry that Hydropothecary was taking the environmental and social impacts of cannabis seriously.

Even with the company's front bench more fleshed out, the workload was enormous. The words "hive of activity" are hackneyed yet fully represent what life was like. Staff showed up early and stayed late, day after day. New ideas would be floated, only to be fleshed out, created, and launched within a day or two. The pace was frenetic in every department, from cultivation and operations to marketing and HR. "Meeting Mondays" became as much an institution as Terry's Friday afternoon "Beer O'Clock." And with the planning of a 250,000-square-foot greenhouse expansion set to be announced in a few months, it was only going to get crazier.

Inside Seb's spartan office in the farm's expanding ModSpace village, the same was true for Seb. As CEO of a public company, he had to balance getting granular on decision making for operations and capital expenditure with hitting the phone or the road to pitch the stock. He wanted direct reports from all his VPs. He had to make snap decisions, moving so quickly that other team members were unaware they had even been made not to mention why.

Clearly, it was time for a change. And Adam knew it was necessary, even for himself. His title was chief brand officer, but that hardly covered the scope of what he did daily: overseeing marketing and communications, doing crisis management, weighing in on product innovation and brand, and adding his voice and insight to hiring. Throughout May, after work, he'd crack open his laptop and read everything he could about corporate structure and management, searching for a solution. Was it to hire another VP? But to do what? Did they need to restructure the company? And what would that look like? He'd read a well-written 2006 article in *Harvard Business Review* that seemed to have the answer. Entitled "Second in Command: The Misunderstood Role of the Chief Operating Officer," it tries to define the COO's value.

"Understanding what makes for a successful chief operating officer is vital because the effectiveness of COOs (or ranking operations executives by whatever name they are called) is critical to the fortunes of many companies — and could be to many more," write authors Nathan Bennett and Stephen A. Miles.

"Finally, there is no single agreed-upon description of what the job entails or even what it's called. Often, companies turn responsibility for all areas of operations over to the COO — this typically includes production, marketing and sales, and research and development. In some firms, the job is to be Mr. Inside to the CEO's Mr. Outside," they continue.

"A-ha," Adam thought. Maybe Hydropothecary needed a COO. It was a natural solution to hire a Mr. or Ms. Inside and unleash the awesome power of Seb's Mr. Outside. Their CFO, Ed, seemed to agree, so Adam asked human resources to draft a job description.

A week later, Adam changed his mind. Again diving into post-dinner research at his kitchen table, this time to play the devil's advocate in order to ensure they were making the right decision, he came upon a website called Organizational Physics, hosting an article entitled "Organizational Design: Why You Should Not Have a President and COO." He clicked on the link and then laughed out loud. The landing page image was of a quote from Rear Admiral Grace Hopper (1906–1992) Adam had seen before: "The most dangerous phrase in the language is 'We've always done it this way.'" Not in cannabis, Adam thought. We're figuring it out as we go. Still, the opening lines of the article kept him reading. It was as if the author were writing about Hydropothecary.

"It's a classic tale. Your company's driven, visionary founder manages to lead your start-up to takeoff and hit rapid growth mode. But then something happens, and everything starts to bog down. Those former start-up struggles and early wins turn into a whole new set of challenges: running the business at scale."

Jay-sus. No kidding, he thought. The article went on to outline why leaders at most companies think that very scenario warrants hiring a president/COO and why they shouldn't. There was the usual stuff about a new hire not fitting into the existing culture and failing to replicate past wins. But two sentences really grabbed Adam's imagination.

"In another common scenario, you'll find that soon after joining, the new President/COO will get into conflict with the founder/CEO about who really runs the business. When this happens, the culture quickly erodes into 'old guard' vs. 'new guard' and execution speed bogs down across the board from all the in-fighting and politics."

Adam immediately emailed the article's link to Seb, who was just returning from meetings in Montreal. For the next two hours, they each read everything they could about the author and founder of Organizational Physics, Lex Sisney. An expert at business scaling and organizational structure, Lex had helped countless companies level up through structures and processes that clearly define roles and responsibilities. Adam found Lex's email address and tapped out a note complimenting his great insights and asking if he'd be interested in helping Hydropothecary. A day later, he and Seb were on the phone with Lex, offering him a consultant's role.

Lex's involvement in structuring the company was pivotal in transforming the inner structure from a start-up to a seasoned company. Later, as the company mushroomed and it became essential to have more cross-functional understanding and fewer direct reports to the CEO, HEXO would hire a COO to ensure the business planning function was operational and that there were no departmental silos. But back then, that they even investigated something about which they knew nothing, like operational structuring, spoke to Adam and Seb's shared mindset. Seb is formally educated, Adam was a B student who never finished any university degree he started. Even so, both men constantly self-educate, reading voraciously both in print and online. As Jay Ewart observed, "They had to learn and move far and fast in a really short time. Along the way, they've used all the resources they could to educate themselves."

7 A.M., JUNE 5, 2017
THE FARM, CHEMIN DE LA RIVE
MASSON-ANGERS, QUEBEC

The results of last month's pesticide investigation were in. The company's pesticide management system established in 2016 had been effective, but that was hardly worth a headline. Despite its proven worth, the company had to expand the voluntary recall to include cannabis bud that had been grown prior to that system. New preventive measures were also put in place, creating a new industry benchmark for health and safety in production.

June 05, 2017 07:30 ET
Hydropothecary Announces Results of Investigation and Expansion of Voluntary Product Recall of Dried Cannabis
GATINEAU, QC — (Marketwired — June 05, 2017) The Hydropothecary Corporation (TSX VENTURE: THCX) ("THCX" or the "Company") has announced the results of its investigation into the low-level presence of myclobutanil at the Company's facility . . .

"Based on the results of our investigation" [says Sébastien St-Louis,] "it is clear that the low-level presence of myclobutanil resulted from older production and appears to have been introduced to a small number of plants by a former employee without Hydropothecary's knowledge or authorization. Current evidence also suggests that the myclobutanil application occurred before our new head grower and current QA team were in place. Finally, it is clear from testing results that no dried cannabis that was produced by our current grow team shows any sign of contamination at reporting levels set by Health Canada."

If the news of an extended recall pointing to the actions of a former employee raised any eyebrows, the moment was quickly overshadowed by the auspicious events of June 5.

8:30 A.M., JUNE 5, 2017
THE FARM, CHEMIN DE LA RIVE
MASSON-ANGERS, QUEBEC

It was time to raise money. Again. To survive in the tumultuous cannabis industry, Hydropothecary had to grow. Again.

And so, at 7:32 a.m., the announcement that it was doing a $20 million raise through a bought deal private-placement basis courtesy of Peter Kirby's Canaccord hit the newswire.

Adam checked his phone and looked at the stock price. It was early, but he was anxious. For every dollar raised, it meant handing out equity. You never want to sell too much or too little. And God forbid that the raise was less than the offer. But he had to trust Seb and Ed. They'd been working on the deal for a while and had the full weight of the board behind them. They needed the additional capital for expansion, and they'd carefully prepared, but there was always a risk. Still, $20 million was a mountain of money. He thought back to a year earlier — it seemed like five years ago — when $3 million seemed like substantial bank. Now, he thought, there was momentum. He rolled the number around in his head . . . $20 million was a big-league number.

Soon after the markets opened, his phone started pinging. And pinging. Congratulations were pouring in from family and friends, investors all. Then came a text from Seb. They'd oversold. Within an hour and a half of markets opening, they'd busted past the $20 million with its twenty thousand convertible debenture units at $1,000 a pop. Ten minutes later, Seb texted again. They were upsizing the offering to $25 million. By 2:04 p.m., a second press release crossed the wire announcing the upsize. In the end, they raised $30 million in a day.

"If you think that the second press release came out quickly," laughs Adam, "you should have seen how quickly the board voted on the resolution to upsize."

It was good news. No, it was great news. Seb had always said that you have to make deals to get more deals because there is a natural momentum to the flow of money. Not only had they moved into a completely different echelon when it came to their capital raise, they were crushing it. The word was getting out. Which, in one way, was a bit of a miracle.

While other departments at the farm were gaining structure and being fleshed out with staff, the communications department was still operating like a start-up. The department was agile, smart, and capable of pivoting on a dime, and there was nothing the comms and marketing team loved more than putting out a tire fire. Untethered from structure and process, they could scramble and make things happen. But, without structure, everything was a fire drill.

"We were all kind of sitting around waiting for the phone to ring with another issue that we could go and manage, because we were good at it," says Adam. "It gave you a badge to do whatever you needed to get it done. It was like you're allowed to kick in a door and get approvals or make an expenditure and paper it up the next day."

The atmosphere was as exciting and dynamic as a newsroom in a crisis, but it also made the comms team deeply unpopular with the more structured departments around them. What they needed was a comms director to implement process and therefore a modicum of sanity. So Adam got to work. Very quickly, he touched base with HR to flesh out a job description and start interviewing candidates. There were good candidates, even great ones from senior federal government positions and agencies, but it was apparent that the farm's distance from both Ottawa and Montreal was a major sticking point. By the time the role was eventually filled, a year and a half had passed.

Billion Dollar Lesson

"Even though there are things you can do really, really well, and you have fun doing them, it doesn't mean you don't have to put in the right structure and the right processes, and then round it out with the right people. I was directly involved in comms for too long, and that's not how you build a sustainable company. Your company won't grow if your founders or key personnel are focused on the tactical operations side of things for too long." — **Adam**

With just 16 months left to legalization on October 17, 2018, hiring at the company went into overdrive. It seemed that no sooner would HR fulfill key roles than demands were made of HR to find more employees. By the end of 2018, human resources predicted they'd be at 250 employees; a year later, the need would grow to more than 1,000 across three locations.

With that expansion came jockeying for space. It seemed like each week, another ModSpace was added to the farm (increasingly looking like a campus,) creating a micro city of temporary offices. Armed with a staff list, Adam and Seb would visit the offices on Sundays, moving desks around to accommodate the influx of bodies, followed by a note announcing the new arrangements. For several months, the marketing department was housed in a narrow basement office not unlike Adam's home office. In the marketing ModSpace, nicknamed the Taj Mahal, the non-functioning toilet was removed and the room repurposed as desk space.

Although space requirements were never on Seb's mind — he was thinking light years ahead — the exercise did serve to keep the pair grounded.

"I had to keep moving things around, asking who's coming in, what do we need. For us, even though we were dealing with the mundane task of office locations, it was very helpful for us to serve and put things in perspective. With a visionary like Seb, being able to ground yourself in the present and do that analysis was helpful," says Adam.

9 A.M., JULY 31, 2017
THE FARM, CHEMIN DE LA RIVE
MASSON-ANGERS, QUEBEC

The marketing team had been busy. Ever since Hydropothecary's peppermint-flavoured cannabis-oil product, Elixir, had become a reality a few months back, the creative output of the department had gone into overdrive in anticipation of its public release. The team had a 50-line spreadsheet outlining every activity they had in the hopper. There were social media posts, packaging design, pop-up banners, and printed materials for trade shows. A script was drafted for customer experience, together with investor and educator fact sheets. That morning, two hundred influencers, clinics, and journalists across the country received elegant, hand-assembled Hydropothecary boxes filled with information, notepads, pens, non-cannabis sample bottles, and chocolates. It was a launch fitting for a truly innovative new product.

Everyone at the company was going flat out. They had launched Elixir, which would go on to win three Canadian Cannabis Awards over two years. They had also launched Decarb. Yet its reputation as a company that priced products higher than the market warranted remained. It was time to change the tune.

For too long, the business development team had been getting feedback from people saying, "Aren't you those really expensive people from Quebec?" despite having introduced the H2 line of dried flower at a mid-range price. H2 proved so popular, in fact, that medical registrations increased dramatically, forcing the customer experience team into bigger quarters.

The negative perception of the $32-a-gram pot remained. And so, in mid-August, at a time when CBD products across the country were at a premium and some LPs were pricing them up to $11 a gram due to demand, Hydropothecary introduced Honeydew. A high-CBD flower, it was an astonishing $7.20 a gram. Adam wanted it seen as it was intended to be: very much a political statement.

"It was basically saying that we care about our medical clients. We're making this accessible to them. We had to modify people's opinions that we were a luxury cannabis company, because we'd dropped that strategy much earlier in our development. At $7.20, it was one of the least expensive products out there. That price was not a decision of profit margins. It was a decision to make a statement."

It's one thing to create demand. It's another thing to meet it.

Two weeks after Hydropothecary launched Honeydew, the company announced another expansion, this time the 250,000 square-foot, state-of-the-art greenhouse with 10 growing zones under a diffused glass roof that would optimize uniform light transmission and light penetration. With plants in each growing zone at different states of growth, the new facility would mean they could ramp up production to 25,000 kilograms a year through continuous harvesting. Sprawling across the existing campus and onto a previously purchased parcel of land next door, B6 was not just destined to be one of the best cannabis greenhouses in North America, it was the physical manifestation of the company's growth and potential. Gone were the flapping plastic greenhouses, ramshackle out-buildings, and decrepit farm equipment. They had been replaced with an entire growing complex of offices, storage, and staff lounges.

Events were happening quick and fast and not just at Hydropothecary. Across the country, more and more licensed producers were appearing, with Statistics Canada recording 80 by the end of 2017. Health Canada nearly doubled the number of licences issued in the second half of that year. Where companies had 50 employees the year before, they'd now doubled or tripled in size. In total, 2,399 Canadians were directly involved in the legal production of marijuana. In fact, Canadians were growing weed at an incredible pace — 80,535 kilograms of dried flower was produced in 2017, compared with 35,912 kilos the year before. And in 2015? A laughable 9,659 kilos were produced. Then there were the medical marijuana industry con-ferences and public expos, online magazines, newsstand titles, and blogs, all popping up to take advantage of the impending green rush.

LATE AUGUST 2017
FINANCIAL DISTRICT
TORONTO, ONTARIO

The one aspect of the green rush that wasn't healthy at Hydropothecary was its relationship with Bay Street. Despite the capital raise, the expan-sion plans, and prospects for the future, Hydropothecary stock price was down. And it stayed flat, too. It turned out to be the topic of discus-sion during a business trip Adam took to meet bankers and investors in Toronto at the end of the summer.

Despite the handshakes and inquiries after family, Bay Street had definitely become a less-than-welcoming place. Whatever ecosystem

Adam and the team receiving the "Best New Product" award at the 2017 Lift & Co Gala.

Construction of the one-million-square-foot Building 9.

LEFT: Large marijuana buds freshly harvested in 2017.

BELOW: Packing medical marijuana for irradiation. 2017.

ADAM MIRON

ADAM MIRON

The first Hydropothecary order packing station. 2017.

A helicopter is being used to remove snow from the roof of Building 6.

HEXO House painted by Tristan Eaton on the Never Jaded Tour.

Wu-Tang Clan perform at a HEXO party on the Never Jaded Tour.

LEFT: Adam in the new HEXO offices in 2019.

BELOW: Adam and Sébastien filming a company update.

Hand processing marijuana joints in Gatineau.

Sébastien speaking at the Molson Coors announcement.

LEFT: The first shipment of HEXO's recreational product leaving the farm.

BELOW: Julie celebrating with staff at the 10/17 all hands meetings.

ADAM MIRON

ABOVE: A gold-tipped joint dipped in Elixir and rolled in Hydropothecary kief for Adam & Sébastien's 10/17 celebration.

RIGHT: Sébastien drives his boat on Lac McGregor.

JULIE BEUN

was in place, it was no longer making room for Adam and Seb. The problem wasn't just the stock price, as Adam would soon learn.

During the visit, he joined several bankers at a bar downtown. It was a tough night for Adam, with plenty of uncomfortable questions about how things were going at the pot farm. At the end of the evening the bill arrived, and a few hands reached out to cover it.

"Well, I guess I'm getting it," remarked one snidely, "because God knows Hydropothecary doesn't pay for anything."

The comment sent a heated blush up Adam's neck.

Months earlier, he and Seb had discussed paying for investor relations with the market makers who provide stock purchase and sale solutions. It was common practice. In fact, it was the kind of thing that bankers and brokers felt was necessary for them to continue participating in deals. But just because it was always done that way wasn't enough to convince Seb to spend money. As far as he was concerned, Hydropothecary wasn't big into promotion. The company was focused on its core fundamentals and playing the long game. So, too, were its competitors. Not much later, Adam and Seb discovered that competitors were spending anywhere between $750,000 and $1 million a month on investor relations. They may have been saving money, but holding out on playing within the rules meant that Hydropothecary was feeling the chill from the bankers. It became obvious the company was being excommunicated from the Bay Street ecosystem. And why not? These two guys from Quebec weren't paying to play, and their stubbornness was one reason their stock was undervalued and not gaining like other LPs.

One thing became crystal clear. If Bay Street was fed up with you, it had remarkable power over the health of your company. After that night, Hydropothecary got into the investor relations (IR) game and regained its traction.

Billion Dollar Lesson

"Was it a mistake not to put that kind of money into investor relations upfront? Not really. We learned from the experience, and we put our flag in the ground. We said that we don't do things just because that's the way it's always been done. In the end, we developed an effective plan that was seriously based on ROI and that fit what we were doing. It's not that Hydropothecary didn't pay for anything. It meant that we gave a shit about our shareholders' money." — **Adam**

CHAPTER 8

9:30 A.M., SEPTEMBER 19, 2017
THE FARM, CHEMIN DE LA RIVE
MASSON-ANGERS, QUEBEC

Via Outlook
A: julie@thehydropothecary.com
De: Peloquin, Tristan (La Presse)
Re: Hydropothecary annonce la certification casher de pro-
duits transformés de marijuana médicale

"Kosher weed? You're joking."

The short and incredulous email from Julie's journalist mate Tristan Peloquin from *La Presse* wasn't the only one. The *Ottawa Citizen* was equally nonplussed. The announcement that Hydropothecary was the first cannabis producer to obtain kosher certification for its processed products — the announcement coming on the eve of Rosh Hashanah — had journalists guffawing into their coffee. One called Julie directly, laughing and saying that it was "the best press release I've ever read." The Canadian Press had a field day. "Quebec Medical Marijuana Producer Certified 'Kosher,' Just in Time for the High Holidays," smirked the headline. The CBC went down the same waggish path, as did *Huffington Post*. Across the country, the novelty of kosher weed was viewed as hilarious and quirky. And yet, it was a very smart move for reasons the leadership team at the company hadn't entirely anticipated.

To most at the pot farm, kosher certification didn't make a lot of sense. Honestly, they wondered, did people actually want their cannabis to be inspected by a rabbi? Was it that big of a market? What was the difference between kosher and regular weed? Would it translate into sales? The discussion went back and forth. Research was done into the best certifying authority. In the end, Hydropothecary chose a local non-profit authority.

A few weeks before the press release crossed the wire, most of the marketing team, together with the product development guys, squashed into a repurposed upstairs boardroom in the farmhouse, now dubbed "Oregon" after one of the early US states to adopt legalization. Few had any previous dealings with a cleric of this sort, so interest ran high. And the rabbi did not disappoint.

He was everything you could hope for from the traditional image of a rabbi: deeply bearded, knowledgeable and interested, curious yet conservative. He had a forthright manner and a natural authority in his way of questioning, softened by a merry twinkle in his eye. Hydropothecary may never have hosted a rabbi before, but the rabbi had never been on a pot farm either. Most of his certification work tended toward edible processed consumer products, but having toured the modern and spotless cannabis facilities, he was willing to go through the rigorous certification process.

He smiled and, making a small supplication with his hands, addressed the group.

"In kosher, we're very careful with what we put into our bodies," he said, pausing to stroke his beard. "The initial process is to confirm that the components of a product are kosher, that there are no animal by-products, no insects, no impurities. Every part of the process is inspected. And we do spot-checks throughout the year."

He went on. "What this is doing is showing the proper etiquette for kosher and being able to care for people. It is saying the product is pure. Kosher is something for people from many backgrounds, including vegans, vegetarians, and religions other than Judaism, who are careful about what they consume. Kosher means the product has gained the trust of supervisors who take very seriously what they should certify."

For cannabis, he added, certification would require an audit of cleaning protocols and a compliance review. Around the table, everyone nodded. But there was a question: Why should medical marijuana be kosher, anyway?

The rabbi nodded. He loved a good theological discussion. There were three dissenting opinions on the subject, he explained, but essentially it boiled down to whether a product is necessary for health and well-being. Marijuana had clear medical advantages and uses, making it kosher by nature. "But if you say to me, Rabbi, there is a plant similar to marijuana and it has intoxicating side effects, but it's not needed medically — you just enjoy it — that's not kosher." He went on to explain that there were kosher-certified wines and spirits, but with marijuana, "we'll need to test the waters. We'll have the conversation and we'll take the pulse of the country."

The real driver, of course, was the optics of having a third-party certification that would hopefully overcome the lingering bad smell caused by the myclobutanil recall. It wasn't a costly exercise, despite involving so many departments, but if another, independent body was reviewing and certifying their processes, so much the better.

But the real surprise was how much the media loved it. *High Times* — the bible of canna culture — ran a front-page story on its website. The Jewish media picked it up and, for the tsunami of digital impressions alone, it was deemed a worthwhile exercise. Plus, it further cemented the company's reputation as an innovator thinking outside the box.

6 A.M., OCTOBER 12, 2017
THE FARM, CHEMIN DE LA RIVE
MASSON-ANGERS, QUEBEC

The mist was still lifting along the banks of the Lièvre adjacent to the Hydropothecary campus when employees started showing up early for work. One after another, the crunch of tires on gravel could be heard, followed by doors slamming and "Salut toi, ça va?" This was a new dawn, but more than that, it was a banner day for Hydropothecary. Today, it would break ground on the next phase of its expansion into a 250,000-square-foot, state-of-the-art greenhouse.

It was a major undertaking, in every way conceivable. The greenhouse itself, to be built by specialist Dutch firm Havecon, would cost $25 million — already fully funded — and feature 10 separate growing zones that would allow for constant cultivation. There would be a staff lounge, loading zones, and real offices. By the time it was brought online and licensed to grow by Health Canada, it would boost the company's production to 25,000 kilograms of dried product annually. For the neighbouring towns of Masson-Angers and Buckingham, it would mean a bonanza of a hundred full-time jobs. That in itself was enough to draw the local media and nearly a dozen politicians from their warm offices into the cold, all eager to be present and photographed at a growing cannabis facility. It was the usual cast of suspects.

In the grand scheme of things, groundbreaking ceremonies are akin to the opening of an envelope. There's nothing to look at — not yet, anyway — but it is about the promise of something great, and a chance to get up on a podium and self-congratulate. That certainly happened, with Seb revving up the crowd, which included his parents, with his showmanship and impressive dramatic timing. The dignitaries, too, all said their piece, mostly in French. In the audience, Adam, still a monoglot despite all this time working in Quebec, picked up phrases here and there. When his old friend Greg Fergus, a Liberal MP, got up on stage and began recounting anecdotes about Adam as a young political mover, he was lost. Everyone laughed on cue and smiled at Adam. Outwardly, he smiled and nodded, completely clueless as to what was being said. But like the post-TSX Venture after-party where Meena and Adam's impressive friends had gathered to celebrate with them, the glow of having such an array of the community filled his heart anyway. It was beyond gratifying to not only be celebrated but to celebrate with these supporters.

The rest of the day was filled with, first, a catered lunch, then media tours through the existing greenhouse and an exhausting number of interviews. Overseeing it all from his great stature was Devan Pennell, who'd joined the company as director of capital projects. A former director of finance for the Ottawa Sports and Entertainment Group who supervised the multi-billion-dollar redevelopment of downtown Ottawa's Lansdowne Park, which features a sports stadium, condos, and a massive commercial complex, Devan was no stranger to thinking big. For that project, he'd been responsible for spending $220 million. After stickhandling Lansdowne, though, he was starting to look around for other opportunities.

Adam and Devan knew each other through Devan's younger brother, a friend of Adam's. Devan had followed Adam and Seb's progress, so he was aware of what the cannabis farmers were up to. In the early days, Adam and Seb had invited Devan to their basement office to go through their business plan.

"Seb ran me through the model, and as a finance guy, I was sort of blown away because it was good. It was bulletproof. I didn't really get all the assumptions, and it wasn't really my area of expertise, but from a modelling standpoint, I was like, 'Holy shit, these guys are on to something,'" he recalls.

Soon after the basement meeting, Devan sent Adam an email, sharing that he was thinking of taking on consultancy clients, Adam had headed over to Ed's office in the ModSpace, knocked once, and walked in. Ed and Seb were elbow-deep in budgets and projections, which was normally a signal to Adam that his interruption should wait. But he pressed on.

"Hey, you remember Devan Pennell? Ottawa Sports and Entertainment Group?" Seb and Ed nodded, clearly unwilling to be distracted from their task. "Well, I think he might be a free agent. You want to chat with him?"

Ed looked up. "Yes. Absolutely." It was a case of the right person at the right moment. Devan quickly became so instrumental to the company, he jumped through a number of titles and competencies within a few years. At one point, his turnstile of titles was even a cause for concern — what would it look like on LinkedIn if his job changed every six months, for heaven's sake? Adam didn't see that as a problem.

"To me, very few people understood how crazy-fast our company was growing and how much we were moving. Devan could do a lot of things. He was a great project manager. He was an accountant. He was a communications person. And he'd been there from the beginning as an investor, attending every AGM we had. I remember telling him at our 2014 AGM in the basement of the Westin hotel, next to the Harper government caucus party: If a guy like you came on board and joined our company, one day you could hold a very, very senior management role."

As VP of the Program Office at the time of writing, Devan admits there was an early period where he didn't see the clear path to a billion-dollar start-up, but he could see that Adam and Seb did.

"Very quickly, I saw the culture and saw the commitment that was being put forth of 'make it or bust'; I could see we're not going to limp into this. We were saying we're going to go hard, and we're going to be ruthless and relentless in our execution. And that's when I went 'Okay, I can do this.'"

(Facilitating his and every other role at Hydropothecary was an incredibly robust spreadsheet called Christopher. It was the work of the company's eager and hard-working accountant, Sean McKenny. The thing was so complex and so complete, Adam had dubbed it "Christopher," after the Enigma-busting computer created by British cryptanalyst Alan Turing during World War II.)

The team at the farm was expanding, as were ideas for the next product innovation. To please investors and create buzz among consumers, Hydropothecary needed to release one new product a quarter, something that would change the game. Decarb and Elixir had done just that. But it needed more, a regular parade of blockbusters. Yet, as long as the various teams were pinballing from one idea to the next without any sense of strategy, it was part guesswork, part footwork through feedback from the sales team talking to clinics and their patients. The product innovation team could table all the great ideas they had, from vapes to personal lubricants, but it more or less seemed like seeing what floated. They needed more of a framework, something that would clarify the direction, content, and scope of what Hydropothecary innovation could look like.

With legalization now less than a year away, speculation about the role of cannabis in edibles and beverages was at an all-time high. The federal government had already signalled that legalization would be a two-step process: basic cannabis products like bud, oils, and powders would be allowed first, on October 17, 2018, followed by edibles, beverages, cosmetics, and vapes after that. In many ways, it was too early and too complicated to predict what the government rollout of phase two would really mean, but Hydropothecary and other LPs had to decide if they were just going to grow lots and lots of weed, only to let American companies turn them into value-added commodities as the Canadian mining and other industries had done, or if they were going to truly own this world-first Canadian cannabis industry by adopting another strategy altogether.

The answer for Adam and Seb was consumer-packaged goods, otherwise known in the industry as CPGs. As a CPG company, Hydropothecary could produce and innovate consumable products like cosmetics and vapes or drinks. It would be a highly volatile and competitive market governed by regulations so tight they squeaked, but that just made the challenge all the more enticing. Plus, in adopting a CPG approach, Hydropothecary would immediately have a strategy and, following that, a structure.

Adam went to work hiring a consulting firm to help Hydropothecary build a world-class innovation lab. The idea itself came quickly enough, but once undertaken, it soon became apparent that neither Adam nor anyone else had a clue about what it would take. The consultants did, however, and peppered the leadership team with the kind of questions that result in real, honest, hard-to-come-by answers. What were their core values? What do they care about? Did they want to be a data-driven R&D lab or a consumer data-driven lab? In the end, it was a year-long process before the sprawling R&D Innovation Lab in Belleville, Ontario, came to fruition.

Billion Dollar Lesson

"We learned so many valuable lessons from our corporate structuring guru, Lex Sisney: Don't build structure around people. Build the structure and fill it with people who match your needs. But don't take too long to do it. One of the mistakes we made was that we took too long to get the innovation lab from paper to reality. We spent a considerable sum of money on building a world-class system and process, really having thought through everything down to job descriptions. It was there, it was ready to go, but until we implemented the plan, it was hard to find the right people. We did hire some incredible talent in the end, but it was a much longer process than it needed to be." — **Adam**

9 P.M., DECEMBER 1, 2017
CANADIAN CANNABIS AWARDS, THE CARLU
TORONTO, ONTARIO

No one knew what to expect.

The name of the event in itself was funny enough — the Canadian Cannabis Awards (CCAs). Even-keeled, good-natured Canada was hosting awards for the best weed in the country. But unlike the Cannabis Cup years earlier in Amsterdam, the CCAs were not being held in an edgy disused warehouse, participants enveloped in a cloud of smoke, or at a neon-pink club hosted by bikini-clad girls with 10-foot-long volcano bags.

No, this was a truly Canadian event: polite, enthusiastic, inclusive, and held at the historic and glamorous Carlu on Yonge Street, in downtown Toronto. And it was being hosted by Lift & Co., a cannabis organization founded by Tyler Sookochoff and known for its cannabis expos and events, as well as for being Canada's first cannabis website for news, views, and reviews. The awards had been held before, but never as a gala or on this scale. More than seven hundred cannabis industry "pioneers" would be in attendance. In other words, it was going to be an absolute pot-luck. Literally.

That much was evident once at the Carlu. Some invitees saw the word "gala" and dressed accordingly in gowns, sparkly cocktail dresses, suits, and tuxedos. Adam, ever the style maven, sported a white tux vest that stood out among the black-tie penguins. He'd had it tailored earlier that week, having discovered it was two and a half suit sizes too big for him. Others who had migrated from the old school 4/20 headspace of cannabis wore what suited them: jeans (but their best ones); graphic tees;

quirky colourful jackets; Converse All Stars; braided, beaded beards; a splash of patchouli; and anything else that, to them at least, said, "This is a special night."

And it was, truly. Having endured the indulgent or incredulous laughter over the years when introducing themselves as legitimately working in the legal pot industry, the gathered army of advocates, activists, corporate suits, policy wonks, and enthusiasts found themselves with their tribe: people like themselves for whom the only real things that mattered were growing the best-quality product, educating the public, and somehow making enough money to continue to expand what was too often the butt of punny "growing industry" jokes. Not one person looked like the other, but everyone beamed with the shared knowledge that, on this night, they were honouring an industry brought out of the shadows. They were noisy, ebullient, and proud to be present.

The Lift & Co. team herded people to their seats for the awards presentation. The main players were all there — Emblem, Broken Coast, Peace Naturals, Tilray, Aurora, and Tweed — together with smaller concerns. It was just an awards night, to be sure, but it was their awards night, their very own cannabis awards, judged by a panel and voted on by their peers and customers. The mood was beyond joyful, so much so that the emcee, then the comedians, struggled in vain to capture the audience's attention. Eventually, they decided to roll out the prizes.

Like the Oscars, a slick video montage played as the nominees were announced for each category. Top Sativa Flower, Top Hybrid Flower, best compassion pricing program, top customer service . . . there was a category for everything. But aside from Top Licensed Producer, the one award that mattered more than anything else was Best New Cannabis Product.

The video started and the Hydropothecary table cheered wildly as the company name appeared on the screen. They were up against some pretty strong competition, but they were also determined to lead the pack with innovation. All eyes on the stage, Julie twisted in her seat to look at Adam. His forehead glistened slightly with perspiration. He'd been up late the night before with Seb, entertaining investors in an effort to build communication with the public markets. That in itself wasn't the cause of the perspiration. The 3 a.m. Chinese food they'd indulged in later certainly was. Seb had flown out earlier that day, in similar shape. Adam gave Julie a quick, pained smile. "Fingers crossed," she whispered.

"Third place goes to . . . Hydropothecary, for Elixir No. 1!"

Around the table, there was a micro-moment of hesitation before they broke out into applause. It was disappointing, no doubt about it. But to be in the top three meant something, right? For a half a second, Adam indulged in the fantasy of standing up, flipping the table, and stomping out.

"Second place goes to . . . Tweed Black Label, for Argyle Softgels!"

Shit, Tweed didn't get the first berth either. Those softgels were a fantastic innovation, so if they weren't handed the laurels, who the hell was left?

"First place goes to . . . Hydropothecary, for Decarb!"

Adam leaped out of his chair like he'd been goosed. "Fuck yeah!" he shouted, clapping. He looked around the table — everyone was shouting and laughing in disbelief. Good old Decarb! Wonderful, convenient Decarb, cooked up over a weekend in the bunker, had landed Hydropothecary at the front of the pack. Adam started for the stage, motioning to everyone at the table to join him. Half got up, half hesitated, embarrassed, but after a second followed him. Adam stood at the podium, glowing in his tux. The emcee leaned in to hand over the mic. "You've got 30 seconds."

Crowding around him, the team draped their arms around each other as if a rugby scrum.

Adam cleared his throat and leaned into the mike.

"If you don't know this, our first customer was my dad. He was the first customer of ours who passed away."

Somewhere in the crowd, someone barked out an ill-timed laugh.

Adam's voice trembled slightly, and the noise of the crowd diminished slightly. There was real emotion behind this.

"Before he did," Adam continued, mastering himself, "our products made a huge difference in his life. And I want to thank everyone here, in the industry, on our team, that made that possible."

Although the speech wasn't heard at the back of the room because of chatter, its poignancy was such that it was used to close out the promotional video Lift & Co. later released. That evening, Hydropothecary was also runner-up for Top High THC Oil. The press release sent out, the gang celebrated late into the night. They had to get up early the next day to head back to Ottawa, but tonight they were on top of the cannabis world.

6:30 A.M., DECEMBER 12, 2017
GATINEAU, QUEBEC

Being on top of the cannabis world can be as fleeting as fame. Blink and a competitor edges past you in the race to grow more weed, get more clients, do more deals. Legalization was on the horizon, and the industry was going to explode. Every LP worth its shareholders' faith wanted to be bigger, more productive, and have a more robust financial outlook than any of the others when the time came. If academics go by "publish or perish," cannabis has "expand or perish."

And so, less than two weeks after putting the award in Adam's ModSpace office at the farm, Hydropothecary publicly announced plans to expand production capacity to 108,000 kilograms a year, by buying adjacent land and building an $80 million, 1-million-square-foot greenhouse.

The timing couldn't have been better. Seb had just testified to the National Assembly in Quebec City about the cannabis industry. Adam had watched the feed and marvelled at how composed and unstudied his business partner was, especially when he was grilled about the recalls. He'd truthfully and honestly responded that recalls were proof the system was working, and that if there weren't any recalls in a brand-new industry, consumers should be concerned. It was a next-level performance.

Seb's leadership and vision were on display that day, as they were in the days leading up to the announcement. The press release was drafted, discussed, reviewed, and rewritten. Inside the ModSpace offices, debate raged over whether to lead with the impressive square footage of the building or the amount of cannabis that would be produced. Many were nervous about assigning an actual number to potential production capacity before trees on the new 78-acre property had even been felled.

But Seb insisted.

He'd done the math and he knew what was possible. He had firm faith that if you believe it and give voice to the vision, it will happen. Just ask Elon Musk. Anytime he talked about the fastest electric vehicle, he faced doubters. Besides, what did 1 million square feet mean to investors? Unless they did the intricate calculations themselves and came up with a number of kilos per year, it was hardly going to move the needle on their stock price. The press release stated they'd be able to produce 108,000 kilograms of dried cannabis a year, then went even further, predicting that the massive building would be built within a year, to be completed December 2018.

Billion Dollar Lesson

"The most powerful learning experiences come from our failures. They come from challenges. If you can't look back at what you just did and say, 'How could I meet that challenge in a better way?' then you haven't learned anything. You might have made it through the challenge on dumb luck, but when you get a challenge, you rise up, you meet it, you look back, and you must ask, 'What did I do?' And then ask, 'How do I approach that problem slightly differently?' Finally, you ask yourself, 'Knowing what I know now, can I take on a challenge that's three times as hard?' And you end up with a more audacious goal." — **Seb**

Madcap as that timeline seemed, it wasn't impossible. The 250,000-square-foot building had been announced the previous summer, with a seven-month timeline. In interviewing greenhouse companies to build it, Devan had two big players laugh outright and say, "You guys are nuts." The third — the Dutch company Havecon — had said the timelines were possible, but it would be expensive and the internal Hydropothecary teams would have to be on top of their game.

"At the time, Havecon said, 'This is crazy, this is the fastest greenhouse we've ever built. And it's going to be one of the more sophisticated ones, because you guys want an R&D-level greenhouse.' The timelines were intimidating, but we knew what we were up against," notes Devan.

What they didn't anticipate was the severity of that winter, which blew cold day after day and snowed to near-record levels. At one point, Devan hired a helicopter to hover over the roof to blow off the snow because the walls were not yet in place to support the structure. It was only when he was in the air and gazing over the expanse of the construction site that he really understood what they'd undertaken.

"You're so focused on the execution and the pieces that you don't often get to see it from a bird's-eye view. It was the first time I got to see it, that just the sheer size of the footprint that we were trying to operationalize, and I remember I was like, 'Holy crap, this is massive,'" recalls Devan.

And so, in the midst of that, Hydropothecary announced the second massive expansion, starting with clearing half of the more than 70 acres it had purchased. And, as with the first expansion, Havecon didn't bat an eye over the very short timeline to execute, because by then the phrase "We execute on our promises" had become part of the pot company lore.

"It's definitely the theme," says Devan. "If someone said, 'No, it can't be done,' we said, 'I don't believe you, let's try. We'll give you everything you need to deliver.' If what they were saying was impossible to achieve in weeks, it was within months. If we got halfway between impossible and possible, we were still way ahead of the curve."

Seb's predictions were just the kind of bold and confident move investors had come to love about him, and they made sure he knew it. With the math already done for them, even the meanest understanding could figure out that applying a multiplier to 108,000 kilograms of marijuana a year meant the company was in a strong position but undervalued. That, together with the awards and speculation that they were about to announce a supply deal with the Quebec government, resulted in a rerate of the company's value.

In many ways, the company was still thinking and behaving like a start-up, with an all-hands-on-deck attitude and energy. Getting the public raise made it feel like they were on the cusp of graduating into the big leagues. Certainly, production, sales, and public awareness all appeared to be increasing, with no sign of abating. There was so much good news to share, Julie pitched the idea of a mini-magazine for their customers. The Hydropothecary story was being written as it happened, in real time. The first issue of *The Hydropothecarian* — a real mouthful in any language — was mailed out to clients on January 15, 2018, and went on to feature the people, news, and highlights of life at the pot farm.

Of course, the marketing and innovation teams were feverishly working on other projects as well. Having come so close to winning an award for Elixir THC mist, the company was about to launch the CBD version, also with peppermint. It would prove to be a bestseller, for a few reasons.

For one, it had the highest concentration of CBD per millilitre then available to medical cannabis patients. Like Elixir THC, it was convenient and discreet. But more than that, it was just the kind of CBD product newcomers to cannabis could wrap their heads around. Where the majority of Canadians knew little about cannabis, and what they did know came from 4/20 stoner culture, few had distinguished intoxicating THC from CBD, the non-intoxicating cannabinoid widely used for anxiety, inflammation, and mental focus. (While both THC and CBD are the subject of clinical trials for various diseases and conditions, CBD has shown great promise for controlling seizures, inflammatory bowel disease, and fibromyalgia, among other conditions.) With Elixir CBD and other CBD products from competitors, cannabis was far more approachable and far less intimidating. It was the right product at the right time: in December 2018, it was named Best New Product at the Canadian Cannabis Awards.

DECEMBER 20, 2017
HÔTEL LE ST-JAMES, OLD MONTREAL
MONTREAL, QUEBEC

Seb looked down the long table at which the board of directors was assembled. He loved Hôtel Le St-James: the vaulted ceilings, the impeccable service, the shining marble floors. In so many ways, it was the epitome of high finance and success. In fact, the St-James had once been the storied Merchants Bank, dating back to 1870; one of the stone walls in its former vault was actually a part of Old Montreal's original fortifications. When Hydropothecary was truly a start-up, the plush surroundings would have felt like a tight new pair of $500 shoes, but today, it felt just about right.

Seb recalled another meeting, a month earlier, and winced. The board had gathered to welcome its newest member. Instructed to find a meeting room near the farm in Buckingham, Seb's diligent assistant had done just that. There were slim pickings — or rather one picking, to be exact — which would cost $62 including tax. Having no other options, she booked a meeting room at the Motel Les Pignons Verts (the "pignons" — the French word for gables — rather extravagantly referred to a green standard-issue motel roof). Walking in with the board members, any one of whom could have bought the motel on the spot, Seb squirmed in dismay. A few jokes were made about the place, followed by overly hearty laughter that did nothing to ease his discomfort. When two elderly women wandered into the room — the meeting room apparently doubled as a shortcut to the motel proper — Seb tried to usher them out. "We're having a meeting, ladies," he offered helpfully. Two white-haired heads swivelled to look at him. "A meeting, here? A meeting! Really! Well, we're just walking through, don't mind us."

But that was a month ago, and today they'd gathered to review what the company was up to. He'd just started speaking when his phone rang. He quickly glanced at the caller ID.

"I'm going to have to take this. Excuse me."

The call was coming at an opportune moment. Of all the board meetings they'd had, this was one of the more pleasant ones. The company was coming out with one great announcement after another, the rerating had been well accepted by the public markets, and they were on the cusp of doing incredible things, or rather, more incredible things. And their strategy of "Quebec first" was about to pay off. For years, they'd been the first licensed producer in Quebec. They'd focused on their relationship with the provincial government, and Hydropothecary was a proudly bilingual company creating jobs in an economically depressed region. And now they were about to send shockwaves through the industry.

"Right, excellent. I'm putting you on speaker."

Seb put his phone on the board table. "Jay's got some news. Do you want to tell everyone what you just told me?"

History was about to repeat itself. Like a few other board meetings in the past, a phone call bearing great news brought everything to a halt. Jay had called to announce that, working with Société québécoise du cannabis (SQDC) CEO Jean-Francois Bergeron, Hydropothecary had just finalized the biggest supply deal in the history of cannabis. And the letter of intent that was being drafted had Hydropothecary's name all over it. (When the finalized deal was announced in March 2018, it would be worth about $1 billion over the five-year term.)

The board meeting immediately erupted in questions.

In an industry where big news happens often and quickly, it's easy to become jaded. One pot company bought another for millions? Check. Someone has raised another $100 million? Ho hum. But when the press release announcing the letter of intent to supply the Quebec market crossed the wire two months later, the industry sat up straight in bed and whistled in admiration.

Hydropothecary would supply the government's cannabis retailer, SQDC, with more than 200,000 kilograms of product over five years, with the built-in expectation that the products supplied would move away from dried flower and toward value-added products. It was part of their overall strategy, Seb noted in another release when the deal was finalized in March:

> Becoming the preferred supplier to the Quebec market out of the gate post legalization is a source of great pride and a vote of confidence in our ability to scale operations to meet our supply commitment. This agreement marks an important step in the execution of our growth strategy, which is focused initially on the Quebec market by expanding our Gatineau facilities and hiring new employees, and then establishing our presence in other Canadian markets.

Challenging as it could be to remain French-first in a business dominated by English Canada, it had paid off. Other companies had set up shop in la belle province, but none was headquartered in Quebec, a fact that very quickly appeared in the press release tombstone describing the company. When it came to competitive advantage, it gave the province the confidence that, even weighed against much larger cannabis companies, Hydropothecary understood the environment and the value of strong ties beyond mere geography. What's more, together with announcing it had selected locally headquartered Shopify as its e-commerce platform, and had strengthened the management team, the deal sent a positive message to the public markets.

This all should have made a major impact on stock prices, except that the announcement came amid one of the more significant dips in the market. Across the board, share prices were taking a beating, Hydropothecary's included. And yet, the news came at the right time nevertheless, because it gave the company a vast amount of buoyancy in a real down-market environment.

But that was still unfolding the March morning of the announcement about the SQDC supply deal. In a boardroom at Hill+Knowlton Strategies' downtown Ottawa offices, Seb was holding court with shareholders, investors, and analysts, explaining the deal, what it would mean for the company, and how it fit into the overall strategy. All the people from investment firms and large institutions with whom they'd poorly communicated about their low costs, healthy margins, and strong infrastructure were now not only present, they were listening intently.

From the back of the crowded room, with its long boardroom table, Adam watched Seb in action. He was amazed, as always, at Seb's ability to see today and next year simultaneously.

Completely unscripted and a master of his subject, he ran through the key points, deftly answered questions, and sounded every bit the CEO of a billion-dollar company. They'd been assessed as a junior player in a mushrooming industry, at least until now. With the SQDC deal, they'd captured the flag. Now for the next one.

Hydropothecary was officially no longer a start-up. It had grown into its big-boy pants.

Billion Dollar Lesson

"We've always stood by the idea that whatever we do in business is part of a long-term strategy. It's great to see deals and news move the needle in terms of stock price, but those short-term gains shouldn't be the goal. You're better off planning and executing a strategy that takes the long view." — **Seb**

2 P.M., EARLY JANUARY 2018
CABARETE BEACH
CABARETE, DOMINICAN REPUBLIC

White sand, blue water, clear skies.

For two days, there'd be nothing but those three things to think about. Adam, Meena, Seb, and Aruna relaxed, wandered over to Calle Principal near Cabarete's waterfront to eat, then moseyed back to their Airbnb to sit and think about nothing. The most exciting thing was a quick call from their now-retired partner, Louis, who'd called from Quebec to wish them a "bonne année 2018" while they were having dinner one night. Aside from that, chilling was the only thing on the schedule.

Sitting by the pool on the third day, Seb started to get restless. Two days of lounging around was all fine and good for others, and while he appreciated it in theory, too much relaxing was the gateway to boredom for him. He and Adam had been discussing how far the company had come, the momentum they were now under, and where they could guide that energy into a trajectory that made sense. There was always a need for fresh capital, of course, and with Hydropothecary having one win after another, it seemed to them that the time was right to shake the pagoda tree, to use the old Indo-British Empire idiom, for obtaining quick money.

Seb picked up his phone. He'd get the ball rolling, holiday or no holiday. The last capital raise they'd done was on a road show, after which the investors took the stock and perpetually shorted it, keeping it artificially low in the interests of making a quick buck. For the next year, it would depress Hydropothecary's stock price, and it was an experience Seb was not eager to replicate. In fact, it wasn't something the company even needed to do, because it was in a much stronger position than it'd ever been.

Twenty minutes after Seb started dialling, Adam looked around. Seb was off on his own, talking and gesticulating, pacing back and forth, looking around and seeing nothing except what was happening in his head. Every now and then, he'd return to their rentals, vibrating with energy. He was single-handedly building momentum for a deal that, a day earlier, didn't even exist as a possibility. The chase was on. Forget paddle boarding or swimming. Holidays are for raising capital.

Adam and the sisters were just starting to think about lunch when Seb bounced into the pool patio, beaming. "Well, it's done. I talked to a bunch of bankers, got them to compete for the deal, beat them up on terms, and got it down to a 4 percent fee."

He looked at the expectant faces, watching for amazement. They were still digesting the news. He twitched impatiently and tried again.

"Guys! It's done! I've raised $100 million. It's gonna happen as soon as we get back!"

Hydropothecary Announces $100 Million Public Offering
News provided by
The Hydropothecary Corporation
Jan 08, 2018, 07:59 ET
/NOT FOR DISTRIBUTION TO NEWSWIRE SERVICES OR FOR DISSEMINATION IN THE UNITED STATES./
TORONTO, Jan. 8, 2018 /CNW/ — The Hydropothecary Corporation ("THCX" or the "Company") (TSX VENTURE:THCX) announced today that it has entered into an agreement with Canaccord Genuity Corp., Eight Capital, and a syndicate of underwriters (the "Underwriters") pursuant to which the Underwriters have agreed to purchase, on a bought deal basis, 25,000,000 units of the Company (the "Units") at a price of $4.00 per Unit for aggregate gross proceeds of $100,000,000. Each Unit will consist of one common share (a "Common Share") and one half of one common share purchase warrant (each full warrant, a "Warrant") of the Company (the "Offering").

Each Warrant will be exercisable to acquire one common share of the Company for a period of two years following the closing date of the Offering at an exercise price of $5.60 per common share, subject to adjustment in certain events.

Hydropothecary had a problem.

Hydropothecary *was* the problem. From the outset, the name Hydropothecary had been a hassle to spell, a hassle to pronounce, a definite hassle to remember. In creating the original email addresses for the company, Adam had even added a layer of complexity by throwing in an extra word, "the": @thehydropothecary.com. Everything from domain names and business cards to printed material was an exercise in sticking to the elegant look and feel while cramming a long and challenging company name onto a tiny space. In both official languages no less.

It was different, that was for sure, and initially Adam loved to tell investors and anyone else who'd listen what it meant and why it was chosen. He even had a last slide on the investor PowerPoint, like an Easter egg in Marvel films, intended to forestall the inevitable "What does 'Hydropothecary' even mean?" The slide showed luxury brands with difficult names. The penny would drop as Adam explained the panache and exclusivity of brands like Hermès. Without fail, some guy would show off his Hermès shoes or belt.

The trouble was that, while it worked on some levels, it wasn't really that effective for anyone not privy to the explanation. And they couldn't afford to spend five minutes of every conversation explaining it until it caught on. At one point, the company was running with both Hydropothecary and Hydropothecaire (pronounced hee-dro-poth-ee-care), to make it more palatable to French sensibilities. It didn't work. After doing their very first Radio-Canada TV interview at the farm, Adam and Seb tuned in to the broadcast that night at Adam's place. The story was introduced, some footage played with a voiceover, and the journalist did his stand-up to camera in French. "Je suis ici à le Hydropot et Cary . . ."

Something had to be done.

Adam decided to have a frank conversation with Sébastien. He laid out the difficulties they had and what they were anticipating, especially as legalization loomed in just a few months. They needed to make a decision, but Adam still felt the hesitancy borne of affection for something he'd created himself. Sébastien was blunt.

"Come on, don't you see it? You're too close to it. If it needs to change, change it."

Sometimes you swing and swing and swing, never really taking a break to grab some water and towel off a little. And sometimes, that's exactly what you need to do to get clarity.

Billion Dollar Lesson

"The larger a company grows, the more complex the deals and organization become. It's easy to get caught up in the minutiae and not seeing the clearer — and bigger — picture around your goals. Stay focused on that, and follow the KIS rule: Keep it simple. Complexity kills." **— Seb**

A few days later, Adam called his hard-working marketing manager into his office in the Taj at the farm. He'd completely covered the peel-and-stick whiteboard with sticky notes on which were written names, ideas, and emotions, as well as sketches. Adam stood up, marker in hand.

"So," he began, "we are going to pick a new name for the company and the recreational cannabis brand. We'll keep Hydropothecary for the medical brand, but we need something else for the recreational brand."

"We're going to rebrand the company?" she spluttered. "Us and who else?"

She had a valid point. Until now, the company had relied on its internal talent, preferring to exercise maximum control over its voice, tone, and branding. Other LPs had adopted the use of outside agencies earlier in the piece, but the "farm job" culture still lingered. Asking for, much less paying for, outside help seemed antithetical to the Hydropothecary way of doing things. Adam had rolled up his sleeves and dived in, pulling his already overworked and overburdened team with him.

If there was a struggle to be had, Hydropothecary was found ass-deep in it. They'd never taken the easy way or the path more trodden, partly because everything about the cannabis industry was new and innovative. It hadn't been done before and there was no playbook. So Hydropothecary did things the Hydropothecary way: stubborn about having a hybrid greenhouse, stubborn about not calling their cannabis products by their better-known street names, stubborn about setting improbably short construction timelines, stubborn about the price per gram, free shipping, and everything else. If it was different and difficult, Hydropothecary did it. Renaming and rebranding the company mid-stream was just the next crazy-assed challenge.

But the scope of such an undertaking would put the small marketing team into an early grave, so a Montreal-based agency was hired to help out. The marketing manager set up meetings, built relationships, got quotes, and managed what were to become the biggest and most rewarding projects in the company's marketing history.

But first, the agency team needed to tour the farm and meet key people like Seb and Ed. They wanted to have the 30,000-kilometre-high conversations about what the company was about, what emotions it elicited, and what the more esoteric vision was. They wanted to dive into corporate, brand, cultural, and societal truths about cannabis. They had a survey aimed at finding out all of that and more.

Not surprisingly, it wasn't a conversation Seb and Ed wanted to have. During a meeting between them and the agency, Adam kept an eye on Seb's reaction. While he could understand the necessity for the exercise, this was not his job, and his face said so. Or rather, it said "I sure as hell better not be paying for this." Ed's was rather more morose. He appeared to listen intently, but his body language telegraphed something else. "Oh my God, just put me out to pasture. I can't handle this. Get me back to my spreadsheets and financial reporting and things that make things."

Adam tried to make the exercise as painless as possible. "The agency wanted to talk about our emotions, but you take a bunch of execs who don't get marketing in the room and they're just thinking, 'Your job is to pick a fucking name. Why are we talking about our feelings?'"

Even so, the next few months were nothing short of fun for Adam and his team. They took regular trips to Montreal, ate delicious things in fancy restaurants, and had a chance to really drink the juice of creativity. After a short spell as a hands-off senior executive, it was also a happy return to what Adam loved best: rolling up his sleeves and really digging into a creative marketing project. More than anything, though, it was an opportunity to stop swinging and swinging and take the time to really figure out what Hydropothecary had evolved into, through external research and cultural truths.

It was a blast, but it also became clear that, like a lot of major agencies, this one was bumping the Hydropothecary file through various people. While it was true that the most senior person had attended the first kickoff meeting, she didn't make a second appearance until much later, when she stopped in casually to take part in a discussion. In fact, so many people aside from Hydropothecary's main point of contact handled the file, it wasn't entirely clear who the account lead was. The other disappointment was how slow the agency was moving, lumbering along like an elephant despite the compressed timeline Hydropothecary faced to get the job done before legalization, just months away.

Eventually, however, the agency had something to show for its work and invited Adam and his team to Montreal for the reveal. The buildup was wonderful. In a meeting room, the agency team had placed a series of 11-by-17-inch pages, each with a new brand name, logo, and colour palette, but covered over with a blank sheet. For each option, the agency lead gave it a big introduction, then peeled away the sheet. It was exciting, to be sure, but it rather felt like Adam and Seb were being sold names by a marketing company, rather than being given names that reflected their company. The final option was revealed, and the agency people smiled expectantly. No doubt about it, they felt they'd crushed the assignment.

Adam took a moment to gather his thoughts.

"Thank you. You obviously went to some lengths to present these names, but none of these really resonates. Can you come back to us with more suggestions, but this time, hit us with them over the phone? And we need this to happen a hell of a lot more quickly than it is."

The agency went back to work and, soon after, set up a phone meeting to discuss more suggestions. Back at the farm, in Adam's office, the team listened to the presentation and looked at each other as the options were rolled out. Once again, the suggestions were not spectacular. The agency had done all this research and background, thought Adam, so why can't it come up with a name that makes sense? Frustrated and increasingly aware of the days ticking away, he decided to come up with a name himself. True, they'd spent hundreds of thousands of dollars on the exercise, and it had been valuable, but if he needed the job done, he'd do it himself.

Once again, the basement start-up mindset took over. For the next few weekends, Adam thought up and discarded potential names, writing them on his basement office whiteboard, only to rub them out again. There were a few possibilities that could be held up against the agency's suggestions, but none that really made his heart sing. It was time to get some inspiration.

Ottawa is home to an astonishing variety and scope of national museums. The National Gallery. The Museum of History. The War Museum. The Museum of Nature. But for sheer hands-on happiness, there is nothing like the three Ingenium museums: Canada Aviation and Space, Canada Agriculture and Food at the only working farm in a capital city, and the Canada Museum of Science and Technology, which had undergone a three-year $80 million renovation. When it finally reopened in the fall of 2017, the lineups went out the main door, which now boasted an impressive million-bulb LED video and sound screen that wrapped around the entrance and showed non-stop dynamic images and videos. Inside, the museum looked nothing like it had before. Gone were the tired old displays — with the exception of the beloved but reskinned Crazy Kitchen — replaced with exciting hands-on activations intended to inspire kids to explore more. The massive train engines were still there, but everywhere else, the museum had cracked open its archives to bring out the best of its collection in the most kid-friendly way possible. (The museums, through the Ingenium Foundation, are also among the most progressive internationally in creating programs for and outreach to young minds. In fact, Science and Tech now has a Maker Studio with a 3D printer and tools for visitors, including students from underprivileged schools, to use, as well as experiments for them to try.)

While Meena took the baby and their eldest daughter on their own exploration, Adam wandered around with Nalina on his shoulders. He was fascinated by how contemporary and next-level the displays were.

Kids in one area raced wooden cars down two separate tracks, while others gleefully threw strips of brightly coloured chiffon into a child-sized wind tunnel. Families marvelled over the sound experience, laughing in delight at making music by hopping into different spotlights. There were mystery boxes with different organs to feel, robotic arms to play with, and a stargazing room that contrasted the Greek vision of the heavenly bodies against the equally ancient star chart of the Ojibwa people.

If this place was designed to excite the imagination, Adam thought as he dodged a throng of chattering kids, it's working. He moved from one display to another, quietly talking to Nalina about what he saw. As he stood at one station, a mother called to her daughter, "Hey, come look at this! It's an exoskeleton!"

Pop!

A light bulb that had been waiting to go off for weeks, even months, flashed in his mind. The way the woman said "exo" was perfect: with an added "h" as a nod to Hydropothecary, "HEXO" could be pronounced easily in English, French, or most any other language. It was simple, it was elegant, and after pulling out his phone with Nalina still on his shoulders, it turned out it was also available as a domain name.

Billion Dollar Lesson

"About a year into the early farm days we realized our mantra was 'Work relentlessly, don't be afraid to pivot, and let the dogs bark,' which was a favourite piece of advice from Rajan Uncle. With that, we weren't often afraid of pivoting — we made some big pivots along the way — but we always were aware that there was risk involved. Changing our name was a perfect example. We knew we needed to make a change, so we changed. Hell, if we were wrong, we'd change again. So, manage the risk but take the chance, believe in yourself, and pivot when you need to." — **Adam**

Now with a strong contender for the new name, Adam went back to the agency. It also had come up with an alternative. Legal checked them out and both passed the sniff test. The next thing was to get feedback from leadership, investor relations, communications, and, of course, the marketing team. This wasn't a democratic vote; it was simply to take the temperature of the room and listen to any concerns. With standing room only in the Taj, Adam presented the PowerPoint devised by the agency. It started with the high overview of the brand, consumer, industry, and cultural truths. It then went deeper into research and archetypes. Both names were presented, and Adam went around the room asking for thoughts and opinions. Almost everyone preferred "HEXO." Leaving the Taj, Adam headed to Seb's office in the next ModSpace over.

Ten minutes later, the company had a new name for its recreational cannabis brand.

From that moment, the real work began. With a launch date of May 24 so they could introduce the new brand at the upcoming Lift & Co. trade show in Toronto, the design team went into overdrive, finessing the colour palette and logo and creating marketing materials. They had a line of branded swag, business cards, a trade show booth complete with a waterfall wall and infinity mirror, new product names, and a big neon sign to hang over the farmhouse porch. Faced with Health Canada regulations about advertising brands, the Montreal agency got clever and presented a tweaked version of HEXO for the brand logo. Under Health Canada regulations, cannabis companies couldn't advertise their brands in publications that anyone under 19 could read. But they could advertise their corporate logos, within certain restrictions such as size and the use of the word cannabis. The company logo became HEXO Corp, while the recreational brand had the "H" and "E" stacked over the "X" and "O." A corporate blue colour but same font and a different configuration. In that way, the company could build awareness for the brand without actually advertising it.

One way or another, Canada was going to get to know Hydropothecary's new name.

On May 23, just as HEXO was readying to announce the new recreational brand at Lift & Co., the Réseau de transport métropolitain

(Montreal Transit Authority) released its rebranded look and feel. It had amalgamated with 14 other bus authorities, together naming themselves exo, and using a similar colour palette and typeface for its branding. Adam loved it.

"I thought, 'Wow, not only are we going to be the biggest player in Quebec, but you're going to walk into any bus or subway stop and everything will say 'exo' in our typeface and colours.' It was a complete coincidence."

Two months later, Adam was on the cover of *Hydropothecarian*, the mini-magazine Julie had developed for medical clients and staff. The story ran under the headline "Stay Curious! The Inside Story on HEXO, Hydropothecary's Adult-Use Cannabis Brand."

While it was important to rebrand, it was equally critical to reassure the company's medical clients that Hydropothecary as a medical brand would still exist for them. That wouldn't change — at least for now. The story Julie wrote on behalf of Adam explained everything, at least what the public needed to know.

> On May 24, at Lift & Co's annual Toronto trade show, Hydropothecary launched HEXO, the company's recreational brand. HEXO is a brand for explorers, the curious and the never jaded, but how did it come about? Hydropothecary's co-founder and Chief Brand Officer, Adam Miron, tells the story.
>
> [The first part of this article was redacted to be as compliant as possible with Health Canada's regulations.]
>
> As Hydropothecary, we have been and will continue to cater to you, our medical patients. We built this company for you, with you, and that will never change. But as a corporation, the recreational market is an opportunity to start from scratch, creating a brand that speaks to cannabis purists and cannabis tourists. A brand that would become iconic. In short, a brand for those who are always exploring, constantly curious and never jaded.
>
> But building a new brand requires more than sitting around a table, brainstorming with our creative team. We dug deep into cultural, industry, brand, and consumer truths. And what we discovered was surprising — yet confirmed what we already believed about our clients.
>
> The cannabis consumer as a dropout and non-productive member of society is a stigma not reflected in the stats.

Research shows that compared to cannabis rejectors, cannabis consumers are more nurturing, socially more active, better educated, earn more and are more likely to travel than cannabis rejectors. For a culture obsessed with productivity, it turns out cannabis consumers are not the couch potatoes they're painted to be.

In the cannabis industry, brands either reinforce stereotypes or reinforce stigma, by hiding from the truth of who they serve. Even companies launching new rec brands are throwing as many ideas at the wall as they can, watching for which stick. With HEXO, we did none of that. Having drilled down to very thoughtful data, we have built a brand that explorers, the curious, the never jaded can be proud of, a brand that truly reflects who they are and allows them to celebrate both their productivity and their lifestyle.

In the months ahead, you'll be hearing more about HEXO both here, and in the news. HEXO is part of Hydropothecary — notice the H — and vice versa.

But one thing will never change, for either brand. We will continue to offer excellence in product innovations and commitment to quality from the same facilities in Gatineau.

As they say here in Quebec, plus ça change, plus c'est pareil!

HEXO by the Numbers

HEXO explorers are the new renaissance. Fuelled by curiosity, they have the power to change cannabis stigmas, be active, productive, social and most of all, are never jaded.

Enjoy outdoors
50% of cannabis consumers vs 36% of cannabis rejectors
Socially Active
36% of cannabis consumers vs 28% of cannabis rejectors
Nurturing
60% of cannabis consumers vs 41% of cannabis rejectors
Hold a master's degree
20% of cannabis consumers vs 12% of cannabis rejectors
Source: BDS Analytics

CHAPTER 9

They were back.

After just 15 months on the TSX Venture, Adam and Seb were back at the Toronto Stock Exchange. And they were about to graduate to the big leagues.

Being accepted to list on the Toronto Stock Exchange is a big deal for start-ups graduating from the venture space. From an administrative point of view, it means reporting more financial statements, and doing it more often. Internal procedural and auditing controls are different, too. But it also means they have the confidence of shareholders and the TSX, which opens up the possibility of investment capital from the billion-dollar pension funds.

As Adam watched Seb's toddler, Chala, press the button (this time not with her bottom) to open the market for trading, his heart swelled. It was an incredibly short space of time from the venture to the main exchange, but it meant HEXO wasn't going away. In reality, it was picking up pace.

Of course, a lot had changed in the past 15 months. They had registered HEXO as the new ticker and ditched THCX. They had a new adult-use brand and a new look. Everyone in the company was pulling in the same direction, heaving away with all their might. Buildings were going up, deals were being done, and they were on track to own the cannabis space in Quebec. They were just getting started, yet here they were, already on the main exchange in Canada. The difference between this and the junior exchange, Adam mused, was like that between an undergrad and a postgraduate degree. Same university, same cafeteria. Completely different set of expectations and achievements.

Everyone felt it.

Where they'd been giddy for days after going public back in March 2017, now their hearts were filled with the quiet glow of satisfaction, coupled with a deepening awareness of the possibilities this change would bring. They were being taken seriously, by serious people. As Chala ran around collecting confetti from the floor and tossing it in the air, Seb and Adam accepted congratulations and handshakes, as well as a few heartfelt hugs.

Adam was mid-embrace with a well-wisher when he noticed the distinguished form of Donald Wright next to Seb. His gaze was direct and compelling. As president and CEO of Cinaport Capital, Wright's opinion carries weight. When he talks, people listen. He quietly waited a few minutes until Adam's conversation ended. He had something particular he wanted to say to Adam and Seb, in private.

"First of all, congratulations. This is a great day for you. Quite an achievement." His voice was low and deliberate. "You know, in the history of Canada, there are fewer than a hundred Canadians who have started a company and lived to see it worth a billion dollars. You are two of them."

Adam and Seb's eyes widened. Was that true? Whoa. Adam's smile melted into a serious gaze. That was incredible. He needed to think about what that actually meant. But Donald wasn't done.

"And gentlemen, one other thing." He was smiling, but his eyes were serious. "Don't be afraid to tell that story."

(A year later, Adam was interviewed by an incredulous journalist who couldn't believe the company, at that time worth more than $2 billion, had started in his basement. "I told him it was true, and he said, 'Well, that's just hard to believe. One day, that story will be well known.' I just nodded and thought to myself, 'Don't you know it, buddy.'")

Up and down the aisles of the Royal theatre in Toronto, HEXO staff quickly moved, dropping branded cotton tote bags stuffed full of HEXO swag onto each seat. Adam stood in the aisle next to Meena. He checked the time on the vintage Rolex he'd bought when he left his previous start-up in media. The doors were about to open. There was a lineup down College Street for half a block — people eager to witness history. After all, RZA — a foundational member of the legendary rap group, Wu-Tang Clan — was going to live score the film *The 36th Chamber of Shaolin* (the inspiration for their 1993 debut album, Enter the Wu-Tang [*36 Chambers*]), followed by a question period. Some had seen the famous 1978 film that was so closely tied to the Wu-Tang Clan story, but none had seen it with the music created live by a Clan member. Better still, it was all free, courtesy of HEXO. Who or what HEXO was, they didn't know, but they were grateful to the mysterious benefactor nonetheless.

A few days earlier, on August 23, HEXO had launched the Never Jaded Tour, a $12 million exercise in brand awareness and risk mitigation. The upcoming legislation on advertising cannabis was going to put licensed producers in a tight spot: they had a great product, but there could be no product advertising, and no brand advertising anywhere that wasn't a strictly 19+ venue.

HEXO may not have been able to directly advertise to the general public, but thanks to the recent rebranding exercise and research, it had identified its "tribe," the demographic of switched-on and savvy cannabis tourists and cannabis purists. HEXO consumers were social, reflective, and active explorers who were always curious, never jaded. They liked live music, theatre, foodie culture, and taking care of themselves. They were into the urban scene, embraced seemingly random events, and were always up to learn more. The Never Jaded Tour would deliver it all to them.

In the spirit of the upcoming legislation, HEXO ensured that all its events and promotions were strictly directed to those 19+ events. From the outside looking in, Never Jaded was just Never Jaded: there was no mention of HEXO. But once the punters entered a venue, HEXO was everywhere. Brand ambassadors were on hand to educate and entertain. The entertainment lineup would include theatre takeovers to screen classic films like *The Big Lebowski* and dinners by rambunctious celebrity chef Matty Matheson. There'd be live concerts by the Wu-Tang Clan (its first reunion show, for its 25th anniversary), Fetty Wap, Our Lady Peace, dvsn, and Z-Trip. There were e-sports tournaments and yoga classes held at the Never Jaded "Flower Shop" pop-up speakeasy in the former Fluevog Shoes store on Queen Street West. Later, the Flower Shop would be the site of an incredibly powerful wall-to-wall-to-ceiling art installation by internationally renowned urban artist Tristan Eaton. It was, in short, a rolling, rollicking, front-loaded cultural circus.

It fit the brand the Montreal agency had developed, but it wasn't its campaign. Whatever the agency's shortcomings, it was undeniable that it had come up with some of the most creative and convincing launch campaign ideas Adam had ever seen. But having been relegated to the agency's E team — not even their B team — Adam was no longer confident the agency could deliver on what it was suggesting. Adam was still mulling over what to do when the marketing manager called him while he was driving through Alberta on the Never Jaded tour that spring. He pulled over and answered the phone.

The manager sounded like she'd just hit a deer and was in shock. "Adam, I need to talk to you," she blurted out, then rushed into a jumbled rant he couldn't understand. Eventually, he figured out that, as a result of her frustration with the Montreal agency, she agreed to hear a pitch by a Toronto events company. It had this crazy idea for a cultural tour, with all these big names and big ideas. She rattled on for a bit, not running out of steam. Finally, Adam interrupted her.

"Okay, I trust you. I mean, do you want to do this? Yeah? Okay, let's take a look. Send over their presentation."

The spreadsheets looked like an ink cartridge had bled out all over the printer. Wild colours, terrible palette, with no actual rhyme or reason that Adam could discern. It was like they were throwing pasta at the wall. Want a Wu-Tang concert? How about Matty Matheson? Yeah, we could do dvsn, he's cool, too. The ideas came thick and fast, and seemed to be all over the place. He wasn't sure where to go with it, but Adam trusted two things: his gut and his marketing manager.

And so, HEXO hired the agency, which turned out to consist of two friends who'd never worked together but shared a hipster co-working space in downtown Toronto and saw an opportunity to hit the next level through a cannabis company. Through their hustle and vision, they created Never Jaded, a brilliant and well-executed campaign that not only went on to win an ADCAN Award for marketing but later landed Adam and artist Tristan Eaton an invitation to speak at the 2019 Cannes Lions International Festival of Creativity.

But as the Never Jaded campaign rolled on, it became apparent there was an issue. It was an expensive branding exercise, but the 43,769 people who'd registered to take part across the country weren't connecting the tour to the brand.

Toronto's *Now* magazine clued in early, in an article dated September 6, 2018. In it, the publication wondered aloud what Never Jaded might be, noting the press release described it as a "collective" and a "social movement," focused on "concerts for the nation's music lovers, interactive art exhibitions, theatre takeovers, and memorable culinary experiences" from Toronto, Vancouver, Edmonton, Ottawa, and Calgary. The potluck of cultural miscellany involved artists like dvsn, Fetty Wap, Murda Beatz, Our Lady Peace, and celebrity chef Matty Matheson — but who was bankrolling the whole thing?

"Never Jaded is under the umbrella of HEXO, a — can it be so simple? — cannabis company," *Now* wrote. "That explains the vagueness, but it's there if you look in the fine print. Cannabis sponsorships are in a legal grey area right now, but that hasn't stopped brands from finding their way in the music market."

Now Toronto got it, but apparently not everyone did. In an effort to be as compliant as possible, HEXO had masked itself too much. At a Calgary Never Jaded event, Adam overheard a conversation between concert goers. They loved the event, loved that it was free. But, someone asked, who actually put it on? Did anyone know? Adam's stomach fell. He emailed HEXO's general counsel and booked a meeting. They were on a call at 5 a.m. the next morning.

"Hey buddy, listen. We have to own this tour. We're wasting time, we're wasting money. This is insane, not being able to put our name out there with this tour. This has to change. I need a detailed explanation of the risk threshold, and I'm telling you right now, we're going to push for this and start labelling these events 'Powered by HEXO.' I need you to get behind that."

Back in Gatineau, the lawyer absentmindedly scratched his well-manicured goatee.

"Okay. You want to take this risk? I'll back you up."

Later that day, Adam called the marketing department. The tour needed to pivot. Marketing needed to design revised ads for the Wu-Tang show and everything that followed it. Taxi toppers around Toronto, building wraps, the digital ad at Dundas Square. They all needed to promote Never Jaded events with the words "Powered by HEXO."

It turned out to be a smart move and the tipping point for the tour.

Years earlier, in the basement office, Seb and Adam wound down after a night of filing forms and problem solving by watching music videos. Adam was fascinated by product placement. One night, they watched a Miley Cyrus video in which a brand's lip gloss made a three-second appearance. "I bet that cost $20 million for that product placement," Adam said. Seb shook his head and laughed. "That's crazy. We'd never do that."

Fast-forward to Never Jaded and they were doing exactly that, live, with the biggest names in hip hop, not to mention rock legends like Our Lady Peace and a world-renowned artist.

"Here we were, partnering with some of the biggest bands in history, with some of the best artists alive," says Adam.

"We weren't far from doing all sorts of things, and all of a sudden all that product placement became within the realm of possibility. We had no idea prior to that how we would put our product in a music video. Now we knew, now we had contacts, and we had access."

There was another benefit of doing the tour: from a marketing point of view, HEXO had really drilled down to the audience, beyond selling cannabis and into the occasions in life when cannabis is consumed, and how and by whom. In doing that, they'd learned a valuable lesson.

"Up until Never Jaded, we were doing great things, but we were horrible about communicating what they were," says Adam. "But, once you were inside a Never Jaded event, with the big shiny HEXO letters, the swag, the branding everywhere, the brand ambassadors, we were doing a spectacular job of telling people about our brand by visually communicating it, all within the constraints of age-gated venues. Never Jaded on the outside, HEXO on the inside. We saw that it was possible, and we knew we'd figured out a way to communicate," recalls Adam.

In the end, Never Jaded was 50 days of activations, 22 tour events attracting more than 13,000 people, 18 concerts, 28 pop-up shop events, and 271,553 webpage views. There were also more than 800,000 digital impressions from advertising in 800 bars across the country, and a total of 8.2 million impressions in paid media.

HEXO had literally wallpapered Canada with 250,000 pieces of branded swag (67,000 went just to Never Jaded events). But what does a quarter million T-shirts, hoodies, ball caps, socks, and toques look like? In theory, that was the HEXO logo on one in every 148 Canadians. More importantly, HEXO now had thousands and thousands of Canadians who knew exactly who they were.

Back at the farm, it had been a busy summer.

The sales team had locked down a supply agreement with British Columbia's Liquor Distribution Branch (BCLDB) on July 11, 2018. Compared with Quebec's SQDC deal, it wasn't as big of a beast because the supply scope was limited to the award-winning Elixir products. But it was meaningful because it expanded HEXO's reach across the country. Ironically, the first BCLDB store was destined for Kamloops, home to Terry Lake, HEXO's then VP of corporate social responsibility, who'd once been mayor of the city. A well-known figure for that as well as for his role as British Columbia's former health minister and minister of the environment, Terry loved that his hometown would play a historic role in legalization.

Kamloops was also home to Adam's mother, Ann, and his stepfather, Phillip. On October 17, a few months after British Columbia announced its first store in Kamloops, Ann and Phillip proudly stood in line at the cannabis store to buy Elixir. When Ann finally got up to the sales clerk to pay, she leaned across the counter conspiratorially.

"You know," she said, barely containing her glee, "my son co-founded HEXO!"

The clerk glanced up, surprised.

"You're Terry Lake's mom?"

A week after the BC supply agreement was announced, HEXO went to market with its most controversial product to date, an intimacy aid called Fleur de Lune. That it was an intimate oil wasn't remarkable in itself — there were plenty of similar things in the American market in California, Colorado, and Washington States. Yet, it was a harder sell than Elixir because both female sexual arousal and the effects of THC are difficult to measure. What's more, media reports of THC pre-lubricants having any effect on the depth, length, or accessibility of orgasm for women was largely anecdotal, highly descriptive, and utterly unrepeatable in any marketing materials. But where there's a will, there's a way, or rather, where there's a demand, there's a market. Named for the ineffably beautiful but rarely blooming cactus moon flower (*Epiphyllum oxypetalum*, also known as Queen of the Night), the imagery of the sensual and slowly unfurling blossom was intended to be about as suggestive as Health Canada's Victorian sensibilities would allow.

As it happened, Fleur de Lune's release coincided with HEXO visiting the Women Grow Leadership Summit in Denver, Colorado. There, intimate oils, cannabis, female orgasm, and the effect of cannabis on intimacy were the subject of deeply serious formal workshops and personal discussions. The marketing manager returned to the farm a few days later. It was really gratifying, she told the team, to sit through presentations about cannabis and exploring sexuality in an open, nurturing environment where there was no judgment.

Although HEXO didn't realize it at the time, Fleur de Lune was a first for the company for a whole other reason. Until then, HEXO had been developing product innovations largely based on THC or CBD content, their effects, and smoke-free innovations. But Fleur de Lune broke new ground altogether because it was the first HEXO product developed for a specific occasion or moment.

By the time the federal government enacted legislation legalizing cannabis edibles, in October 2019, much of the Canadian cannabis industry had already pivoted away from solely marketing high-THC or high-CBD dried flower products and was instead gripped by the idea of creating unique products for specific occasions. There would be a cannabis drink, topical, edible, or vape to help you sleep, relax, perform, focus, fly high, or deepen intimacy. From a marketing point of view, it was a simple approach that Canadian consumers could understand, much like the original Hydropothecary Time of Day products were. And it was going to be a game changer.

1:15 P.M., AUGUST 1, 2018
BNN BLOOMBERG, QUEEN ST. WEST
TORONTO, ONTARIO

The SQDC deal, led by Jay and Seb, had been a great victory. Now, with the biggest supply deal in the history of cannabis under their belts, Seb and his team started to wonder: if HEXO could negotiate a $1 billion deal with a provincial organization, could anything stop them from doing the same with another organization, say a Fortune 500 company? And if they could create joint ventures with Fortune 500 companies playing in the consumer-packaged goods space, wouldn't that fit perfectly with the forthcoming edibles legislation set to come online in the autumn of 2019?

HEXO wasn't the only cannabis company thinking that way. Canopy Growth had formed a strategic partnership with US alcohol giant Constellation Brands. And there were plenty of other global Fortune 500 companies looking at Canadian cannabis companies with a speculative eye. It was to be expected: In 2019, a Zion Market Research report would speculate that by 2025 the global cannabis beverages market would generate US$4.5 billion.

Already HEXO had seen an enthusiastic adoption of smoke-free, easy-to-use cannabis products like Elixir and Decarb. If it could come up with a half a dozen other unique value-added products that moved away from dried bud and the spectre of smoking, it would be hard for the competition to keep up, theorized Jay McMillan. "We could do that across Canada, then again in other markets. Where there is a flower market to start, it's not going to be a flower market forever. We needed to give consumers the option, different methods of consumption with different experiences, so they can incorporate products into their life-styles in a way they weren't doing with dried flower."

The time was perfect for HEXO to find a partner with whom to hold hands and leap over the edge into the cannabis-infused beverages space. But it had to be the right match. Aside from corporate approach and brand values, HEXO's leadership was particularly concerned with cultural fit. While HEXO was now a big and growing company, it'd only recently been tempered in the fires of the start-up crucible. The result was a ballsy, visionary, and innovative billion-dollar start-up that was not only coming of age but still dreaming of things just beyond its grasp, at least for the moment. Whoever it partnered with would have to have the same audacious goals and passion for aggressive execution.

"We didn't see us tying ourselves to a strong 'corporate suit' culture," recalls Jay of some early discussions. "And some companies were only looking at cannabis beverages speculatively, and saying, 'Yeah, we'll do a regional play, we'll try to invest, and we'll see what happens.'"

One major corporation stood out. Molson Coors Canada had been in discussions with other LPs, but the conversations ended for various reasons, including the news prematurely finding its way to the media. So, when the legendary Canadian beer company's investment bankers approached Seb, he was ready to listen.

Over the next weeks and months, through countless conversations, it became evident that both companies not only spoke the same language, shared a Québécois heritage, and had the same global ambitions for can-nabis but could also work very well together.

Billion Dollar Lesson

"When you're in business school, it makes no fucking sense when they're talking about mission and values. When you're a small entrepreneur, it makes no sense. Now if you asked me that question, the first thing I really want to talk about is values. They're the fundamental basis for every strategic decision. They're the guardrails for everything you do. It may sound like business mumbo jumbo, but understanding that has taken me a lifetime to learn." **— Seb**

Adam, still buzzing across the country on the Never Jaded Tour, had come to the same conclusion. Tooling down Highway 2 from Edmonton on his way to a Calgary event, he dialled into a conference call with the Molson Coors Canada's VP of Innovation. Everyone was still in the early stages of speculating just how far cannabis beverages could go and how they could overcome various hurdles to make them happen. One thing they could agree upon was their impatience to get into the space.

"Adam, I just want to make cool shit and get it out there quickly," the VP said. At the other end of the phone, Adam laughed inwardly and thought, "Oh boy, this thing is going to work!"

By the time Seb and Molson Coors Canada CEO Frederic Landtmeters appeared together on BNN Bloomberg TV on August 1 to announce that they planned to create a standalone joint venture, the two companies were marching lockstep. They would create innovative and shelf-stable cannabis-infused beverages that would offer a predictable consumer experience and quick onset time, just like a beer or a glass of wine. They'd start with base functional drinks like zero-calorie diet pop or energy boosters and incorporate cannabis. They'd already started looking at technologies that would overcome the biggest hurdles US cannabis drinks companies had faced, such as mixing oil-soluble cannabis into a water base without the two separating.

"The capabilities Molson Coors brings to the table simply don't exist in the cannabis space today," Seb told BNN. "There's so much overlap on values, but also strategic objectives." He struggled to master his boyish grin, somehow containing himself enough to look calmly delighted. Beside him, Landtmeters was po-faced and to the point. "What we have done is look at the increased acceptance of consumers of cannabis, and that will increase going forward. As soon as we saw the opportunity was there, we made a choice not to be a spectator."

The announcement made, the rest of August flew past at a rapid pace, propelled along by the communications team issuing press releases in rapid-fire succession. Each marked a huge moment in the company's development, but few inside the departmental trenches had the time to stick their heads up over the parapets to assess the impact. Sure, teams were keeping tabs on competitors' moves, in terms of product developments, market reach, investor relations, and share of voice, but there was no time to draw a breath and marvel at either the growth or the astonishing achievement of turning a $35,000 investment into a billion-dollar company in five years. The pace was eye-watering, yet the milestones were all there, splashed across the newswire. The first harvest in the 250,000-square-foot B6 expansion came in on time, on August 9 that year. A week later, the company reached two hundred employees and announced on August 16 it would be hiring another three hundred by the end of 2018.

Four days after that, the Ontario Cannabis Store released the news that it had a supply agreement with HEXO for its Elixir line, as well as Fleur de Lune. With supply agreements in place with Quebec, Ontario, and British Columbia, the sales team turned its attention to Alberta, where they'd already made a strategic $10 million investment in the independent corporate cannabis retailers Fire & Flower. By the time the company's shareholders officially voted to change Hydropothecary Corp. to HEXO Corp. on August 29, the company had already been living with HEXO as the recreational cannabis brand since May. That it was now also the corporate name seemed like a lunch-bag letdown.

GATINEAU, Quebec, Aug. 29, 2018 (GLOBE NEWSWIRE) — The Hydropothecary Corporation ("HEXO" or the "Company") (TSX:HEXO) is pleased to announce that it has changed its corporate name from "The Hydropothecary Corporation" to "HEXO Corp." effective today.

The change of the Company's name to "HEXO Corp." follows the Company's previously announced launch of "HEXO" as its new brand for the adult-use cannabis market, while continuing to use the "Hydropothecary" brand for the medical cannabis market.

"As we look to expand globally, we sought to find a name that would resonate around the world. Something that is strong, easy to pronounce, and easy to recognize. Something that has the ability to become truly iconic," said Adam Miron, co-founder and Chief Brand Officer of the Company.

SEPTEMBER 2018
THE FARM, CHEMIN DE LA RIVE
MASSON-ANGERS, QUEBEC

If August was hectic, September roared into the pot farm with a vengeance. Legalization was a month and a half away and, as they say, shit was getting real. Every day, another newspaper or TV headline would speculate about a looming cannabis shortage. And every day, LPs and provincial authorities would temper those stories with mitigating interviews. "Part of our planning was calculating how much product the province would require for an estimated number of stores at the launch of legalization," noted an Alberta Gaming, Liquor and Cannabis spokesperson in a *Calgary Herald* article. The remark was masterful in saying very little, but it also reflected the uncertainty everyone was feeling. It was, after all, difficult to judge exactly what Canadians would do the day after legalization. Would "cannabis purists" already consuming black market weed suddenly bail on their favourite supplier in favour of publicly standing in line at a government-run outlet? Would Mom and Dad decide that the intervening 30 years since they last smoked pot as uni students was long enough for them to try again? Most importantly, had the industry done enough education about cannabis to overcome the lingering stink of dope stigma to persuade curious Canadians to become cannabis tourists?

These were questions no one had real answers to, and everyone in the industry knew it. In May 2018, CIBC released a report suggesting that Canadians would be consuming at least 800,000 kilograms of medical and recreational marijuana annually, yet even at full production, the commercial industry would be able to supply only 350,000 kilograms — "nowhere near enough to supply the adult-use market," the report added, rather unhelpfully. Conversely, Statistics Canada released its own figures that seemed to suggest Canadians wouldn't be all that keen on experimenting, with 79 percent saying they weren't about to start using marijuana, legal or not.

Whatever their fellow citizens thought or felt about pot, LPs across the country were nevertheless ramping up cultivation and post-harvest production of dried products, oils, soft gels, and pre-rolls. At HEXO, the cultivation team was expanding daily, with dozens of new faces joining weekly to work in the greenhouses.

Construction on B9 was still ongoing, with the mud, trucks, and crews creating a nuisance as well as an energy of their own. The supercritical CO_2 machines worked around the clock, extracting cannabis oil destined for Elixir bottles. The operations team toiled 24/7 from September to December, with the director himself once doing a straight 36-hour stint, with just a catnap in his office to see him through. Production was happening at a lightning pace, in part because of their work with Segra, a company that specializes in industrial-scale cannabis micropropagation, or plant-tissue culture. Rather than traditional cloning from mother plants, micropropagation generates exact copies of the original plant without the risk of pathogens, fungi, and other issues that can plague other production processes. The end result was a quick and effective scaling up. Over in the marketing department, the team was frenetically producing in-house educational videos for SQDC and OCS budtenders, and finalizing product names, labels, and packaging. The mood was upbeat and excited. Every person on campus and at the corporate offices in downtown Gatineau was acutely aware that they were making history.

But as with everything else with HEXO, it was not enough to make history in the past tense. History is happening today, created by the bold. Seb's vision of a global Fortune 500 consumer-packaged goods company needed a lot of room in which to flourish. And it needed a framework.

Internally, HEXO's leadership team had been discussing a hub-and-spoke strategy for some time. Pioneered by the transportation industry, the hub-and-spoke model would put HEXO at the heart of a global network of consumer brands by global Fortune 500 corporations involved in everything from cosmetics and vapes to topicals and edibles. HEXO would supply the cannabis and the technology, Fortune 500 companies like Molson Coors Canada would supply the consumer base and distribution, among other things.

"There are two things that are the bones of great Fortune 500 brands," Seb would tell his leadership team at their regular Tuesday strategic sessions. "You can't build a brand if you don't have a good product. And you have to have great distribution." He'd stress the adjectives: *good* product, *great* distribution.

"Canadian cannabis has five years to build these international brands and to do that, we need great distribution," he would continue. "How are we going to recreate the distribution of some of the top 500 consumer-packaged goods companies? We can't. It's tens of billions of dollars to do that."

Early on, someone would pipe up that they had great distribution in Canada already. Seb would jump on it like a cat on a dust mote.

"Yes, we've got that on lockdown," Seb would reply. "But we need international because the story doesn't survive in Canada alone. The company survives, but the story doesn't. Right now, we're pretty much fully valued based on the Canadian opportunity of today. We need to do more. The capital market push will get bigger and bolder and stronger. The minute you slow down because you're not growing, you're dead. You'll be gobbled up by someone who does figure it out."

Like the Molson Coors joint venture — named Truss, in a reference to a supportive roofing frame — consumer products would be jointly developed and "powered by HEXO" cannabis, but put on shelves by leveraging Fortune 500 corporations' expertise, consumer brand knowledge, and distribution.

Billion Dollar Lesson

"There are cannabis companies that believe that, as CPGs [consumer-packaged good companies], they can make a better beer than Molson Coors, a better chocolate bar than Nestlé, a better face cream than L'Oréal, better coffee than Folgers. It ain't happening. By partnering with Fortune 500s, you're solving two things: product quality and product distribution. Both will fundamentally build your brand." — **Seb**

It was apparent that it was no longer enough to be a producer of cannabis-only products. If HEXO was to truly stand on the international stage, it needed products "powered by HEXO" to be in legal cannabis stores *and* on grocery store shelves, too. And to do that, it needed a Health Canada licence to actually house cannabis for product development in a facility big enough to launch Seb's ambitions. As luck would have it, there was such a facility not far down the Trans-Canada Highway, in Belleville, Ontario.

A year earlier, in October 2017, the Ontario Superior Court of Justice had approved the final liquidation of Sears Canada's last remaining assets, including a 2-million-square-foot distribution centre in the small town of fifty thousand people. The former darling of Canadian retail had been decrepitly staggering along for some time: where the distribution centre once had been a major employer to some 3,000 people drawn from the wider Bay of Quinte Region, it had dwindled to 597. So when HEXO announced on September 10 that it was moving into 580,000 square feet of it to create a R&D cannabis centre of excellence, one could imagine the City fathers swooning. Jobs lost to shrinking industry would be replaced: HEXO had already asked the mayor to bring back the city bus route that ran to the facility in anticipation of the new employees' needs.

The news spread like a brushfire throughout Belleville, but it had been a long time in planning at HEXO. Back in September 2017 when HEXO leadership had set up a partnership with the Metro Supply Chain Group to distribute all cannabis in Quebec for the SQDC, they'd been doing a deal for a gorgeous warehouse adjacent to Autoroute 50, which ran right through Montreal. Better than a billboard, the HEXO sign would be seen by tens of thousands of commuters every day. The warehouse was 200,000 square feet, and for about three hot minutes the team thought it might have been overkill. But within very short order, the operations team had outgrown the space, so Seb and Devan had set out to find a bigger facility. They wanted to stay in Quebec, following their self-imposed Quebec-first strategy, but finding the right industrial property turned out to be more of a challenge than they could have imagined. Buildings were too small, too old, too remote, too costly. At one point, they found a 400,000-square-foot former food-production factory.

"On paper, it was a beautiful facility and we were excited," Seb recalls. "We walk in and we think this is something we can finally do a deal on." Yet good as it was, low ceilings and "mould as old as my grandfather," as Seb describes it, meant it would never pass Health Canada's vigilant rules.

Just as they came to the conclusion that Montreal was no longer in the cards, a solution came in the form of investor Vincent Chiara. Months earlier, Vincent had told Seb about an enormous property in Belleville. Seb had laughed and said, "The fuck we're going to do with that," but now it didn't sound so ludicrous. He called Vincent back to ask if the property was still for sale.

"Already bought it," Vincent chuckled, but he agreed to work out a deal to lease HEXO 500,000 square feet. But first, they needed to see it. Arriving one day in Vincent's personal helicopter, Adam and Seb were gobsmacked by the sheer size of the building. "Jesus," thought Seb. "You could fit our entire operation in Gatineau in this building It's a fucking airport."

The deal was done soon afterward, and then had to be redone.

"Not two or three months go by and I'm thinking, 'This is stupid. It's too fucking small.' So we redid the deal, Vincent cancelled a deal with another small marijuana company, and we're optioned for the entirety of the facility. We'll do technology and regulatory access for Fortune 500s who need to participate in the market in Canada. As we fill Belleville with hub-and-spoke partners like Truss, they'll all be there under a licensed roof," noted Seb.

At a packed information session at the local Travelodge the week of the announcement, Adam spoke to townspeople delighted by every word he said. HEXO was growing, he noted, and they'd chosen Belleville for the company's first foray outside Quebec, as a strategic and logical way to establish a presence in English Canada.

"Once we get up to full speed, we anticipate two hundred jobs, but things move fast," Adam told the *Belleville Intelligencer* newspaper. "The company's growing — who knows where we go from there. I mean, we're looking at growth in all sorts of different places and different sorts of components of this industry and sector, but it's two hundred jobs for now, and who knows where it goes. The sky is really the limit."

If Belleville housed any skeptics of the cannabis industry, he added, HEXO would change their minds. "It's a brave new world . . . and this societal shift we're going through is quite the experience. I think that's why we put so much emphasis on quality, that's why we put emphasis on credibility. We're proud of what we do, but we're also very proud of the way we do it."

The deal to take over the massive Belleville building also represented something else for HEXO. As a hub for product development, as well as a facility destined to have completely automated production and state-of-the-art cannabis transformation technology, Belleville was the embodiment of HEXO's Big Hairy Audacious Goals. Hundreds of thousands of square feet would be under fully automated cultivation, with giant bales of weed being moved, sorted, transformed, repacked, and prepared for shipping with no human hands ever touching it. With a team of scientists, chemists, engineers, and labourers, HEXO would no longer be just a pot producer in Quebec but would be stepping into an entire new era of next-gen innovation.

It was, quite simply, the single most ambitious thing HEXO ever decided to do. The deadlines to outfit the building, hire employees, and establish processes were so tight they squeaked. But that was hardly news. After all, this was the cannabis industry.

Billion Dollar Lesson

"Growth must constantly be front of mind. But you have to make sure you are fully financed for whatever growth you are about to tackle. Don't do it until you can afford it. Don't start spending it until it's in the bank." — **Seb**

12 P.M., SEPTEMBER 24, 2018
THE FARM, CHEMIN DE LA RIVE
MASSON-ANGERS, QUEBEC

Trucks rumbled up and down the dusty, potholed, suspension-wrecking Chemin de la Rive from morning to night. For what felt like decades but had only been 18 months, HEXO had played host to dump trucks, excavators, diggers, and pickups industriously bouncing through wheel ruts on their way around the campus. So, when an unmarked white semi-trailer slowly navigated its way down the service road shortly after lunch, it was completely and utterly unremarkable.

And yet, today was the day. And that truck was *the* truck, the one that would carry HEXO's inaugural shipment of recreational cannabis to market. More specifically, it was headed straight to the first SQDC retail store in Montreal.

At least, that's what the company put out on social media. In truth, the first shipment leaving Masson-Angers was headed to British Columbia and either the Kamloops storefront or shops opening later across the province. That information was kept quiet — the ink on the SQDC contract was still wet and no one at HEXO wanted to upset the elephant they'd bedded down with — so diplomacy reigned.

Still, the first SQDC shipment (which actually happened a week later, on October 4) was significant and a major milestone. And now the countdown was on. In just six weeks, on October 17, Canada would become the first G8 country to legalize cannabis for adult use.

"Every industry believes it's the fastest paced," one of HEXO's executives would later note in an article. "But the cannabis world is something else."

The words were prescient. Two days after HEXO sent its first shipment, the company issued a press release announcing its first international move. Months earlier, a former managing director at Deutsche Bank had contacted Seb, telling him about a cannabis company in Greece looking for a partner to get into the German medical market. Seb's reaction — Why the hell do I need to go to Greece? We don't have time for that — changed after he flew in to meet the people behind the company, Qannabos. The operation fit in with HEXO's vision of having a Eurozone processing centre, even if the Greeks' focus on medical did not. In the end, a partnership was formed to establish a Eurozone processing, production, and distribution centre designed to create a foothold in the EU. The deal fit right in with the company's hub-and-spoke approach. Qannabos would bring its brands powered by HEXO, as well as its infrastructure and know-how to the European market, in anticipation of legalization still to come. Unlike other LPs that had signed supply deals with individual European countries, however, HEXO planned to establish a 350,000-square-foot licensed space for manufacturing, processing, and distribution. It would be a low-cost supply when HEXO entered the United Kingdom and France in the early 2020s, while giving Qannabos the capital injection it needed. While it was hard to predict which of the more than 30 countries already with medical cannabis legislation would be the first to enter the recreational market, the company would be ready.

In the cover story of the December 2018 issue of *Hydropothecarian*, Jay explained the benefits of manufacturing cannabis in-country as opposed to importing it. "Most licence holders are shipping across the world, and it's not simple. But if you have products and approval from within the EU, it will mitigate logistical hurdles, give us dramatically better operational efficiency, and let us deliver our award-winning customer service."

And so, HEXO had set its stage for legalization and beyond. If the past five years were one long qualifying lap to determine pole position in the race to international cannabis dominance, October 17 would be the start of the actual race. HEXO was ready.

Billion Dollar Lesson

"Being an effective cannabis CEO is about more than the deals, though they are critical. Part of the role is creating deals that can flex with changing regulations. Be prepared for whatever the regulations look like, so you can participate." — **Seb**

Belleville was happening. The news about Greece was out. So, too, was the formal announcement made on October 4 that the HEXO/Molson Coors Canada joint venture, Truss, was a reality and would have its own board of directors, staff, and offices in Toronto. And across the country, HEXO products were at that moment being unpacked from their secure

shipping containers and lined neatly on retail shelves, like soldiers awaiting the call to action.

The only thing left was to wait for the day Canada would take the
lead in altering forever the way the world viewed this magical, wonderful
weed called cannabis.

7 P.M., OCTOBER 16, 2018
NATIONAL GALLERY OF CANADA
OTTAWA, ONTARIO

'Twas the night before legalization and all through the auditorium, pun-
dits, advocates, and thought leaders took to the Walrus Talks stage to
discuss cannabis. The Walrus Talks Cannabis speaker event had been
perfectly timed for the eve of legalization. At this moment, on the prec-
ipice of a major cultural shift, it was time to reflect. The speakers were
as diverse as the crowd: renowned criminal defence lawyer Annamaria
Enenajor; First Nations Tax Commission chairman Manny Jules; CEO
of HollyWeed North Cannabis, Renee Gagnon; and CBC radio host
and advertising pundit Terry O'Reilly, among others. The packed auditorium listened intently, but the mood was far from reflective. Every
seat was taken, not by members of the public wondering what the fuss
was about but by advocates, industry leaders, amnesty agitators, cannabis
company reps, and early medical adopters who'd risked imprisonment
for their medicine. Looking around, the one common feature on everyone's face was the anticipation of positive change.

When they were asked to stand and be counted among cannabis
users, they happily obliged. The audience was then asked to stay up
if they'd consumed marijuana recently. People tittered but remained
standing nevertheless. In a middle row was a crew from HEXO, led by
Terry Lake.

Had anyone used cannabis that month? They could sit. And what
about that week? Please take a seat. As bodies dropped, the HEXO
crew laughed nervously. They were all still upright. One of them leaned
over to Terry. "Well, CBD is cannabis. It counts." The speaker drove

home the point. Had anyone consumed cannabis that day? In the end, only three were still standing, blushing furiously and relieved to take their seats.

It seemed that despite all the work, education, and effort the industry had collectively put in over the past five years, owning cannabis consumption still made people nervous. The ghost of stigma lingered even among cannabis consumers.

8 A.M., OCTOBER 17, 2018
THE FARM, CHEMIN DE LA RIVE
MASSON-ANGERS, QUEBEC

Forget the entrenched idea about 4/20 and its illicit stoner culture. Today, the Canadian cannabis industry had its own legal, transparent, and visionary number to rally around. All the long hours, the deals, the disappointments, and successes were coming to fruition.

October 17, 2018, would forever more be the unofficial Canadian Cannabis Day. But how would it be celebrated? For weeks, Adam, Seb, and anyone else who even side-eyed a journalist heard the same smirking assumption that the Masson-Angers site would be undetectable by NASA because every one of their employees would be blazing away in a cloud of puff. And every time, they'd give the same answer: no, it will be business as usual. You don't work for five or six years to open a store, only to have everyone take a holiday on opening day, right? Even so, the question would be tediously redirected, sometimes with incredulity. "You mean to say that you won't be getting high on the first day it's legal to do so?" Clearly, the interviewer had never worked in a stringently regulated environment or considered the sheer stupidity of asking why people wouldn't be tripping balls while at work. Eventually, HEXO's comms department put out a press release.

October 17: Business As Usual At HEXO
17 oct. 2018 06h30 HE | Source: HEXO Corp.
GATINEAU, Quebec, Oct. 17, 2018 (GLOBE NEWSWIRE) —
Today, October 17, 2018, is destined to become the day Canada

made history for legalizing adult-use cannabis. Celebrations are planned across the country as all Canadians adapt to the change. However, HEXO Corp's employees remain focused on delivering on the company's commitments.

"October 17th will be a historic day for Canada. We remain resolute in honouring the commitments that we've made to our customers, investors, partners, and to all cannabis supporters," said Sébastien St-Louis, HEXO Corp's Chief Executive Officer and co-founder.

"As a community, we are working to protect public health and safety. At HEXO, that means an uncompromising commitment to quality, to innovation, and to providing our clientele with an exceptional cannabis experience and incomparable service."

In truth, October 17 was a day like any other. Deadlines were looming. Projects that wouldn't come online for six months were duly given space on whiteboards, with sticky notes flagging key deliverables. Everywhere, employees still moved quickly, but perhaps with a bigger grin. Inside the Taj, each member of the marketing team was given the corporate credit-card number and a $100 budget to buy as many different products from various LPs as they could from the online Ontario Cannabis Store. The products would be delivered to homes, the time it took to ship would be noted, and the unopened packages would then be brought to the office to be unpacked and inspected.

The buzz in the office was real, particularly when Adam popped in. He'd just arrived the night before from Saskatoon, fresh off the last moments of the Never Jaded Tour. Despite the jetlag, he was pumped. He had a few meetings, followed by a special celebratory gathering in the afternoon to introduce the company to their partners at Molson Coors Canada. Everywhere he looked, he saw industrious people bustling about, punctuated by shouts of laughter. A creative and energetic hive, the Taj generally attracted visitors, but today was bopping. In every greenhouse zone, workers in lab coats, hairnets, and blue shoe covers chatted and high-fived over the shared sense of accomplishment.

In short, it was business as usual.

The line to get through the single security door at the back of the newly operational B6 facility was nearly two hundred people deep and moving slowly.

It felt even slower given the weather. It was a typical mid-October day for Masson-Angers, unpleasantly overcast, cool, and windy. Yet, aside from a few regretfully uncovered arms and bare legs, no one seemed to care. Today was the day. Canada was going legal, and HEXO was graduating from being a cannabis producer to being a world-class cannabis consumer-packaged goods company.

One by one, every employee who could be spared from their duties filed through the door, first swiping their security tag and entering their code, then opening the door and closing it behind them before the next person could do the same. It was taking forever, but security on cannabis farms was a 360°, 24-hour commitment. Eventually, someone from legal made an executive decision and overrode the tedious process by ordering the bay doors to be opened.

Inside the concrete and steel shipping bay, people buzzed around having quick conversations, their voices giddy with the excitement of both an afternoon off and the promise of a special gift. There were so many new faces, too. The company had been growing quickly and departments building out so robustly, it was no longer a big group of old friends gassing about what they were planning for the weekend.

As she entered the utilitarian space with the rest of the marketing team, Julie spotted Ines — one of the original originals whose tenure dated back to when the farm grew ornamental plants — and rushed over for a hug. "Salut Ines, ça va, toi? You're looking well! I haven't seen you in a year! How is that even possible? And who the hell are all these people?"

Ines grinned, bobbed her head, and shrugged her shoulders, all simultaneously. "Tu as raison, Julie," she said in her charmingly blunt way. "Ce n'est pas comme au bon vieux temps! Ha ha! Yep, no more the good old days!"

No kidding, Julie thought, making her way through the throng to the stage that had been temporarily set up for the day. This certainly was no longer like the good old days of pulling into the farm, parking next to ramshackle barns, and squelching across the muddy yard to work in an uninsulated storage shed, fitted out with card tables and folding chairs. All that had been demolished and excavated, and in its place stood the shiny new B6 greenhouse, with its 10 growing bays, each roughly the size of the entirety of B5, HEXO's first purpose-built greenhouse. Where wild turkeys once boldly marched across the yard in search of flower seeds and insects now stood 250,000 square feet of next-generation cannabis production.

The crowd inched closer toward the stage, like teenagers at a high school dance. On the left stood the assembled HEXO big wigs. With them were a handful of strangers, hands comfortably in pockets, chatting with the management team as if shipping bays were their natural and favourite milieu.

With every event, there's always a moment before *the* moment marked by a simultaneous exhale. It's the microsecond when a crowd becomes collectively aware that this is it. All eyes expectantly turned to the stage, the lights dimmed, and a projection on the blank wall burst into life with a montage of impressive images and drone footage, showcasing the pot farm in a light few had seen before. To a persistent drumming beat, the sizzle reel expertly raced through the best of HEXO's achievements, the music rising to a crescendo, then ending with a throb. Immediately, every person present shouted in joy, roaring their approval and clapping till their palms turned red. This is us! We're really . . . we're really fucking incredible!

In a single superman leap, Seb was up on stage, mike in hand and a big grin on his face. The clapping went on and on. He put a hand in the air for quiet, then, alternating between English and French, proceeded to pump up the crowd all over again. This was a historic day in a historic era for Canada, he shouted over the applause. And HEXO is a pioneer in Quebec, Canada, and soon the world!

In front of a projection with the words "Innover maintenant pour l'avenir" (Innovate now for the future), Seb spoke for a few more minutes, then one by one introduced the strangers: the chairman of Truss, new Truss CEO, and Frederic Landtmeters, Molson Coors Canada's president and CEO, who was standing with Adam. Everyone in the crowd craned their necks and inspected the men with interest. They'd been hearing about them for some time. It was good to put faces to the names. Speeches made, Seb threw wide his arms and announced there was a special gift from Molson Coors for all present. He asked the crowd to face the big roller doors and shouted, "Open them up!"

Just beyond the fenced area, in a parking area, was a Molson Coors truck packed with hundreds of Coors Light eight-packs. Whooping in delight, the crowd rushed to the truck and lined up to claim their prize.

Ironically, HEXO was celebrating the historic day with a case of beer and Seb's stern warning not to drink and drive.

8 P.M., OCTOBER 17, 2018
ADAM'S HOUSE, CENTRETOWN
OTTAWA, ONTARIO

The house was finally quiet.

Adam had arrived home from work in time to make supper for his girls and by 7:30 p.m. had tucked them into bed and retired to his music room. Before long, he saw through the window Seb bound up his front steps, knock once, and let himself in. Adam and Meena had moved into a multi-million-dollar home in a tony neighbourhood a year before, so the broken-down wooden slats at Spruce Street were a distant memory — but Seb's boundless energy was still the same.

"Hey, how was your day?" Adam asked as Seb walked into the music room. Then, as they had for years, the two men sat down at the kitchen table and, over the course of an hour and a half, swapped funny stories, shared concerns, and went over operational issues. Although he had publicly said legalization day would be business as usual, it was actually quieter than normal for Seb. Having put so much energy and focus into their plan, he told Adam, "I had fuck-all to do today. I barely got a phone call, and I think I answered three emails." He'd even gone home around 4:30 p.m. and spent the early evening with his family.

"Want to go out back?" Adam held up a joint. Seb laughed out loud. "Yeah, sounds good."

It wasn't just a joint. It was a glowing, golden, and magnificent next-level rocket ship of every cannabis product HEXO had, and it looked like a pot Cornetto. Adam had painstakingly made it a few days earlier, dipped it in cannabis oil, rolled it in kief, and popped it into a gold tip. To keep it upright, he stuck a toothpick in the bottom and jabbed it into an apple.

Sitting outside in the cold autumn air, they lit up. The thing was too massive to manage in one sitting, and neither was interested in getting obliterated. Even smoking a joint was a once-a-month indulgence for Adam, who'd also eschewed alcohol and animal protein the year before. The point was to relax, return to the music room, and when the time was right, spin Pink Floyd's *Dark Side of the Moon*.

Back in the music room, they settled into the butter-soft tan leather armchairs. They looked at each other for a moment. True, they were in different houses and operating at a different scale. Their basement start-up was now a billion-dollar corporation headed for international waters. But they were the same people, having the same conversations, and sharing the moments they'd always relished.

Finally, Adam broke the silence.

"Okay. So, what's next?"

Seb smiled cryptically.

"What's next? Adam, we're just getting started."

EPILOGUE

Standing behind the wheel of his $200,000 custom wake boat, Seb's grin grew wider and wider with every agile skip of the craft over the deep water. The sun was shining, and for once after a very wet spring and early summer, it wasn't raining. It was a perfect day to take out the boat, which was a new acquisition, together with the modern wood-and-steel lake house he'd purchased the previous October.

Seb loved Lac McGregor, with its 1,345 acres of wooded inlets, expansive bays, and hidden coves. He'd grown up here, in a way, having spent so many weekends over the summer at a cottage nearby. Slowing down the boat slightly, he called out to Adam and Julie, who were lounging in the sun on the bow's white leather cushions.

"See that white pillar there?" He pointed to an unremarkable inlet guarded by a single buoy attached to the post. "That means don't go there, too shallow. It's also right near the cottage. You know? *The* cottage."

Adam laughed out loud. Talk about serendipity. The "cottage" was the original spot where, just six years earlier on a Canada Day long weekend, their friend Max had first floated the idea of starting a cannabis company to Seb.

There was another intersection, too. On their way up to Val-des-Monts, Adam and Julie had passed by a brand-new SQDC outlet on Gatineau's Boulevard de la Gappe. It was the fourth Quebec cannabis store, and the first located outside Montreal.

"Shit, look at that," Adam shouted as they blasted past it up Autoroute 50 in his new black Escalade. "Is it even open yet?" Julie quickly grabbed her phone to check. "Yup, opened at 10 a.m. Sweet. And it's filled with our product, right in our neighbourhood!"

It was a blissful day, made more so by the wonderful coincidences of timing and place. The plan was to spend the afternoon out on the water, talking and reminiscing. But first, Seb wanted to open up the engine and maybe show off a little.

"Hang on!" he shouted over the wind. In the front, Adam and Julie grabbed the safety bars. "NO, I MEAN HANG ON!" and with that he cranked the wheel and sent the boat roaring into an impossibly tight circle, spraying up a 4-metre plume of water like a peacock's tail. Whooping and laughing, they did it again in the opposite direction, skipping over the wake before setting off to find a quiet spot in the middle of the water to talk.

The mood was ebullient. And rightfully so. Between the October 17, 2018, legalization date and the summer of 2019, HEXO had emerged not only as a significant Canadian cannabis company but as a real contender on the world stage.

They'd listed on the junior New York Stock Exchange, with plans to up-list to the parent exchange later in the summer.

In March 2019, however, their Canada-wide expansion began in earnest, with an all-share, $263 million acquisition of Newstrike, a cannabis LP known for its partnership with beloved Canadian icons the Tragically Hip. (The relationship, formed before the death of Gord Downie, was the brainchild of founding CEO Jay Wilgar. Newstrike's weed, branded UP, would be grown in greenhouses with piped-in music. "It was a novel means of sustaining the Tragically Hip's legacy into the future," noted the *Toronto Star* at the time. The company's relationship with the band would continue into Newstrike's acquisition by HEXO years later.) The acquisition would also add distribution agreements in eight provinces. Overall, HEXO's production capacity would jump from

108,000 kilograms annually to 150,000 kilograms, part of Seb's plan "to become one of the largest cannabis companies in the world," he noted.

The positive news for 2019 didn't end there: They'd had their first harvest in the million-square-foot greenhouse, their posh new corporate offices in B6 were operational, and their Greek partners had secured a medical licence for Europe.

The plan for the next few years would be even ballsier than the previous few. Seb had thrown down the challenge to his leadership team to bring the company to $5 billion in revenue in 2023. It was a lot to have achieved in six years, and the scope was even grander for the next decade. But they weren't doing it alone.

Leaning back in the captain's chair of the boat, Seb looked like a lion sunning itself: deceptively relaxed, but ready to spring into action. While he hadn't visualized exactly this moment, on this lake, with these people, he'd always seen the bigger picture and had been driving toward bigger and bigger goals. They'd come to fruition because he and Adam were surrounded by people who not only shared that vision but were willing to make sacrifices to attain it.

"It's not the money," he finally said, his voice only just heard over lapping waves and distant bird calls. "I know I've already got more money than I ever thought I'd need. This has really been about building the team, getting people to drive and work together toward a common goal."

He paused a minute to reflect.

"Next thing that is important to me is that our kids grow up, you know, not to be assholes. The smiles on their faces, it's amazing. They're learning about the world, and when you see it, it's incredible."

Adam watched him for a second. "What about where your head's at, what you're looking for in happiness?"

Seb turned to him, looking thoughtful.

"You know, we just came back from that trip to Israel, and we really started to talk about the plan to give back, using this little power we have to actually make a positive difference for people. But to really make a difference globally, we need to be a Fortune 500. We're still tiny. I mean, we're rich from the perspective of who we are — people who grew up poor. But we have no power to change the world. Not yet.

"But we're going to get there, Adam. I'm really excited, not just focusing on the team but on the long-term strategic planning, getting really smart. We have all the right tools. When you look at all this," he said, sweeping his arm around him, "we had nothing back then. We had absolutely nothing. The team was bare bones. We didn't have a competitive advantage. We didn't even have a licence for two years."

Billion Dollar Lesson

"Avoid shiny things. Be very clear about what your business is, where the revenue is actually going to come from, and focus on that until that business line is proven and profitable. Then chase something new." — **Seb**

Julie and Adam nodded. It was all true. They could remember one time when Hydropothecary couldn't even make payroll because of a bank issue and had to use Louis's cash.

"Now we have some of the best infrastructure on the planet. We have one of the best teams on the planet. We are going to battle with a loaded gun, where before we only had a stick. Well, that's okay," he said, cocking his head. "It's all about where you point your stick."

He started the boat again, gently guided the wheel, pointing the nose in the direction of the lake house. His broad shoulders flexed as he moved. There were so many walls they'd torn down to get where they were, but at no time did they think becoming a billion-dollar start-up was inevitable. They'd dreamed of being a $20 million family-owned company, for sure. But getting to a billion dollars? That journey itself was the goal, with its hassles, challenges to overcome, ditches to be dug, and deals to be made.

Seb sat straighter in the seat and opened up the throttle a bit. "You know, we need to stay at the helm, accelerate, and keep driving. We're on a path of such momentum. HEXO becoming a $5 billion or $10 billion company is happening, with or without us. It's happening," he repeated, half to himself.

"You know what it feels like?" Seb asked, turning to look directly at them. "It feels inevitable. We have a real shot at being a Fortune 500."

Just like in the early days, Seb had picked a bearing and started rowing. As had Adam. But for the first time in six years, he wasn't headed in the same direction as his brother-in-law.

2:45 P.M., OCTOBER 2, 2019
ADAM'S STUDIO
OTTAWA, ONTARIO

The light was perfect, even for a grey autumn day.

Adam's new creative studio — so new the furniture and pictures were still randomly pushed up against the walls — was a 1,000-square-foot space with two northwest facing walls framed by massive windows. The view was beyond ordinary, the studio overlooking an industrial park notable for car detailing, body shops, and wholesale auto parts. But the studio itself was more obscure still. It was located next to a garage and accessible by a set of stairs at the back of a curious combination of coffee-shop/fancy-wheel-rim business run by a tall, slim Chinese guy and a cheerful South Korean woman who made killer Americanos and sold *hanguk bbang* pastries.

The coffee was great. But the abundant natural light was the selling point if this was to be a studio. That and it was a secure, quiet place to reflect. Adam had made some big — nay, monumental — decisions that summer, and reflection was a featured part of his new life plan. This spot would do, at least until he found the right property. And he was looking.

Just after returning from a family trip to Europe, Adam called Julie and suggested they grab a coffee. She lived in a tidy rural village not far from Ottawa, and her little white Victorian house was a few steps away from both a well-loved café and an ice creamery known for its in-house creations. A coffee and vegan chocolate dessert later, they hopped in Adam's Escalade and drove to a wooded acreage near the Ottawa River, not far from where Julie had grown up. As they cruised down Fifth Line Road, she chattered away about her teenage years in the area, the people who lived along that stretch of road, and the decimation of the nearby community of Dunrobin by a tornado a year earlier. She didn't know why Adam was looking at a big undeveloped property, but she figured he'd tell her when he was ready.

"So, the plan is this," he began as he parked in front of a "For Sale" sign poking up out of an overgrown ditch. He pulled out his phone and found an aerial view online. It was actually two properties, amounting to a couple of hundred acres. Part of it was still untouched, part had been cultivated for crops. There was a swamp, too. It was raw, to be sure, but he wanted a property big enough to be private, yet accessible by road.

"Okay. So, are you building out here?" Julie asked, privately marvelling at the thought of Adam in rubber boots, riding a tractor.

"Sort of. I will build, but it will be a studio. A live music space. A retreat where you can go and create and hang out. It's something I've been thinking about a lot. I need a place to create. I need to build. I just don't know what yet."

During the wild start-up years, the cannabis industry had been a greyhound running at breakneck speed, heart pounding and ears back. It was a thrilling ride, in a white-knuckle are-we-fucking-nuts kind of way. It was not for conservative thinkers or the risk-averse, but for pioneers, fearless adventurers, travellers, visionaries, and blue-sky thinkers. Decisions made in the morning were transformed into action by the afternoon, and creative ideas conceived of on Monday were hardened into marketing campaigns by Friday. For every new regulation the government imposed, there was a pivot and a sense of opportunities rather than obstacles. It was, in short, a business designed for hot-blooded entrepreneurs.

But to quote the title of S.E. Hinton's seminal coming-of-age novel . . . that was then, this is now. Not only did the environment and appetite for cannabis change between 2013 and 2019, it was a different dog running a different race. The course had evolved and the stakes radically and almost unrecognizably altered.

It was still fast-moving and would undoubtedly stay that way as it matured into something more akin to the alcohol industry in terms of deals, volume, scope, and scalability. But as it grew from start-up to an industry on the cusp of stepping out of the regional play and onto the world stage, the old ways of doing things, the "farm jobs," the atmosphere of pitching in regardless of the task, and the bloated canna-dollar budgets supporting the race to riches were no longer appropriate.

The kind of people needed to helm Cannabis 2.0 were different, too. On a regular basis, news would filter through the grapevine of yet another executive, C-suite blue suit or founder either splitting from the original company or leaving the industry altogether. Serious money-bucks investors had arrived on the scene, demanding more robust sales, plumper bottom lines, and a leaner operating environment. The corporatization of cannabis has been, in many ways, not only inevitable but absolutely necessary for its growth.

HEXO was no different from any of its competitors. As its corporate structure firmed up, roles and responsibilities changed and restructuring took place. (In October 2019, HEXO "aligned its operations with its 2020 expectations," notes a press release, in the process shedding some two hundred jobs, shifting priorities, and shuttering some facilities.) Some departures were not unexpected, some were.

But when Adam announced he was leaving the company he co-founded, the earth moved in Masson-Angers.

Billion Dollar Lesson

"I think there is a difference between making an emotionally driven decision and keeping a good amount of EQ present when making a call. This is a skill I had to develop over the years, but you have to keep the people in mind when making a decision. That balancing act is a key focus in business and one that constantly needs to be assessed." — **Adam**

HEXO Corp Chief Brand Officer Adam Miron steps down from position, stays on as key Board member
18 juil. 2019 06h30 HE | Source: HEXO Corp.
GATINEAU, Quebec, July 18, 2019 (GLOBE NEWSWIRE) --
HEXO Corp ("HEXO" or the "Company") (TSX: HEXO; NYSE:

HEXO) announces that HEXO co-founder, Adam Miron, has decided to step down from his position as Chief Brand Officer. These changes are effective today. Adam Miron co-founded HEXO six years ago with Sébastien St-Louis and has played a key role not only in building the company, but as an innovative leader in the cannabis industry. Adam will retain his seat on the HEXO Board of Directors and will continue to serve as president of the Board of Directors of HEXO MED, the Company's Greek affiliate.

"Building HEXO has been one of the greatest privileges of my life," said HEXO co-founder, Adam Miron. "I am a builder. What I see today is an established company with amazing leadership across all functions. I would like to thank the entire team and all our supporters for making this possible."

MID-MORNING, JUNE 24, 2019
TOSSA DE MAR, CATALONIA, SPAIN

The moment he made the decision to leave HEXO hit Adam square in the back like a rogue wave. Literally.

After lugging a day's worth of baby equipment, food, towels, sunscreen, and hats down the 500-metre elevation from his and Meena's Airbnb — sold to them as "just 500 metres from the ocean" with no mention of the quad-killing vertical hike — the family settled in for a day of relaxation.

They'd driven down from Cannes, where Adam had shared a speaker's stage with world-renowned urban artist Tristan Eaton a few days earlier at the Cannes Lions International Festival of Creativity. En route to Tossa de Mar, in Spain's Costa Brava, they'd stayed in Montpellier. It was a surreal experience: sitting in their villa, looking out of a Juliet-balconied window at homes owned by Bono and Elton John, Adam took a conference call with the marketing manager, who was huddled over her computer in her worn-out little office in a ModSpace portable back at the farm.

The Montpellier flat was also on a streetcar line in the centre of town, and that night, with the perfumed Côte d'Azur air wafting in, Adam and Meena lay on their bed, listening to different music playing in each vehicle as their doors opened and shut down below. It was a moment of utter bliss. Throughout the trip, they'd talked endlessly about whether Adam was actually contributing anything to the company now that it was fully staffed up, if he should leave, and if he did, what would he actually do then? The discussion flowed back and forth in the way such things do between a couple totally at ease with each other. Still, as their rental car ate up the kilometres on the way to Spain, Adam was no more set on an answer than when they'd set out. But that night in Montpellier was the start of a tipping point. They were in an exquisite place with their children. There was no timeline or agenda, aside from having the pleasure of each other's company. And they were wealthy beyond what they'd ever imagined.

What more to life was there?

On the pebbly Tossa de Mar beach, Adam had his answer. There was more to life, but it wasn't going to be found at HEXO. Like other cannabis company founders, his usefulness to the company in a real sense was exhausted. Yes, he'd stay on the board and contribute his wealth of knowledge and expertise, but for a long time he'd been waiting for the right moment to exit gracefully. He'd been waiting for the right team to be in place. For the right leadership. The right products.

As he sat on the beach, helping his bright-eyed daughters sort through pretty pebbles they'd collected, a wave crashed over his back and with it came the wet slap of reality: there was no point in waiting any longer, because there was no such thing as a perfect moment to leave. He'd heard about "stretchers" in business: stories about company founders who stay in charge longer than they should and so are figuratively a burden on a stretcher everyone has to carry around. He'd secretly been worrying about being that burden for two years. So, that night, as fireworks exploded over the town in celebration of Spain's St. Jean Baptiste Day, he told Meena.

"Okay, I think I'm going to do it. I think I've made up my mind to leave. When I get back, I'm going to sit down with Seb and be like, 'Are you okay with this?'"

As she had done years earlier in Bali when Adam told her they were going to need a lot more money to start the company, Meena looked steadily into his eyes and said, "Okay. If you're sure, I'm sure." Now Adam just needed a plan for what he'd do next.

Back in Ottawa a few days later, the conversation with Seb went as anticipated. Not only did Seb — at the time one of the last original cannabis CEOs still in the game — support Adam's decision, he applauded the fiscal responsibility he was showing by stepping away. The leadership team front bench had filled out with talented individuals doing all the jobs Adam used to do and, with the new COO changing the culture in a very real way, the timing was about as right as it was going to get. All that was left to discuss was a timeline for his leaving.

"I'm thinking I will give it 6 to 12 months to transition, then I'm out," Adam told Seb. Both of them felt a twinge of anxiety upon hearing the words spoken aloud. They'd operated as two parts of the same brain for so long, knew each other so well, that the thought of severing the connection sent a frisson of fear into their guts. Still, as Adam pointed out, they'd always defined success differently from the average punter who worked hard, put in his hours, and felt rewarded with a pay raise and a corner office.

"If you're amicably and financially able to walk away from the company you've started," he said, "that's success. But if you're stuck at the top of your company and you can't leave, even though you're making a million dollars a year and your company is worth $100 million, that's not my definition of success."

But, as their discussion turned to the actual operational and financial health of the company, they soon came to the conclusion that there was no reason to wait even that long. In short, there was no time like the present.

And so, two weeks later, on July 18, at the age of 35, Adam Miron retired.

Of course, retirement is entirely subjective. Adam retired from HEXO's day-to-day operations, to be sure, but not from life. There were no 4 p.m. early-bird retiree suppers in his immediate horizon, nor were there any snowbird trips planned to Floridian golf courses. In the days that followed the announcement, Adam's phone buzzed constantly with offers to join boards, meeting requests for angel funding, and emails with job offers. (Soon after he retired, he was also named Entrepreneur in Residence at Kamloops's Thompson Rivers University.) It was overwhelming, because without his ritual planning and knowing what he was going to do at any point in the day, he was having trouble figuring out what to wear, much less if he needed to shower first.

And so Adam got to work with hundreds of sticky notes in a half-dozen colours and a blank wall. What would his days look like, now that he was free to do as he pleased? One sticky-note colour was for fitness, another for family, a third for new projects, and so on. As he arranged and rearranged his day planner, he started to review the fourth quadrant of his *ikigai* chart. (Among other ways to define his purpose in life, Adam had recently embraced *ikigai*, a Japanese concept that means "reason for being." By working through an *ikigai* chart, one is able to find the source of what makes one's life fulfilling and worthwhile.)

"I'm a builder," he thought. "I'm good at starting companies and even better at starting companies in which there's a strong operator in the lead."

But that wasn't enough to filter through the dozens of offers he was receiving, now that his social equity — his availability as a resource to others — had risen. He needed another variable in his decision-making protocols. And he knew just what it was.

Back in the bright creative studio over the coffee shop, Adam searched for a way to answer Julie's question about what he was going to do with the space and by extension, the rest of his life. He loved to have a good plan, but he needed a reason to have the plan in the first place. The job offers, the board seats, the investment opportunities were flattering, but what was the "why" — why should he do one or any of them?

"I realized that I have a very simple filter: standing at the door of my house with my suitcase in my hand and my three girls holding onto my legs and saying, 'But, Daddy, why do you have to leave again?' And if I could explain to a six-year-old why, in a truthful way that made sense, then I was going to do it. But it had to pass the test. And telling kids 'Because I'm going to make more money' is not a respectable answer to give a six-year-old. Because then she says, 'Oh, don't we have enough money?' and she's crying."

Adam took a sip of his Americano and fiddled with his phone as a text came in. Another opportunity for the newly minted, self-made multi-millionaire, perhaps. Adam got up to stretch his legs, talking as he did.

"So, yeah, that doesn't pass my filter. Might for someone else, but it doesn't for me. And that's when it hit me. What is the most impactful thing I can do? What would pass the test? Creating a system that would lead to impactful change, that one day, should my kids choose, would mean they'd be involved in a program that would help other people's lives."

But rather than just making a donation, he added, he'd take a leadership role and become an advocate and philanthropist, adding inherently to the value of cash with public awareness. And what would that look like, Julie wondered aloud.

"I don't know yet. But it's coming. But the important thing is that, after all these years of start-ups and business and going away and the tears at the door, I know what I'm supposed to be doing. And I can now articulate to a six-year-old, through her tears, that Daddy has to leave because we're going to be able to help a lot more people."

Julie stood up next to Adam, and nodded toward a line of 24-by-36-inch canvases drying on a drop cloth on the floor. After many years, she'd recently started painting again herself. She looked over the canvases, some of which were spray-painted by him, others obviously the work of smaller hands. "So what's the deal with the art? I didn't even know you were into it."

He nudged one of the canvases with his foot. "Yeah, I'm not very good, but I was worried that I'd lose my creative brain. At HEXO, I had this wonderful opportunity to be creative with product names, colours, branding, interior design of the corporate offices . . . I don't want my brain to slow down."

"As if," Julie thought, but it did seem like those blank canvases propped up against the wall meant more than a chance to paint. It seemed to her that they represented opportunity, as yet unexpressed, for Adam's next adventure. He'd start with something raw and unformed, as he had with HEXO, and shape it by the power of his will, determination, and energy into something remarkable.

As if he was reading her mind, Adam finished the analogy.

"Your art's very good, by the way, I've seen it on Facebook. Mine isn't . . . but for me, it's not about the art. It's about . . . well, I fully intend to stop buying more canvases, because I'm going to paint these, whitewash them and do it all over again."

Julie laughed with delight. As in his start-over-again business life, so too in art.

For six years, building a cannabis company had consumed them all. Adam and Seb had leaned on each other, on their abilities, and their faith in the gods of industry. They'd struggled and survived. Despaired and succeeded.

Yet making piles of money had only been a goal, not a purpose. For Seb, it was about gathering an army, scaling a mountain, planting his flag on the peak, and readying to conquer again.

But that wasn't Adam's purpose: he had been industriously building, creating and doing his whole life, setting goals and surpassing them, but never really with an end in sight. He'd come to realize he didn't need to have an endgame. In fact, he didn't even want one. It was enough to have built HEXO from infant to its teen years and then move it out the door. He'd always imagined he'd start a billion-dollar company. Now that he had, he wanted to start over. Build, create and do, over and over.

Adam looked up from the canvases and grinned boyishly at Julie. After years of ups and downs, he could sum it up in shorthand and know she'd get it.

"You know what they say, right?" he said as they turned off the lights and headed for the door. "It really is all about the journey."

Standing at the top of the stairs behind him, Julie rolled her eyes. Hard.

"It's all about the journey. What fucking bullshit," she thought. She knew Adam. It was more about the driving curiosity, the determination to build, the real desire to be a man of note.

As he left, she followed him, as she had done for six years, and stood beside him in the parking lot. She glanced over as she fished for her car keys. Something was brewing behind those sharp brown eyes. And even if he didn't see it clearly at that moment, even if he was still adjusting to being a retired fricking multi-millionaire millennial living the dream, even if he still had questions, she could sense it.

Adam had picked his next destination and was already rowing like a madman.

ACKNOWLEDGEMENTS

It may take a village to raise a child, but it takes an army to write a book. Although this book was written in an all-seeing, all-knowing voice by one author, several people contributed to the shaping of the narrative with their insights, shared memories, reflections, and intonations.

To that end, Adam spent hours retelling the story, sharing his memories, reflections, and insights.

Sébastien filled in the black-and-white business events with his expertise and a deep understanding of commerce.

HEXO's first publicist, Julie, interviewed, researched, and wrote the book, relying on her own recollections, supported by six years of detailed meeting notes, dozens of interviews, and seemingly random (to others) ephemera and colour details journalists obsessively gather and store in the back of their minds' filing cabinets.

Other voices, too, can be heard and deserve gratitude and recognition. Particular thanks goes to: Adam and Seb's wives, Meena and Aruna: without you, your insight, support, love, and unwavering leonine ferocity, HEXO wouldn't exist as it does; it is your faith, as well as your ability to dream to the stars with them that shows scalability is truly infinite.

Friends and family who held our hands and leapt over the edge with us, committing not just their money but their passion, support, and love:

without you, without friends + family — i.e., framily — nothing is possible. You bless us.

All the experts upon whom we have relied upon, leaned on, and exhausted with late-night phone calls and endless emails: You have never let us down. You know who you are.

The City of Gatineau, Mayor Maxime Pedneaud-Jobin, and Gatineau municipal councillors, the Province of Quebec and its leaders: your early and ongoing support has made our region a leader in Canada's marijuana industry.

To the Government of Canada: for its vision and foresight in creating an opportunity for Canadian entrepreneurs to create a multi-billion-dollar industry.

Finally, this journey began with the pioneers of legalization, the early advocates of medical cannabis who risked criminal charges, and outliers who raised their voices for change. The entire cannabis industry owes you a debt of gratitude.

To Our HEXO Family

From our first three employees who hopped on board in 2013 to a thousand true believers now, you have all helped build this company with love, sweat, and effort.

Our growth from the basement on Spruce Street in Ottawa to a major Canadian and international corporation did not happen by mere chance. We started with a vision and nurtured it. Encouraged by its growth, we dreamed bigger and bigger. For every scheme we put in place, for every failure we experienced, we learned from mistakes and built bolder and more epic plans. We relentlessly implemented and executed on them. We brought together the smartest people we could find, the most talented minds, and the most dedicated workers. We became a family and, as a family, we all pulled in the same direction.

Whether you are the hundreds of hands diligently cultivating our plants or part of the team fanning out across the globe in search of new opportunities, each of you has our gratitude for your part in our incredible success. Every minute of every day, we are perfectly aware that you, above all else, have made HEXO the incredible success it is. *Merci.*

Seb & Adam

A Note from Sébastien St-Louis

My father was a "warrior poet" — a strong-willed and stubborn man who spent the final two years of his life battling cancer and heart disease with more resilience than could be expected of any man and who left this world on his own terms.

He never did anything he did not want to do; coming to terms with the end of his life was no exception.

The last time emergency responders came to our home, he spurned the use of a stretcher, walked to the ambulance, turned to my mother, told her he loved her, and waved goodbye with a wry smile — something he had never done on many ambulance trips to the hospital during those hard-fought years. In his final hours, as my mother and I each held vigil by his bedside, I placed my hand on his chest and felt the last beats of his heart. I knew he had found his peace.

My father was a great teacher. A voracious reader and accomplished writer himself — though he mostly only wrote for his and my mother's eyes — he would appreciate good literature with the critical precision of the sharpest editor and, more importantly, the flair of a poet. I know he would have enjoyed reading this book and I have no doubt his insights would have made it an even better read. We'll each have to take joy in the fact that instead of writing the story with me, he lived it with me.

He was a deeply sensitive soul — though he consistently tried through the years to convince himself and others otherwise — who would find pleasure and fulfillment in reading a good book and living a quiet life.

In his youth, roused by a deeply rooted sense of justice, my father led a student revolution for French-language rights in his hometown of Sturgeon Falls in Northern Ontario. It was a difficult fight with overwhelmingly unfavourable odds. He was defending his heritage and an entire way of life, which required an unrelenting battle against local discrimination, as well as school board and provincial govern- ment resistance. At the peak of the fight, Prime Minister Pierre Elliot Trudeau came to Sturgeon Falls, shook his hand and told him to "keep going." My father beamed with pride whenever he recounted that story.

Billion Dollar Start-Up was written while my father was ill, yet his battle and my recollections of life with him provided me with an inspiring reminder of why what we do at HEXO is so important.

Thank you, Pa, for teaching me to think, to lead, and when necessary, to fight. You're a warrior poet.

I love you. Enjoy your peace and quiet.

ABOUT THE AUTHORS

Considered to be one of the sharpest CEOs in Canada's exploding cannabis industry, Sébastien St-Louis is well known in investor circles. He has advised Canadian business owners and CEOs across multiple industry sectors while structuring and closing more than $200 million in financing when at both Export Development Canada and Business Development Canada. As CEO of HEXO, Sébastien has been a fearless leader who has driven the corporation's success in Canada and onto the international stage.

Adam Miron is a well-known figure in political and media circles in Ottawa and across Canada. A natural and gifted raconteur, Adam speaks at more than a hundred public events a year and has appeared at Collision and the renowned Cannes Lions International Festival of Creativity. As co-founder and chief brand officer, Adam is the architect of award-winning national product and marketing campaigns.

Julie Beun is a gifted author, respected journalist, and communications professional whose international experience spans more than 30 years and two continents. Working with Adam and Seb since July 2014, she was HEXO's publicist, chief writer, and content strategist from the earliest days to 2019. She has had a privileged front-row seat to HEXO's remarkable journey from the basement to a billion-dollar company.

INDEX

choices, 32; preparation for legalization, 220

244–45; pace as chief brand officer, 169; political statement with low priced Honeydew, 175; 'Powered by HEXO' label, 212; purpose after the cannabis company, 235–47; response to recall, 139; retired from company, 241–46; security concerns, 88; seeking seed-to-sale tracking software, 111; studio, 239–40; 33 birthday celebration, 144, 146; video call with Seb (India–Canada), 27–28; views on customer service, 52; wanted to sell marijuana to people like him and Seb, 99

Miron, Gaston, 14, 50; Adam's ability to help, 119–22, 128; bankruptcy, 52; childhood and early life, 48–50; death and funeral, 130–33; Hydropothecary's first registered client, 122, 188; lung cancer, 93–94, 119–21, 130–31

MJBiz Conference, 115

MMAR licence (from Health Canada), 57

MMPR (Marihuana for Medical Purposes Regulations), 8, 22

Moët & Chandon champagne, 156

Molson Coors Canada, 216–17, 220–21, 229; overlap of values with HEXO, 217

money woes: broke again after paying out Louis, 89; May 2015, 116–17; on cancellation of CCC deal, 133–35; stretching Rajan's money: asked people to go on half pay, 137–38; time to raise money, June 5, 2017, 172; under-resourced, post going public, 155–56

Montreal investors, 111

Motel Les Pignons Verts, 193

Munzar, Michael (board chair), xii, 58, 90, 100–101, 132, 145, 153; cash injection after CCC deal cancellation, 135; investment in company, 43; meeting with Seb in Bridgehead coffee shop, 42

Musk, Elon, 190

myclobutinal. See under pesticide

Nalina (Adam and Meena's daughter), 92

name (for company), 26, 29, 31–33; Hydropothecary, 198–99, 203, 205, 218; new name for recreational brand (HEXO), 200–201, 210

National Assembly in Quebec City: Seb's testimony, 189

National Gallery of Canada, 227

National Post, 110, 123

Never Jaded "Flower Shop" pop-up speakeasy, 210

Never Jaded Tour, 229; entertainment lineup, 210; failure to connect tour to the HEXO brand, 211; HEXO advertising and branding, 209–10, 212–13

Newstrike, 236

Northern Lights, 99

Nymox Pharmaceuticals, 100

October 17, 2018: business as usual, 229; unofficial Canadian Cannabis Day, 228

OG Kush, 99

One King West Hotel: celebration after going public, 156

Ontario Cannabis Store: supply